Human–Computer Interaction Series

Editors-in-chief

Desney Tan
Microsoft Research, Redmond, WA, USA

Jean Vanderdonckt
Louvain School of Management, Université catholique de Louvain,
Louvain-la-Neuve, Belgium

More information about this series at http://www.springer.com/series/6033

Robert J. Moore · Margaret H. Szymanski
Raphael Arar · Guang-Jie Ren
Editors

Studies in Conversational UX Design

 Springer

Editors
Robert J. Moore
IBM Research-Almaden
San Jose, CA, USA

Raphael Arar
IBM Research-Almaden
San Jose, CA, USA

Margaret H. Szymanski
IBM Research-Almaden
San Jose, CA, USA

Guang-Jie Ren
IBM Research-Almaden
San Jose, CA, USA

ISSN 1571-5035   ISSN 2524-4477   (electronic)
Human–Computer Interaction Series
ISBN 978-3-319-95578-0   ISBN 978-3-319-95579-7   (eBook)
https://doi.org/10.1007/978-3-319-95579-7

Library of Congress Control Number: 2018949051

This Springer imprint is published by the registered company Springer Nature Switzerland AG
The registered company address is: Gewerbestrasse 11, 6330 Cham, Switzerland

Contents

Part IV   Agent Design

Contributors

Raphael Arar IBM Research-Almaden, San Jose, CA, USA

Reza Asadi College of Computer and Information Science, Northeastern University, Boston, USA

Daniel Avrahami FXPAL, Palo Alto, CA, USA

Amos Azaria Ariel University, Ariel, Israel

Jan Balata Faculty of Electrical Engineering, Czech Technical University in Prague, Prague, Czech Republic

Gregory A. Bennett Linguist | UX Researcher, San Francisco, CA, USA

Timothy Bickmore College of Computer and Information Science, Northeastern University, Boston, USA

Heloisa Candello IBM Research, São Paulo, Brazil

Gary Hsieh University of Washington, Seattle, WA, USA

Rafal Kocielnik University of Washington, Seattle, WA, USA

Igor Labutov Carnegie Mellon University, Pittsburgh, PA, USA

Toby Jia-Jun Li Carnegie Mellon University, Pittsburgh, PA, USA

Zdenek Mikovec Faculty of Electrical Engineering, Czech Technical University in Prague, Prague, Czech Republic

Tom M. Mitchell Carnegie Mellon University, Pittsburgh, PA, USA

Robert J. Moore IBM Research-Almaden, San Jose, CA, USA

Brad A. Myers Carnegie Mellon University, Pittsburgh, PA, USA

Stefan Olafsson College of Computer and Information Science, Northeastern University, Boston, USA

Claudio Pinhanez IBM Research, São Paulo, Brazil

Alexander I. Rudnicky Carnegie Mellon University, Pittsburgh, PA, USA

Pavel Slavik Faculty of Electrical Engineering, Czech Technical University in Prague, Prague, Czech Republic

Margaret H. Szymanski IBM Research-Almaden, San Jose, CA, USA

Ha Trinh College of Computer and Information Science, Northeastern University, Boston, USA

Chapter 1
Conversational UX Design:
An Introduction

Robert J. Moore and Raphael Arar

The trajectory of user interface design has come a long way since the inception of computing. Interfaces have evolved from the command-line interfaces (CLI) of teleprinters, computer terminals and early personal computers in the 1970s and 1980s (Stephenson 1999) to graphical user interfaces (GUI), invented at Xerox PARC and popularized by Apple and Microsoft, which are now ubiquitous (O'Regan 2016). More recent interfaces such as the Natural User Interfaces (NUI) of smart phones that recognize human gestures (Wigdor and Wixon 2011), as well as Augmented Reality (AR) and Virtual Reality (VR) interfaces that uniquely mix our physical and digital worlds (Sherman and Craig 2002) have also flourished in the past decade. And 3D user interfaces (3D UI) (Bowman et al. 2004), found primarily in video games, with their humanoid avatars and rich virtual environments today look more like major motion pictures than like their predecessors, such as Pong.

As these interfaces continue to position humanity in the blurry divide between perception and imagination, advances in artificial intelligence have allowed the design community to look back at initial approaches to interface design and user experience. With the command-line, users had to learn to speak the computer's language. But today, with natural language interfaces (NLI) (Androutsopoulos et al. 1995), computers are learning to speak the user's language. It is through this evolution that the discipline of user experience (UX) design emerged. Designers shifted their focus from the technology alone to that of the full experience of a human interacting with the technology. This human-centered approach to design has now become the basis of how new interfaces and digital experiences are conceived and developed.

User interfaces inspired by conversation, perhaps the most natural form of human communication (Nishida 2011), have been around for decades (Frohlich and Luff

R. J. Moore (✉) · R. Arar
IBM Research-Almaden, San Jose, CA, USA
e-mail: rjmoore@us.ibm.com

R. Arar
e-mail: rarar@us.ibm.com

© Springer International Publishing AG, part of Springer Nature 2018
R. J. Moore et al. (eds.), *Studies in Conversational UX Design*, Human–Computer
Interaction Series, https://doi.org/10.1007/978-3-319-95579-7_1

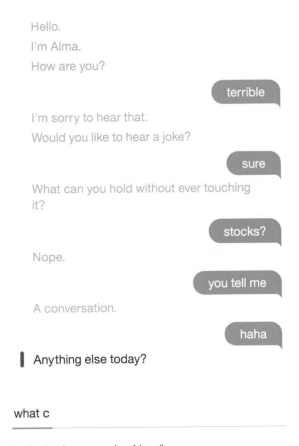

Fig. 1.1 Example of a simple conversational interface

1990); however, a new generation of chatbots and virtual agents has emerged with recent advances in natural language processing and machine learning. Today, natural language interfaces, powered by companies like Apple, Amazon, Google, Microsoft and IBM, have moved out of the industry research labs and into the pockets, desktops and living rooms of the general public. With persistent Internet connections and statistical algorithms, virtual agents are much better at understanding human language today than they were 25 years ago.

Natural language interfaces are very different from graphical and mobile user interfaces (Androutsopoulos et al. 1995). When they are text-based, they tend to consist of simple visual elements borrowed from instant messaging (IM) or short message service (SMS) interfaces, with their text-entry boxes and chat histories. When they are voice-based, they have no visual elements at all! The user experience with natural language interfaces consists primarily of the words and sequences of utterances (Fig. 1.1).

Although natural language processing (NLP) has given us powerful tools for analyzing spoken and written bits of human language, it has not provided designers with models of how those bits of language should be sequenced in order to create an interaction that works like a "conversation" (Moore et al. 2016). Natural conversation is a complex, speech-exchange system (Schegloff 2007), which Harvey Sacks called a "machinery" in its own right (Sacks 1984). Creating a user interface that approximates this machinery requires modeling the patterns of human conversation, either through manual design or machine learning. Rather than avoiding this complexity, by producing simplistic interactions, we should embrace the complexity of natural conversation because it "mirrors the complexity of the world" (Norman 2011). The result will be machines that we can talk to in a natural way, instead of merely machines that we can interact with through new unnatural uses of natural language.

With the proliferation of natural language interfaces, there is growing demand for a new kind of user experience (UX) design. Like the world wide web in the late 1990s, natural language interfaces today are in the hands of the general public, but they lack standards, interaction conventions and often quality when it comes to how to sequence utterances and preserve context. But web design evolved as formal knowledge of graphic design, with its typography, color palettes, layouts and logos, was applied to the user interface problem. In a similar way, natural language interface design can evolve by applying formal knowledge of human conversation, with its turn-taking systems, sequence organization and repair devices. Conversational UX design must draw from the social sciences, such as sociology and psychology in addition to linguistics. Conversation Analysis (CA), in particular, which emerged out of sociology, offers over 50 years of empirical studies of naturally occurring talk-in-interaction in a wide range of settings and languages. CA studies provide formal, qualitative patterns of how people naturally talk. While the proposal to apply these patterns to the design of dialogue interfaces is not be entirely new (Frohlich and Luff 1990; Norman and Thomas 1990), it has become especially timely as new conversational technology platforms are becoming ubiquitous and more mature.

Conversational UX designers must be conversation experts, that is, keen observers of how people talk. They must be able to articulate the mechanics of human conversation so they can design it, instead of simply knowing it tacitly like everyone does. For example, a conversation expert may describe the function of the word "oh" to mark speakers' realizations (Heritage 1984) or how the phrase, "to the what?," in response to "I'm going to the workshop," elegantly elicits a repeat of a single word "workshop" (Schegloff et al. 1977). Conversational UX designers use such observable patterns of the machinery of human conversation in building conversational machines.

This book explores the intersection of conversational UX design, of both text- or voice-based virtual agents, and the analysis of naturally occurring human conversation (e.g., Conversation Analysis, Discourse Analysis and Interactional Sociolinguistics). In it we discuss how humans naturally talk to each other, demonstrate designs of conversational systems and propose new approaches to conversational UX design.

1.1   What Is UX Design?

User Experience (UX) Design is not a new field; however, its acceptance and popularity as a discipline has occurred more recently due to the rise of software and digital experiences. The term "User Experience" was coined by Don Norman in the 1990s at Apple, and since then, its importance has been demonstrated in countless papers, books and presentations. The field has its roots in ergonomics, the study of people's efficiency in their working environment, and it largely applies to a person's overall experience with a digital product or service.

As the number of our digital outlets continue to rise, the field broadens to encompass every digital touchpoint imaginable. Think about your experience at an ATM, on a video-call or in an automated grocery checkout register. All of these experiences have been designed with the goal of producing a more intuitive and natural experience. In an effort to make our digital experiences as "human" as possible, conversation reigns supreme. Now that technology has advanced to handle more natural-language-based interactions, the experience of a human conversing with a computational system needs to be architected and designed.

1.2   Interaction Styles and Conversation First

All conversations are interactions but not all interactions are conversations. Today's chatbot platforms enable the designer to create a variety of different styles of interaction. Because they use natural language classification (NLC), these platforms are an advance over earlier voice control systems that only recognized a limited set of pre-specified command phrases. NLC enables recognition of a much wider range of phrases. However, how NLC is used together with the agent's utterances and other UI elements can produce very different user experiences.

Below are idealized examples representing four distinct interaction styles that we have observed in today's chatbots and virtual agents: system-centric, content-centric, visual-centric and conversation-centric styles. They are not mutually exclusive, but each emphasizes a different aspect of the interface.

System-centric interaction styles are like interactions with web search engines, but also with voice control systems (Example 1; A is the automated agent; U is the user).

(1) System-Centric Style

```
01 A:  Hello, I am MedicareBot. To find answers to Medicare
02     questions, type your question in natural language.
03     Include whether you have Original Medicare or Medicare
04     Advantage. For example: "Original Medicare coverage
05     for influenza vaccination."
06 U:  Original Medicare coverage for diabetes screenings?
07 A:  Medicare covers tests to screen for diabetes as well
```

```
08      as services and supplies to help treat the disease.
09      Medicare will pay for 100% of its approved amount for
10      the test even before you have met the Part B deductible.
11 U:   thanks
12 A:   There are no results for this question. To find answers
13      to Medicare questions, type your question in natural
14      language. Include whether you have Original Medicare or
15      Medicare Advantage. For example: "Original Medicare
16      coverage for influenza vaccination."
```

In this type of interface, the agent only recognizes one class of user actions: queries or commands. They cannot recognize other kinds of actions for managing the conversation itself, such as appreciations, "thank you," or clarification requests, "what do you mean?". The interaction is entirely user-driven, where the agent merely responds to commands from the user but does not initiate courses of action on its own. In addition, system-centric interfaces can handle only two-turn sequences, as in web search or voice control. Each next user action is like starting a new conversation: the agent forgets what it was talking about only a moment before. Consequently, users cannot refer to or build upon the words in prior turns as a context for their current turns as in natural conversation. While system-centric styles certainly recognize natural language, they do not engage in natural conversation.

Content-centric interaction styles are like interactions with frequently asked questions (FAQ) web pages (Example 2).

(2) Content-Centric Style

```
01 A:   Hello, I am an automated Medicare Assistant. I can
02      answer questions about Medicare insurance. What is your
03      question?
04 U:   am I covered for diabetes screenings?
05 A:   Medicare covers tests to screen for diabetes as well
06      as services and supplies to help treat the disease.
07      Medicare will pay for 100% of its approved amount for
08      test even before you have met the Part B deductible.
09      You will pay no copay or deductible for these tests
10      if you see doctors who take assignment. Doctors and
11      other health care providers who take assignment cannot
12      charge you more than the Medicare approved amount.
13      Medicare Advantage Plans cover all preventive services
14      the same as Original Medicare. This means Medicare
15      Advantage Plans will not be allowed to charge cost-
16      sharing fees (coinsurances, copays or deductibles)
17      for preventive services that Original Medicare does
18      not charge for as long as you see in-network providers.
19 U:   thanks
20 A:   You can ask a question the same way you would ask your
21      doctor
```

Interactionally, content-centric styles may be the same as system-centric ones. They are entirely user-driven and limited to a single class of user actions and to two-turn sequences. Where they differ is in their turn design: the content-centric style is characterized by long, document-like responses to user questions. This length is due to a primary concern for accuracy and thoroughness. As a result, every potentially related detail, example and contingency is built into an extended monologue. Due to the unnatural length of the agent's responses, content-centric interaction styles are incompatible with voice-based interfaces. This length also tends to limit opportunities for back-and-forth since all details are mentioned upfront. In content-centric systems, the agent recognizes topics, rather than conversational actions, as they direct all inquiries or requests pertaining to a particular topic to a single response.

Visual-centric interaction styles borrow heavily from web and mobile interfaces, all of which rely on the principle of *direct manipulation* (Shneiderman 1982) instead of text commands or natural language (Example 3; buttons represented by brackets).

(3) Visual-Centric Style
```
01 A:  Hi, I'm Melanie, your virtual nurse! I can answer your
02     Medicare questions. To start, which plan do you have?
03     [Original Medicare] [Medicare Advantage] [ Other ]
04     ((U clicks/taps Medicare Advantage))
05 A:  Okay, Medicare Advantage. What is your question?
06 U:  am I covered for diabetes screenings?
07 A:  Medicare covers tests to screen for diabetes as well
08     as services and supplies to help treat the disease.
09     Medicare will pay for 100% of its approved amount for
10     the test even before you have met the Part B
11     deductible. You will pay no copay or deductible for
12     these tests if you see doctors who take assignment.
13 A:  Was this answer useful?
14     [ Yes ] [ No ]
```

With visual-centric styles, graphical elements, such as buttons or lists, are mixed into the interaction alongside natural language utterances, and dialog techniques from web and mobile interfaces, such as "Was this answer helpful?" or thumbs up/down buttons are incorporated. Visual-centric styles, rely heavily on buttons and visual elements, and are not designed to work well with the text inputs and outputs alone. Unlike system- and content-centric styles, visual-centric styles tend to be more agent-driven, although they allow some mixed initiative. The agent tends to lead the user down a somewhat linear path. For example, after the agent answers (2nd position) a question from the user (1st position), it immediately initiates a new action pair (3rd position; line 13), like "Was this answer useful?" or "Would you like to find your nearest provider?," instead of allowing the user to respond to the answer. Because such agents do not leave an opportunity, or slot, for the user to indicate if the answer was adequate or if there is an understanding trouble on the part of the user or the agent, we call this kind of design, "hijacking 3rd position."

Finally, conversation-centric interaction styles are more like a natural human conversation than the other styles (Example 4).

(4) Conversation-Centric Style

```
01 A:  Hi, I'm Alma. I'm here to answer any questions you
02     have about your Medicare insurance. How can I help
03     you?
04 U:  I have a question about diabetes screenings
05 A:  Okay, what's your question?
06 U:  am I covered for them?
07 A:  Diabetes screenings are covered at 100% of the
08     approved amount so there is no copay or deductible
09     if you see doctors who take assignment.
10 U:  what do you mean by take assignment?
11 A:  Oh. Assignment means that your doctor, provider or
12     supplier agrees to accept the Medicare-approved
13     amount as full payment.
14 U:  ok thanks
15 A:  You're welcome! Is there anything else I can do
16     for you?
```

First and foremost, conversation-centric styles can handle some level of *conversation management*, that is, they can recognize actions that function to manage the conversation itself. For example, "what did you say?," "none of your business," "okay," "never mind" are all operations on other utterances in the interaction. This is a major part of what makes an interaction a *conversation*. In addition, the responses in a conversation-centric interaction are relatively short, or bite-sized. This enables efficiency and speed as conversations happen in real time, either through voice or text. It also enables more back-and-forth utterance exchange instead of longer monologues. And conversation-centric styles are fully mixed-initiative and non-linear. Either the user or the agent can lead, and the user can always redirect the conversation. Consequently, they also rely more on the user to decide what to do next.

While any of these interaction styles can be useful for enabling users to access information, they do not equally demonstrate competence in the activity of human conversation. Some advantages of conversation-centric interfaces are: (1) they can return specific answers instead of lists or documents that may contain the answer, (2) they efficiently pare down content to bite-sized pieces which can be expanded through more back-and-forth as needed, (3) they can adapt to the user's level of knowledge and preferred style of speaking and (4) they work on a wide variety of devices, including voice-only devices and display-based devices of all sizes.

We advocate a *conversation-first* approach to the design of natural language interfaces, which is analogous to the mobile-first strategy in web design. While mobile-first design begins with the small screen of the mobile device and scales up to larger displays (Wroblewski 2011), conversation first begins with, just verbal input and output, whether voice or text. The UX designer must enable the user to converse with the agent through the words alone, without buttons or visual aids. Voice interfaces, or platforms like the Short Message Service (SMS), force one to design for short utterances rather than for buttons, long lists or documents. Once the conversation is fully functional, it can be enhanced, as needed, through coordination with visual aids, just as a human speaker may use menus or charts to supplement his or her talk. As a result, users can talk to an agent through multiple communication channels, although the experiences will vary in their affordances, similar to human conversation when the speakers are face-to-face or physically distributed. A conversation-first design strategy involves a focus on (1) conversation-centric interaction styles, including support for conversation management, (2) core functionality through the words alone, whether voice, text or both and (3) compatibility with multiple platforms, from voice-only and simple chat to desktop and large displays. In this manner, starting with conversation enables a designer to consider progressive enhancement (Gustafson 2015), so that greater functionality can be increasingly implemented as the modalities of conversation evolve.

1.3 Speakers' Design Principles

Designing natural language interfaces for conversation first will require formal knowledge of the mechanics of natural human conversation. This includes design principles that human speakers exhibit themselves when they talk. Work in Conversation Analysis has revealed three such speaker-design principles: recipient design, minimization and repair.

1.3.1 Recipient Design

In natural conversation, speakers tailor their talk to their particular recipients in multiple ways, adapting to their perceived level of knowledge (Sacks and Schegloff 1979; Sacks et al. 1974). For example, they choose different topics and levels of detail depending on who they are talking to and what they believe that person knows. Speakers' first priority in general is to enable *this* recipient to understand.

While this kind of tailoring or personalization of the agent's utterances at the turn-level is still a hard problem with today's natural language interfaces, it is feasible at the sequence level. That is, the sequence of turns in the interaction can vary widely with different users. Where an expert user may prefer speed and precision (e.g., "flights from SFO to JFK on Apr 17-30"), a novice user may need more hand-holding and back-and-forth (e.g., "I'm going on vacation!"). User-centered design, when it comes to conversational interfaces, in part involves providing multiple paths or trajectories through the same conversation space. Like user-centered design, recipient design is a broad principle. It refers to a "multitude of respects in which the talk by a party in a conversation is constructed or designed in ways which display an orientation and sensitivity to the particular other(s)" (Sacks et al. 1974).

1.3.2 Minimization

While recipients' understanding is generally the first priority in conversation, speakers also display a sensitivity to efficiency. Talking takes time and in the context of a conversation, it takes up someone else's time. In addition, conversation always occurs in some social setting, in which people are trying to get things done, either through the talk itself, in conjunction with the talk or in spite of the talk. Speakers thus tend to try to use just enough words to enable the particular recipient(s) to understand, given the social context (Sacks and Schegloff 1979). Unnecessary details not only waste time, they can make the point of the speaker's utterance harder to grasp. However, minimization is secondary to recipient design. If the shortest way to formulate a particular utterance is unlikely to be understood by this recipient (e.g., "IATA code of origin"?), it should be expanded as needed (e.g., "Which airport do you want to leave from?").

For conversation-centric interfaces, designers should strive to keep the agent's utterances as short as necessary. With voice interfaces, it quickly becomes clear if the agent's utterances are too long because the production of speech takes a relatively long time, but designers should also resist the temptation to make the agent's text utterances too verbose. Although reading is faster than listening, users may not read agent's entire responses if they're unnecessarily lengthy.

1.3.3 Repair

While speakers strive to tailor their utterances in an efficient manner, they also rely on the fact that those utterances can be repaired if they fail. If an utterance is too short or otherwise poorly formulated for the recipient, the speaker relaxes the concern for minimization in order to redo all or part of the utterance, either repeating or paraphrasing it, depending on what the source of the recipient's trouble appears to be (Sacks and Schegloff 1979; Schegloff et al. 1977). Conversely the recipient can also redo all or part of the problematic utterance. A robust repair mechanism, enables people to adapt to inevitable ambiguities, errors and missing bits of information that occur in natural conversation.

In order to benefit from the repair devices of natural conversation, UX designers must build them in. Intents and dialog must be created to handle user utterances like, "what did you say?", "what do you mean?", "what do you mean by origin?", "can you give an example?", "no, I mean one way" and more. Through conversational repair, designers provide users and agents with resources for recovering from troubles in speaking, hearing and understanding. It also frees designers from having always to recognize users' intent on the first try.

Taken together, recipient design, minimization and repair provide an efficient and flexible machinery for natural-language-based communication. Recipient design maximizes the chances of initial understanding, minimization maximizes efficiency and repair enables for subsequent understanding if miscalculations are made. Conversational UX designers can then adopt this kind of strategy: return concise utterances to the user first, but enable the user to expand the content if necessary. In other words, if most users do not require simple terms and instructions, do not return them to everybody. Instead teach users to elicit definitions, paraphrases, examples, instructions, etc. if and when they need them.

1.4 Conversation Types

Human conversation consists of a generic speech-exchange system (Sacks et al. 1974) that is continually adapted by speakers to different activities and situations. Similarly UX designers need to adapt generic conversational UX patterns to particular use cases. Is the virtual agent like a friend or a customer service representative or a teacher or someone else? The use case will determine the range of conversational UX patterns needed to support it. The following are just four broad kinds of conversational use cases.

Ordinary conversation is the kind you have with family, friends and even strangers. Ordinary conversations consist of the broadest range of activities from delivering news to checking up to seeking help or advice to teaching to small talk and much more. Sometimes the purpose of ordinary conversation is simply to open a social connection with another person for its own sake. In conversation analytic theory, ordinary conversation is considered the most flexible type of conversation from which other types are adapted for particular purposes by adding special constraints (Drew and Heritage 1992).

Service conversations are the kind you have with customer service agents or organizational representatives. The roles are fixed: One person, such as a customer, member or citizen, requests service; the other person, usually a stranger, provides services on behalf of an organization. Services may consist simply of answering inquiries or taking actions or guiding the other through troubleshooting. Service conversations have distinctive openings: service providers typically do a greeting, self-identify, identify the organization and offer service, rushing through the transitions, so that the service seeker's first turn can be his or her request, problem or reason for calling. Other times such openings may include a series of questions for verifying the service seeker's identity. Szymanski and Moore (Chap. 2) analyze talk in this kind of conversation.

Teaching conversations are the kind you have within a classroom setting or with a tutor. One person (or more) seeks knowledge; the other presents knowledge and tests understanding. In teaching conversations, the teacher routinely asks the students questions to which he or she already knows the answers. Teachers may withhold the answers in an attempt to elicit the correct answers from the student (McHoul 1990). Whereas correcting other people is typically discouraged in most other kinds of conversations for the sake of politeness (Schegloff et al. 1977), it is required in the teaching conversation for the purposes of learning.

And *counseling* conversations are the kind you have with a therapist, counselor or advisor. One person seeks advice; the other listens and provides advice. The counselee may report a problem of a personal nature or a long-term goal and seek advice on how to manage it, rather than requesting that the other person manage it directly. In psychotherapy, the therapist asks questions and the patient answers them. The therapist may withhold judgment and let the patient lead the conversation without interrupting or changing the topic. Or the therapist may formulate what the patient previously said in order to suggest an alternative meaning (Antaki 2008).

Each of these types of conversations and more depend on the same conversational machinery, such as turn-taking, sequence organization and repair, but the activities and settings in which they take place contain distinctive patterns and slight adaptations (Drew and Heritage 1992). Conversational systems likewise should be built on a shared, basic machinery so that users can rely on familiar practices but also accomplish the distinctive business of the particular application.

1.5 About This Book

The following chapters contain contributions from researchers, from academia and industry, with varied backgrounds working in the area of human-computer interaction (HCI). Each chapter explores an aspect of conversational UX design. Some describe the design challenges faced in creating a particular virtual agent. Others discuss how the findings from the literatures of the social sciences can inform a new kind of UX design that starts with conversation. The book is organized into four sections, each with its own theme. Themes include: human conversation, agent knowledge, agent misunderstanding and agent design. Throughout the book, the term "agent" is used to refer to the automated system. We use this term both in the sense of an active participant in an interaction and, in many use cases, in the sense of a particular role in a service encounter, that is, the one who provides a service.

1.5.1 Section I: Human Conversation

With conversational interfaces, the interaction metaphor is natural human conversation. Therefore the UX patterns for conversational interfaces should be informed by the interaction patterns that humans display in natural conversation. Designers will naturally rely on their commonsense knowledge of how human conversation works, but they can take a more systematic approach by observing naturally occurring human conversation or by consulting the social sciences that specialize on that topic. How are naturally occurring human conversations structured? How do speakers design particular turns-at-talk? What are the fundamental structures of human conversation and social action?

In Chap. 2, Szymanski and Moore demonstrate how the analysis of human conversation can inform the design of UX patterns for conversational interfaces. They analyze customer service telephone calls using methods of Conversation Analysis and highlight some practices in natural human talk. For example, customers frequently do not follow the human agents' lead in the openings of calls, instead initiating their own trajectories. In answering agents' questions, customers routinely lack information needed by the agent or provide hints that enable the agent to figure out the answer. And customers naturally display cues regarding their level of satisfaction in the ways they close the telephone call. Conversational UX designers must understand these kinds of natural, service encounter practices and provide for many of them in their automated service agents.

In Chap. 3, Bickmore, et al. offer a review of the literatures applying knowledge of human conversation, especially from the field of Discourse Analysis, to the design of virtual agents, including embodied virtual agents with (digital avatars) and older Interactive Voice Response (IVR) systems. They outline recurrent errors made by virtual agents, as well as their limitations. The authors focus on the healthcare domain in which errors by virtual agents can have significant consequences where, for example, incorrect drug dosages are given to patients or emergency-indicating information from the user is missed by the agent. In addition to the errors made by medical virtual agents, the authors also outline several strategies for avoiding them.

1.5.2 Section II: Agent Knowledge

While conversational agents must be able to recognize the range of human actions in conversation, they must also be able to access knowledge about the world in order to be useful. Responses of the form, *I know what you are requesting, but I don't have that information*, while critical for demonstrating recognition of the user's intent are ultimately dissatisfying. In order to respond in a knowledgeable way, virtual agents typically must be integrated with backend APIs that provide access to data. What are the challenges and best practices for integrating conversation flows with backend APIs?

In Chap. 4, Balata and Mikovec demonstrate a novel way of integrating a voice-based, conversational agent with navigation knowledge for visually impaired pedestrians. As a result, unlike popular driving navigation applications, users can talk back to the system, asking navigation-relevant questions that are interspersed with location-triggered navigation instructions. The authors describe their strategy of using an "on-demand level of detail technique" to allow the user to control the level of detail of the navigation instructions and to avoid overwhelming him or her with information. This approach nicely demonstrates a form of *recipient design*, at the sequence level, as well as *minimization* on the part of the agent. Moore (Chap. 9) demonstrates a similar method of allowing users to control the level of detail through sequence expansion.

In Chap. 5, Kocielnik, Hsieh and Avrahami describe how to design conversational UX for an agent that is integrated with a user's live health data, such as step count, heart rate or calories burned, as well as knowledge on best practices for improving health. They review the literature on how human health coaches teach people to reflect on their own health-related behaviors and to modify those behaviors to improve health. The authors then offer conversation designs for how an automated agent could perform the role of health coach. In doing so, they discuss some of the technical challenges in analyzing users' freeform text and provide strategies for handling unrecognized user utterances.

1.5.3 Section III: Agent Misunderstanding

A distinctive feature of natural language interfaces is that they routinely fail to recognize out-of-scope actions that users attempt, much more so than a human would. Because the range of actions the user may attempt is unconstrained, it is impossible to prevent users from doing so. The result is misunderstanding on the part of the agent, often for commonsense actions, as Bickmore et al. discuss (Chap. 3). How should the system respond when it does not recognize what the user just said or did? How should the system handle unsupported or out-of-scope user actions?

In Chap. 6, Li et al., demonstrate one kind of solution to the problem of agent misunderstanding: enable users to teach the agent new actions. In their SUGILITE application, the conversational agent performs smartphone tasks for the user, such as ordering coffee from the Starbuck's app. However, when the user makes a request that the agent does not know how to do, it offers to learn the new action. Users can then teach SUGILITE new sequences of actions through a programming-by-demonstration method. More generally the ability for users to teach virtual agents new phrases, actions or information is a critical component of general conversational competence.

In Chap. 7, Candello and Pinhanez demonstrate a different approach to managing agent misunderstanding: multiple agents. They describe a system for wealth-management advice, which employs three distinct conversational agents, or "gurus." One agent knows about savings accounts, one knows about investments and one moderates the conversation. When one agent fails to understand an inquiry, users may recover from such "dialogue failures" by redirecting the inquiry to another agent or by another more knowledgeable agent self-selecting and responding. Furthermore, to manage the utterances of multiple agents, as well as those of the user, Candello and Pinhanez present a method that somewhat resembles the turn-taking model in Conversation Analysis (Sacks et al. 1974). Because no single agent can know everything, the ability to hand the user off to other agents with the needed knowledge or functionality is an important aspect of conversational competence, especially as standards and ecosystems of agents emerge.

1.5.4   Section IV: Agent Design

Conversational UX design is emerging as a distinctive area within UX and UI design. However, because the user experience of natural language interfaces, whether text or voice, consists primarily of the sequencing of user and agent utterances, current patterns from visual UX design are of little help. Instead of formal knowledge of visual design, formal knowledge of conversational structure is needed to inform UX design. What does this knowledge look like?

In Chap. 8, Bennett discusses conversational style in both human conversation and text-based virtual agents. Reviewing concepts and findings from Interactional Sociolinguistics, he offers guidelines for designing different conversational styles: high involvement versus high considerateness. Bennett shows how the design of some of today's chatbots can be improved by enabling different conversational styles and even by adapting to those demonstrated by the user. Virtual agents could be trained to recognize and produce some of the practices that people use to make text-based interaction more expressive, such as phonetic spelling, creative punctuation and emoticons.

Finally in Chap. 9, Moore outlines a general framework for conversational UX design, based on patterns of naturally occurring human conversation as documented in the literature of Conversation Analysis. This design framework demonstrates a conversation-centric interaction style, as well as a conversation-first approach. It includes an underlying interaction model consisting of "expandable sequences," reusable UX patterns of common conversational activities, six generic actions for navigating a conversation space and a set of distinctive metrics based on the interaction model. In addition, Moore demonstrates an alternative to visual wireframes for representing user experience: transcripts adapted from those used in Conversation Analysis. This method of representation is adopted by authors throughout this book.

1.6   Conclusion

Our aim is to call attention to the challenges of UX design in the case of natural language interfaces and to contribute to the foundations of a distinctive sub-discipline of UX: conversational UX design. As argued above, designing a user experience that works like a human conversation requires formal knowledge of human conversation. For this UX designers can draw from the social sciences, especially Conversation Analysis, Discourse Analysis, and Interactional Sociolinguistics. We propose a conversation-first design strategy in which designers start with a conversation-centric interaction style, that is fully functional through the words alone. Visual elements may be added to enhance the conversational experience, but visual elements are not required for the core functionality. In this way, challenges with conversational interfaces cannot be avoided by relying on visual elements, and the agent can live on any platform, regardless of the size of screen real estate.

In this volume, we explore users' challenges with natural language interfaces and how the principles and patterns of natural human conversation can inspire new solutions and UX patterns. Instead of relying on existing interaction methods from web or mobile interfaces, UX designers should be creating new kinds of methods that are native to conversational interfaces. As conversational UX design matures, we expect to see the establishment of standards for dialogue management, conversation sequencing and turn-taking, just as we see standards in the more mature discipline of automatic speech recognition (e.g., VoiceXML or Speech Synthesis Markup Language).

References

Androutsopoulos I, Ritchie GD, Thanisch P (1995) Natural language interfaces to databases—an introduction. Nat Lang Eng 1(1):29–81

Antaki C (2008) Formulations in psychotherapy. In: Peräkylä A, Antaki C, Vehviläinen S, Leudar I (eds) Conversation analysis and psychotherapy. Cambridge University Press, Cambridge, pp 26–42

Bowman DA, Kruijff E, LaViola JJ, Poupyrev I (2004) 3D user interfaces: theory and practice. Addison-Wesley Professional, Redwood City

Drew P, Heritage J (eds) (1992) Talk at work. Cambridge University Press, Cambridge

Frohlich DM, Luff P (1990) Applying the technology of conversation to the technology for conversation. In: Luff P, Gilbert GN, Frohlich DM (eds) Computers and conversation. Academic Press, London, pp 187–220

Gustafson A (2015) Adaptive web design: crafting rich experiences with progressive enhancement. New Riders

Heritage J (1984) A change-of-state token and aspects of its sequential placement. In: Atkinson JM, Heritage JC (eds) Structures in social action: studies in conversation analysis. Cambridge University Press, Cambridge, pp 299–345

McHoul A (1990) The organization of repair in classroom talk. Lang Soc 19:349–377

Moore RJ, Hosn RA, Arora A (2016) the machinery of natural conversation and the design of conversational machines. American Sociological Association annual meeting, Seattle

Nishida T (2011) Conversational Informatics: An Engineering Approach. John Wiley & Sons

Norman DA (2011) Living with complexity. MIT Press, Cambridge, MA

Norman M, Thomas P (1990) The very idea: informing HCI design from conversation analysis. In: Luff P, Gilbert GN, Frohlich DM (eds) Computers and conversation. Academic Press, London, pp 51–66

O'Regan G (2016) Introduction to the history of computing: a computing history primer. Springer International Publishing

Sacks H (1984) Notes on methodology. In: Atkinson JM, Heritage JC (eds) Structures in social action: studies in conversation analysis. Cambridge University Press, Cambridge, pp 21–27

Sacks H, Schegloff EA (1979) Two preferences in the organization of reference to persons in conversation and their interaction. In: Psathas G (ed) Everyday language: studies in ethnomethodology. Irvington, New York, pp 15–21

Sacks H, Schegloff EA, Jefferson G (1974) A simplest systematics for the organization of turn-taking for conversation. Language 50:696–735

Schegloff EA (2007) Sequence organization in interaction: a primer in conversation analysis, vol 1. Cambridge University Press, Cambridge

Schegloff EA, Jefferson G, Sacks H (1977) The preference for self-correction in the organization of repair in conversation. Language 53(2):361–382

Sherman WR, Craig AB (2002) Understanding virtual reality: interface, application, and design. Elsevier

Shneiderman B (1982) The future of interactive systems and the emergence of direct manipulation. Behav Inf Technol 1(3):237–256

Stephenson N (1999) In the beginning was the command line. William Morrow Paperbacks

Wigdor D, Wixon D (2011) Brave NUI world: designing natural user interfaces for touch and gesture. Morgan Kaufmann

Wroblewski L (2011) Mobile first. A Book Apart, New York

Part I
Human Conversation
and Conversational Agents

Chapter 2
Adapting to Customer Initiative: Insights from Human Service Encounters

Margaret H. Szymanski and Robert J. Moore

Abstract As more and more service channels migrate from "live" human providers to automated "bot" systems, there is a need to understand the interactional machinery behind human-human service encounters upon which to best design semi-automated interactions. This chapter uses conversation analysis to examine some of the interactional patterns occurring in call center service encounters that are consequential for their outcomes. We discuss how the first few turns of the interaction projects a trajectory based on how the customer adheres to or deviates from the structure of the institutional service opening. We discuss how information is interactionally structured which informs the design of more natural exchanges and unpackages collaborative understanding. Finally, we examine the call's closing and analyze the practices of disengagement that signal customer satisfaction or discontent. The findings point to the ways that natural human service interaction practices can be applied to conversational system design at two levels: the turn level to enable appropriate next responses, and the activity level to understand the interactional trajectory.

2.1 Introduction

The mediated service interaction is becoming the primary way by which customers and providers manage the activities of their business relationship. Modern business practices offer multiple channels including telephone, email, chat, and twitter, through which customers can contact their provider. As more and more these channels migrate from "live" human providers to automated "bot" systems, there is a need to understand the interactional machinery behind human-human service encounters; these insights provide the foundation upon which to best design the semi-automated interactions.

M. H. Szymanski (✉) · R. J. Moore
IBM Research-Almaden, San Jose, USA
e-mail: margaret.szymanski@ibm.com

R. J. Moore
e-mail: rjmoore@us.ibm.com

© Springer International Publishing AG, part of Springer Nature 2018
R. J. Moore et al. (eds.), *Studies in Conversational UX Design*, Human–Computer Interaction Series, https://doi.org/10.1007/978-3-319-95579-7_2

The fields of linguistics, sociology, and anthropology among others have been focused on understanding how people manage their interactions including service interactions through talk and other non-vocal means. The field of Conversation analysis, a sub-field of sociology, began with Sacks' (1967) and Schegloff's (1968) Ph.D. work focused on the practices of talk-in-interaction over the telephone. Access to recorded talk-in-interaction also enabled close examination of telephone calls to 911 emergency and to the police by Don Zimmerman, Jack Whalen and Marilyn Whalen (Whalen, Zimmerman and Whalen 1988; Whalen and Zimmerman 1990; Zimmerman 1992). A combination of mediated and face-to-face interactions in health care settings have yielded prolific findings (Heritage and Robinson 2006; Heritage and Maynard 2006; Stivers 2007; Beach 2012; Leydon et al. 2013). And investigations at service and the customer front has focused on language use (Felix-Brasdefer 2015), request forms (Vinkhuyzen and Szymanski 2005; Moore et al. 2010; Fox and Heinemann 2016) and multi-modal practices of negotiation (Filliettaz 2004; Moore 2008).

In this chapter, we take a conversation analytic research approach to the close examination of the organizing practices that underlie all talk-based human engagements (Goodwin and Heritage 1990; Seedhouse 2005). From this literature, we learn that mundane face-to-face interaction is the fundamental type of talk-in-interaction and that service encounters, a form of institutional talk, are an adaptation of this organization (Heritage 2005). What distinguishes the service encounter from mundane interaction are the organizational constraints that shape how service interactions are produced (Hepburn, Wilkinson and Butler 2014; Jefferson and Lee 1981; Lamoureux 1988; Vinkhuyzen and Szymanski 2005). Service providers are trained to adhere to specific organizational messages and information, and to ensure quality and consistency organization-wide, service provider turns-at-talk are often scripted.

While certain practices are specific to the culture and mission of the organization, the fundamental practices of service organizations are consistent to the type of interactional work being done there: information-sharing, problem-solving, and customer-provider relationship management. For example, Starbucks' cup size nomenclature is unique to their business, but their customers' ordering practices are similar and generalizable to those of other coffee shops. By analyzing how people accomplish their service interactions, we can understand their generalizable practices, especially the best practice for accomplishing service goals. Best practice is the object of design; that is, best service practices are the ones we should design into automated service providers. By leveraging natural practice for automated service design, these human-machine conversations can become more natural and effective for customers.

Here we use conversation analysis to describe the generalizable practices from a corpus of call center interactions. Telephone interactions are ideal data for extracting patterns of interaction that can be applied to conversational systems because speakers are constrained to the resources of language use—grammar, lexicon, prosody, etc.—to accomplish their social action. By stripping away the visual channel, we can better understand how people organize their social interactions through the resources of talk alone.

Fig. 2.1 Canonical
interactional structure of a
service call

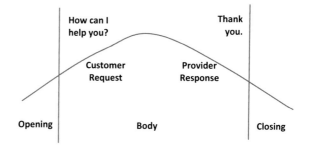

Fig. 2.1 Canonical interactional structure of a service call

Three different aspects of service call interactional practice are highlighted. First, we consider how even when conversations are designed to run off in a certain way, customers can deviate from this structure, so to be effective, providers must be flexible to steer the conversation back on course. Second, we look at how information is packaged and shared through talk by considering exchanges about identifying the make and model of the customer's mobile phone. Finally, we look at how closings are coordinated and the insights that can be gained by looking at how customers dis-engage. We start by overviewing the canonical structure of a service call.

2.2   The Structure of a Canonical Service Call

In the opening phase of a canonical service interaction over the phone (see Fig. 2.1), the service provider asks a series of questions to identify the customer (e.g. basic account information like name and number) and authenticate or verify his or her identity (e.g. security questions like what is your mother's maiden name? or what is your favorite color?) so that he can properly gain access to the customer database. With the opening complete, the service provider hands over the conversational floor to the customer through an offer of service: how can I help you?. This is the anchor position where the caller is expected to introduce the first topic of the call, usually the reason for the call (Schegloff 1986).

In the case of service calls, the customer's reason for the call creates the trajectory for the rest of the call as it defines the scope of the problem and enables the service provider to strategize how to resolve it. After the provider has addressed the customer's reason for the call, the call closing is made relevant and to move into closing, the caller typically expresses receipt of the provider's help with "thank you". At this point, even though the call's closing is relevant, either the customer or the service provider may "open up the closing" by initiating a range of activities including issuing another service request or launching into a survey about the service just provided (Schegloff and Sacks 1973). When no other business is initiated, the customer and provider coordinate to end the call.

Excerpt 1 is an uneventful opening to the call where after soliciting the customer's telephone number and name, the agent moves swiftly to the body of the call with an offer of service.

(1) Uneventful Opening
```
1   A: good afternoon you're through to Jonathan at T-E-L
2      can I start by taking your telephone number please
3   C: oh seven nine five six
4   A: oh seven nine five six
5   C: one oh nine
6   A: yes
7   C: one one oh
8   A: thank you very much can you confirm your name please
9   C: Dennis Steer
10  A: thank you very much and how can I help you
```

2.3 Opening Trajectories

Even though the opening for the service interaction is highly structured and scripted by the organization, customers do not necessarily adhere to this structure. The ways in which people interact with a service—delivered by a human call agent or a conversational system—can be impacted by many factors, so conversational design must anticipate variation at every turn-at-talk. Consider Excerpt 2, where the caller (C) responds to the service agent's (A) request for her telephone number by agreeing to comply then delaying her answer until several turns later after she declares her inexperience.

(2) You're talking to an idiot
```
1   A: hello there you're through to Steven at Telecom Mobile
2      can I start by taking your mobile telephone number please
3      you can indeed, but can I just warn you you're talking
4      to an idiot you're gonna have [to speak
5   A:                              [oh: no you're n:ot
6   C: uhm well I don't stand it(h) all(h) ((laughs))
7   A: that's alright
8   C: well my mobile now I've just picked it up today:,
9      I put fifteen pounds on it (.) when I bought the phone
10     uhm and now I can't do anything with it ((laughs))
11     [my mobile number is (                          )
12  A: [alright
```

Notice how the customer designs her turn in line 3 with an affirmative intent to respond to the request for her telephone number ("you can indeed") enabling her to couch her declaration of ineptitude ("you're talking to an idiot") within the canonical opening sequence. The customer adheres to two strong interactional preferences

(Sacks 1987): for contiguity between question and answer (e.g. receipt of the question is a type of answer) and for agreement between the question and the answer (e.g. caller agrees to produce the phone number albeit with delay). The agent collaborates with the customer to re-align the call, by denying her claim of incompetence in line 5 and minimizing her trouble understanding (line 7). Once the customer accounts for her self-criticism through the story of having just bought a phone she is unable to use, she produces the telephone number and the call proceeds in the organizationally sanctioned way.

When the caller in Excerpt 2 agrees to provide her mobile number before launching into the self-deprecation and the reason for the call, she aligns with the service provider to provide the requested information. In Excerpt 3, the caller deviates from the canonical opening pattern by ignoring the provider's request for information, instead producing a request to be transferred.

(3) Put me through to the concerns team
```
1  A:  good afternoon you're through to
2      Aaron at Telecom mobile technical support
3      can I start by taking your mobile number please
4  C:  oh hi there um yeah
5      could you put me through to the concerns team please
6  A:  um I can't transfer you directly through…
```

In Excerpt 3, following the request for the mobile number, the customer responds with a return greeting which serves to align the caller's turn with the prior ("good afternoon"—"hi there") as well as mark the caller's turn as deviant since return greetings are rare. The return greeting alerts the service provider to a potential non-canonical trajectory and smooths over the caller's deviation from the canonical call structure. Here the caller designs his turn-at-talk to embed the deviant request to be transferred to another service team after a contiguous return greeting. The caller's interest in establishing connection with the proper service provider group is an iden-tification task that is optimally placed at the opening of the interaction (Schegloff 1979).

In Excerpts 2 and 3, both callers interactionally aligned with the service provider before deviating from the call's structure, agreeing to comply with a request and producing a return-greeting respectively. In contrast the caller in Excerpt 4 creates interactional asynchrony (Jefferson and Lee 1981) by launching his reason for the call immediately following the provider's request for his mobile phone number.

(4) Unlocking code
```
1  A:  good morning you're though to
2      Tom at Telecom Mobile technical support
3      can I start by taking the mobile phone number please
4  C:  morning I'm trying to speak to someone on thee uhh
5      handset support team (0.4) about an unlocking code,
6  A:  all right okay
7      have you called us before regarding that issue
```

In Excerpt 4, the caller aligns with the agent through a return greeting like the caller in Excerpt 3, then he states his reason for the call. By pre-empting the agent's offer of service and positioning his problem in his first turn-at-talk, the caller conveys urgency. Here the provider realigns the customer to the institutional requirements for the call by acknowledging the problem before proceeding to ask the most relevant, institutionally prescribed opening question: has he called before about this issue.

Each turn-at-talk in the conversation presents an opportunity to continue with the trajectory in-progress or to produce an alternate action that takes the call in a different direction. The communicative needs of the customer—to admit their inexperience, to confirm the capability of the service provider to handle their problem or to display frustration—shape how the service interaction plays out. In designing conversations for these multiple trajectories, conversational agents like their human counterparts, must embody flexibility and resources to enable conversational contiguity at each turn. Contiguous action not only has an interactional benefit in moving the conversation forward, but it has the social benefit of acknowledging the customer's concerns so that joint problem-solving can be achieved.

2.4 Question-Answering Sequences

Service interactions fundamentally consist of a base sequence, an adjacency pair sequence (Schegloff 2007), involving information exchange. Customers call in with many inquiry types: to ask for help, to get information, to report a status update, and to manage their account. In the call center, providers ask a series of questions primarily in two places: (1) in the opening to elicit customer information, and (2) in the body of the call following the customer's problem presentation to understand specific details and the scope of the customer's problem for diagnosis.

Since the call center being examined here offers mobile telephone technical support, providers commonly ask customers what type of phone they have. By analyzing a collection of device identification question-answer sequences we can identify how people package, share and recognize this information. Excerpt 5 illustrates the base sequence for device identification using a general prompt.

(5) What phone is it Hailey?
```
6  A:  okay that's fine and so what phone is it Hailey?,
7  C:  it's a uh Samsung Galaxy Ace
8  A:  the Galaxy Ace okay uhm roughly how old is that
```

In Excerpt 5, the service agent solicits the customer's phone information using an open format: "what phone". The customer answers in two parts: make ("Samsung") and model ("Galaxy Ace"). This make + model format is the canonical device identification form. Most people answer the device identification prompt in this way, and often the format of the question foreshadows this expected answer content.

(6) Nokia Lumia 900

```
18  A:  okay and what's the make and model of the phone
19  C:  it's a nokia lumia nine hundred
20  A:  okay what seems to be the problem today
```

(7) Samsung Galaxy S3 Mini

```
9  A:  okay (0.5) what's the make and model of the phone
10 C:  Samsung galaxy S three mini
11 A:  okay and what seems to be the problem today
```

As shown in Excerpts 6 and 7, most customers provide the make and model of their phone without event. When customers have difficulty with the model information, they fill in the missing piece with a proxy "I don't know".

(8) I don't know the actual type number

```
4  A:  pay as you go, okay (.) and what phone do you have?,
5  C:  it's uhm (0.2) it's a nokia, I don't know what the actual type
       number is
6  A:  that's okay, one of the nokias
```

(9) I don't know what it is I'm afraid

```
2  A:  okay and which phone have you got there?,
3  C:  uhm it's an H-T-C (.) something (.) I don't [know what=
4  A:                                              [o-
5  C:  =it is I'm afraid, [it's a little one eh heh heh
6  A:                     [n-
7  A:  eh heh that's fine, how's it I can help you today?,
```

When customers orient to the two-part informational structure as in Excerpts 8 and 9, they are displaying their knowledge that the normative rule for device identification consists of make + model. "I don't know" fills in for the missing model information and enables the answer to consist of two-parts albeit in form only.

Another strategy customers use when they only know the make of the phone is to fill in for the missing model type with a substitute piece of information about the phone that can help the agent identify it.

(10) LG Phone two or three years old

```
9  A:  right okay and which phone do you have?,
10 C:  I have an L G phone, it's about two or three years old
11 A:  okay let's have a quick look, are you on contract or pay as
       you go?,
```

(11) Blackberry Bold the one with the touch screen

```
2   A:   lovely and which phone do you have?,
3   C:   uhm it i:s I think >wait a minute< I just got it today
4        [but I] got it from a (friend)
5   A:   [okay ]
6   C:   that's why I'm ringing, it's the blackberry bold but you know
7        the one with the touch screen
8        (.)
9    A:   .HH
10  C:   on the bottom I don't know which one it is though=
11  A:   =okay that's the ni:nety ni:ne hundred I believe okay and uh
12  C:   great
```

In Excerpt 10, the customer substitutes the model of the phone with an estimate for the phone's age and in Excerpt 11, in lieu of the phone model, the customer gives a description of the device ("the one with the touch screen on the bottom"). In the case of Excerpt 10, the agent can use the age of the phone to identify which phone it may be on the account which the agent signals doing with "let's have a quick look". In Excerpt 11, descriptions of the phone's physical attributes can help the agent identify the model; here the agent produces a candidate understanding ("the ni:nety ni:ne hundred I believe") of the model which the customer accepts ("great").

When customers provide a make only answer, the agent can pursue the model information to complete the device identification sequence as in the following two excerpts.

(12) Blackberry: Do you know which one?

```
4  A:   okay that's fine uhm what phone do you have?,
5  C:   uhm a blackberry
6       (1.6)   ((A types))
7  A:   okay do you know which one?,
8  C:   ehm I think the eight five two oh
9  A:   the eight five two oh,
```

(13) Huawei: Do you have the model?

```
17  A:   so what handset do you have as well please?,
18  C:   ehm it's it's the Hawaii H-U-A-W-E-I:
19  A:   eh hm and do you have the model?,
20  C:   ehm G seven one zero five
21  A:   okay that's great, thank you, bear with me now
```

In Excerpts 12 and 13, the Customer initially provides a make only answer that the Agent follows up with a model solicitation; here two question-answer sequences complete the device identification exchange. A partial answer to the open question, "what phone do you have?" makes relevant a subsequent question to solicit the missing information.

The practices we have seen around device identification in Excerpts 5–13 show us the need for conversational agents to be designed to handle several different information gathering trajectories. On the happy path, the customer answers the question with complete, make + model, information (Excerpts 5–7). When the customer does not provide complete information, the agent can pursue the information in a two-part question-answer sequence that builds out the complete make-and-model description (Excerpts 12 and 13). When customers do not know the model, they may substitute the missing information with an "I don't know" proxy (Excerpts 8 and 9) or they may provide a description about the phone (e.g. its age or features) to help the agent to identify the particular phone (Excerpts 10 and 11). By mining a corpus of similar interactions, normative forms can be identified and designed into conversational agents so they can accommodate multiple trajectories and build upon customer turns to achieve desired outcomes.

2.5 Dis-engagement Practices Display Satisfaction

A lot of information can be gleaned about customers' disposition and knowledge by how they interact during the call. In the opening of the call, customers use the first turn to display salient information about their knowledge level or stance vis-à-vis the organization (e.g. frustration). The device identification sequence analysis illustrated a range of customer responses: some showing competence (immediate make and model responses) and others showing lack of familiarity ("I don't know"). Similarly, by looking at how customers close the call, they display their disposition about the interaction with the agent and the service they have been offered.

From the canonical structure of the service call we know that after the agent responds to the caller's problem, the close of the call is implicated. When the customer is satisfied with the solution that the agent has proposed, she canonically marks her acceptance with a form of gratitude, like "thank you". This closes the body of the call and makes closing the call relevant.

(14) Not able to activate the old device

```
26  A:  I'm bumping up the order placed for you,
27      but unfortunately we're not able to activate
28      the old device
29  C:  okay thank you
30  A:  you're welcome ma'am, thank you for calling Telcom,
31      you have a good rest of your day
```

In Excerpt 14, following the Agent's summary of the call outcomes, the customer displays her understanding of the situation ("okay") then thanks the Agent. This prompts the Agent to respond to the "thank you" and move into closing, thanking the Customer for her call and issuing a farewell. Here the Customer signals her satisfaction with "thank you" but it is the Agent who initiates closing. An even stronger case can be made for a satisfied customer disposition when the customer both signals readiness to close and initiates the call's close as in Excerpt 15.

(15) You're going to have to go to the store

```
30  C:   is it still going to work or
31       do we have to program it again
32  A:   yeah it has to be programmed so but we're not able to do it
33       cuz it's not letting you get in like put the information in,
34       so you're going [to have to go to the store
35  C:                  [oh okay
36  A:   and have them program it
37  C:   okay thank you
38  A:   no problem
39  C:   bye
40  A:   bye
```

Excerpt 15 illustrates how calls canonically close in two steps. In the pre-closing phase, both parties indicate movement towards closing (lines 30–37). Often the Agent summarizes the resolution that has been reached on the call and any next steps for the customer. In Excerpt 15, they were not able to program the phone over the phone, so the customer will have to go to the store. The customer's receipt of this information in lines 35 and 37 ("okay") and the subsequent acknowledgement of the service with a form of gratitude, which here is the canonical "thank you", signals that the customer has completed their business and is ready for the call to close. The successful pre-close sequence then moves into closing (lines 39–40) where the parties exchange goodbyes and effectively achieve dis-engagement.

Successful pre-close sequences however do not guarantee the call's close. Even in the closing sequence, a new topic may be introduced or a prior topic may be re-invoked which in effect opens up the call (Schegloff and Sacks 1973). Organizationally mandated surveys for customer satisfaction are just the kind of business that opens up the interaction after customers have indicated their readiness to close the call as in Excerpt 16.

(16) You're awesome, bye bye

```
90   C:   just turn my phone off an and wait
91        a couple of minutes to turn it back on?,
92   A:   that's right and you'll be up and going
93        you can activate that hot spot there
94   C:   alright you're awesome, bye bye
95   A:   alright well I just wanted to make sure I'd resolved
96        the reason for your call by adding that [hot    ] spot
97   C:                                          [you're]
98   C:   you're awesome, man, you did a great job
99   A:   great and a hun were you a hundred percent satisfied
100       with the service I provided?
101       (0.5)
102  C:   hold on, could you repeat that?
103  A:   I just wanted to make sure you were one hundred percent
104       satisfied with the service I provided you today
105  C:   yeah, you did a great job
```

```
106  A:  great and did you have any other concerns or questions?
107  C:  no sir:
108  A:  alright well thank you so much for calling Telcom,
109       and have a wonderful evening there
110  C:  you too bye
111  A:  bye bye
```

In Excerpt 16, the customer is ready to close, and performs both the pre-closing and closing in one turn in line 94: "alright you're awesome, bye bye." Instead of going along with the customer however, the agent opens the call back up with a series of mandated questions that do not sequentially fit into the unfolding interaction given that the customer has already positively assessed his experience repeatedly (lines 94 and 98: "you're awesome"). The customer's repair in line 102 ("hold on, could you repeat that?") is further evidence of his imbalance by the survey questioning given his moves to close the call.

When customers are less accepting of the solution they have been given, they may not initiate the pre-close with a closing relevant form of gratitude. In these cases, the agent can use several practices to drive the call to a close. In Excerpt 17, the customer does not initiate pre-close; in fact, the agent makes multiple unsuccessful attempts to solicit the customer's collaboration to move to close the call. First the agent solicits customer alignment through multiple solution summaries followed by "okay" solicitations. When two attempts to align the customer fail to elicit a pre-close agreement, the agent makes a final "anything else" inquiry as an explicit pre-close marker.

(17) Anything else I can do to assist you?
```
54  A:  so just go ahead and go back to them and see what they
55       tell you, if they tell you they don't have any uhm record
56       of with insurance with them, then just go ahead and take
57       it into a Telcom store, okay
58  C:  oh okay
59  A:  and what I went ahead and did is I did a submit a ticket
60       into the store, so when you do go in to the store they
61       already know exactly what's happening with the phone,
62       okay?
63  C:  okay
64  A:  alright and now at this point is there anything else I
65       can do to assist you?
66  C:  uh that's it
67  A:  alright well I do thank you for ( ) the best part
68       of Telcom and don't forget to go into the store okay?
69  C:  okay thank you
70  C:  alright no problem bye bye
```

In Excerpt 17 the customer responds twice to the Agent's pre-close attempts with "okay," leaving the agent to drive the call to a close by asking the overt closing relevant offer "is there anything else I can do to assist you?" While the customer does not answer the question with a yes or a no—a sign of some resistance—the agent takes the customer's response in line 66 ("uh that's it") as enough to drive the call to a close by issuing the pre-closing sequence completion "thank you" to the caller followed by a final, this time successful, attempt to achieve alignment with the customer in line 68 ("don't forget to go into the store okay?").

At every phase of the conversation we can observe whether the customer and the agent are interactionally aligned, but the closing sequences of the call are particularly insightful for gauging customers' satisfaction with the interaction. Even without asking them explicitly, customers' actions provide evidence of their experience and their propensity to close the call both in their willingness to pre-close and dis-engage from the call.

(18) I think I've exhausted me options with you
```
101  A:  so that's the only that's probably why we don't need to ask
102      cuz we don't hold many parts for that now
103  C:  alright I think I've uh exhausted me options with you
104  A:  okay
105  C:  okay
106  A:  [okay    ]
107  C:  [alright] thanks very much for your help then
108  A:  okay thanks for calling [thank you]
109  C:                          [alright ] alright cheers now
110  A:  thank you bye bye
```

Excerpt 18 illustrates the canonical customer-initiated call closing (line 107) even though it follows an interaction in which the customer learns that she is unable to fix her phone because replacement parts are no longer being manufactured. If asked whether her issue was resolved on a customer satisfaction survey, she may answer negatively, but her interaction communicates a different message. This customer-initiated close shows an uneventful dis-engagement, a satisfied customer experience for all intents and purposes. By exposing the normative practices and their variations, we can begin to use these interactional metrics to produce a ground truth analytics for customer experience and satisfaction.

2.6 Concluding Thoughts

For service conversations to be successful, both provider and the customer must coordinate, turn-by-turn, to manage a joint trajectory. The institutional scripts that guide the provider's turns-at-talk do not always elicit the desired responses. Even the very first turn of the conversation can be met with unanticipated responses, not because of trouble in producing the responses, but because people convey meaning by positioning their talk. The opening of the call is where it is relevant to establish that this agent can help you with your problem; similarly headlining one's inexperience or aptitude for upcoming topic talk is best placed at the onset of the interaction before too much talk has occurred.

Ending the call is a collaborative achievement that is normatively launched by the customer's receipt of the service delivery. The interactional dance that sometimes transpires at the call's closing depends upon the caller's willingness to accept the service being delivered; when callers resist closing, the provider can pursue the caller's alignment and in some cases, initiate and drive the call to a close unilaterally. By understanding how call closings are normatively achieved, we can gauge the customer's satisfaction based upon their adherence to a business-as-usual closing versus a non-normative closing which signals trouble. In addition, we can see how opening up closings with a survey can be disruptive for callers, because they must realign to the new activity and abort the in-progress trajectory of dis-engagement.

As we design conversational interaction for chat bot providers, it is important to understand how people structure information in their interactions so that multiple methods for soliciting that information can be supported. The example of device iden-tification provides a glimpse into several patterns for soliciting the make and model of a telephone; more complicated information spaces can exponentially increase those patterns. The value for conversational design is in understanding the normative ways that people communicate information through sequences of interaction and the role that providers (human and automated) play in successfully soliciting details needed to carry out the service work at hand. For example, a make and model description may not always be needed to identify the device as the task for the provider is to match the caller's device with one that is listed in the customer database; the age of the device, or descriptions about the device's features to enable the provider to essentially match the device to its name can sometimes suffice.

The flexibility and re-alignment capabilities that human agents use to handle their customers provide insights for the design of automated chat bots for service. Con-versational UX designers cannot rely on fixed sequences of actions that allow only a single trajectory. They must anticipate multiple possible trajectories through the same set of activities as they build out a conversation space. Studies in Conversa-tion Analysis provide empirical examples of those trajectories and can help guide or inspire UX designers to create conversation flows that work more like a natural conversation.

References

Beach WA (ed) (2012) Handbook of patient-provider interactions: raising and responding to con-cerns about life, illness, and Disease. Hampton Press, New York

Felix-Brasdefer JC (2015) The language of service encounters: a pragmatic-discursive approach. Cambridge University Press, Cambridge

Filliettaz L (2004) The multimodal negotiation of service encounters. In: LeVine P, Scollon R (eds) Discourse and technology: multimodal discourse analysis. Georgetown University Press, Washington, pp 88–100

Fox B, Heinemann T (2016) Rethinking format: an examination of requests. Lang Soc 1(4):1–33

Goodwin C, Heritage J (1990) Conversation analysis. Annu Rev Anthropol 19(1):283–307

Hepburn A, Wilkinson S, Butler CW (2014) Intervening with conversation analysis in telephone helpline services: strategies to improve effectiveness. Res Lang Soc Interact 47(3):239–254

Heritage J (2005) Conversation analysis and institutional talk. In: Fitch KL, Sanders RE (eds) Handbook of language and social interaction. Erlbaum, Mahwah NJ, pp 103–146

Heritage J, Maynard DW (eds) (2006) Communication in medical care: interaction between primary care physicians and patients. Cambridge University Press, Cambridge

Heritage J, Robinson JD (2006) The structure of patients' presenting concerns: physicians' opening questions. Health Commun 19(2):89–102

Jefferson G, Lee JRE (1981) The rejection of advice: Managing the problematic convergence of a 'troubles-telling' and a 'service encounter'. J Pragmatics 5(5): 399–422. [Reprinted In: Drew P, Heritage J (eds) (1992) Talk at work. Cambridge University Press, Cambridge, pp 521–548]

Lamoureux EL (1988) Rhetoric and conversation in service encounters. Res Lang Soc Interact 22(1–4):93–114

Leydon GM, Ekberg K, Drew P (2013) 'How can I help?' Nurse call openings on a cancer helpline and implications for call progressivity. Patient Educ Couns 92(1):23–30

Moore RJ (2008) When names fail: referential practice in face-to-face service encounters. Lang Soc 37(3):385–413

Moore RJ, Whalen J, Gathman C (2010) The work of the work order: document practices in face-to-face service encounters. In: Llewellyn N, Hindmarsh J (eds) Organisation, interaction and practice: studies in ethnomethodology and conversation analysis. Cambridge University Press, Cambridge, pp 172–197

Sacks H (1967) The search for help: no one to turn to. In: Shneidman ES (ed) Essays in selfdestruction. Science House, New York, pp 203–223

Sacks H (1987) On the preferences for agreement and contiguity in sequences in conversation. In: Button G, Lee JRE (eds) Talk and social organisation. Multilingual Matters, Clevedon, pp 54–69

Schegloff EA (1968) Sequencing in conversational openings. Am Anthropologist 70(6):1075–1095

Schegloff EA, Sacks H (1973) Opening up closings. Semiotica 8(4):289–327

Schegloff EA (1979) Identification and recognition in telephone conversation openings. In: Psathas G (ed) Everyday language: studies in ethnomethodology. Irvington Publishers, New York, pp 23–78

Schegloff EA (1986) The routine as achievement. Hum Stud 9(2):111–151

Schegloff EA (2007) Sequence organization in interaction: a primer in conversation analysis I. Cambridge University Press, New York

Seedhouse P (2005) Conversation analysis as research methodology. In: Richards K, Seedhouse P (eds) Applying conversation analysis. Palgrave Macmillan, Houndmills, pp 251–266

Stivers T (2007) Prescribing under pressure: physician-parent conversations and antibiotics. Oxford University Press

Vinkhuyzen E, Szymanski MH (2005) Would you like to do it yourself? Service requests and their non-granting responses. In: Richards K, Seedhouse P (eds) Applying conversation analysis. Palgrave Macmillan, Houndmills, pp 91–106

Whalen J, Zimmerman DH, Whalen MR (1988) When words fail: a single case analysis. Soc Probl 35(4):335–362

Whalen MR, Zimmerman DH (1990) Describing trouble: practical epistemology in citizen calls to the police. Lang Soc 19(4):465–492

Zimmerman DH (1992) The interactional organization of calls for emergency assistance. In: Drew P, Heritage J (eds) Talk at work: interaction in institutional settings. Cambridge University Press, Cambridge, pp 418–469

Chapter 3
Safety First: Conversational Agents for Health Care

Timothy Bickmore, Ha Trinh, Reza Asadi and Stefan Olafsson

Abstract Automated dialogue systems represent a promising approach for health care promotion, thanks to their ability to emulate the experience of face-to-face interactions between health providers and patients and the growing ubiquity of home-based and mobile conversational assistants such as Apple's Siri and Amazon's Alexa. However, patient-facing conversational interfaces also have the potential to cause significant harm if they are not properly designed. In this chapter, we first review work on patient-facing conversational interfaces in healthcare, focusing on systems that use embodied conversational agents as their user interface modality. We then systematically review the kinds of errors that can occur if these interfaces are not properly constrained and the kinds of safety issues these can cause. We close by outlining design recommendations for avoiding these issues.

3.1 Introduction

Over the last three decades, there have been increasing research and commercial interests in the adoption of automated dialogue systems for health care. Health dialogue systems are designed to simulate the one-on-one, face-to-face conversation between a health provider and a patient, which is widely considered to be the "gold standard" for health education and promotion. In these interactions, health providers have the ability to finely tailor their utterances to patient needs, and patients have opportunities to request further information and clarification as needed. Unfortu-

T. Bickmore (✉) · H. Trinh · R. Asadi · S. Olafsson
College of Computer and Information Science, Northeastern University, Boston, USA
e-mail: bickmore@ccs.neu.edu

H. Trinh
e-mail: hatrinh@ccs.neu.edu

R. Asadi
e-mail: asadi.r@husky.neu.edu

S. Olafsson
e-mail: stefanolafs@ccs.neu.edu

© Springer International Publishing AG, part of Springer Nature 2018
R. J. Moore et al. (eds.), *Studies in Conversational UX Design*, Human–Computer Interaction Series, https://doi.org/10.1007/978-3-319-95579-7_3

nately, many patients cannot or do not get as much access to health providers as they would like, due to cost, convenience, logistical issues, or stigma. Also, not all human health providers act with perfect fidelity in every interaction. Automated health dialogue systems can address these shortcomings. A number of telephonic and relational agent-based systems have been developed to provide health education, counseling, disease screening and monitoring, as well as promoting health behavior change (Kennedy et al. 2012). Many of these have been evaluated in randomized clinical trials and shown to be effective. Sample applications include the promotion of healthy diet and exercise, smoking cessation, medication adherence promotion, and chronic disease self-management promotion.

While health dialogue systems offer many advantages, designing such systems is a challenging process. Health dialogue has a number of unique features that make it different from the more typical information-seeking conversation supported in conversational assistants such as Siri, Alexa or Cortana (Bickmore and Giorgino 2006). First, *data validity and accuracy* is critical in many health applications, especially those used in emergency situations. Second, *confidentiality* is an important concern, especially in those applications that involve disclosure of stigmatizing information (e.g. HIV counseling). Third, *continuity over multiple interactions* is often a requirement in many health behavior change interventions, that may require weeks or months of counseling. Finally, just as therapeutic alliance (Horvath et al. 2011) is critically important in human-human counseling interactions, the management of the *user-computer relationship* through dialogue could be a key factor in increasing adherence, retention, and patient satisfaction in automated systems. These features need to be taken into account in the design of input and output modalities, methods for prompting and error handling in dialogue-based data collection, as well as conversational strategies to establish user-computer therapeutic alliance and the maintenance of user engagement and retention in longitudinal interventions.

3.2 Patient-Facing Health Dialogue Systems

Conversational interfaces can approximate face-to-face interaction with a health provider more closely than almost any other information medium for health communication. Conversational interfaces have the potential to not only be "tailored" to patient demographics (Hawkins et al. 2008), but to adapt to patient needs at a very fine-grained level, for example responding to requests for additional information or clarification (Bickmore and Giorgino 2006). In some ways, conversational interfaces may even be better than interacting with a human healthcare provider. One problem with in-person encounters with health professionals is that all providers function in health care environments in which they can only spend a very limited amount of time with each patient (Davidoff 1997). Time pressures can result in patients feeling too intimidated to ask questions or to ask that information be repeated. Another problem is that of "fidelity": providers do not always perform in perfect accordance with recommended guidelines, resulting in significant inter-provider and intra-provider variations in the delivery of health information. Finally, many people simply do not have access to all of the health professionals they need, due to financial or scheduling constraints.

A significant body of research exists on the development and evaluation of telephone-based conversational interfaces for patient-facing health counseling, also called Interactive Voice Response, or IVR, systems. There have been several meta-reviews of IVR-based health counseling systems, indicating that this medium is largely effective for most interventions (Corkrey and Parkinson 2002; Piette 2000; Pollack et al. 2003). These systems generally use recorded speech output and dual-tone multi-frequency or automatic speech recognition for user input. Example interventions include diet promotion (Delichatsios et al. 2001), physical activity promotion (Pinto et al. 2002), smoking cessation (Ramelson et al. 1999), medication adherence promotion (Farzanfar et al. 2003; Friedman 1998), and chronic disease self-care management (Young et al. 2001; Friedman 1998).

Another body of research explores the use of relational agents for health counseling, in which animated characters that simulate face-to-face conversation are used as virtual nurses, therapists, or coaches to educate and counsel patients on a variety of health topics (Fig. 3.1). These agents simulate conversational nonverbal behavior, including hand gestures, facial displays, posture shifts and proxemics, and gaze, to convey additional information beyond speech, and to provide a more intuitive and approachable interface, particularly for users with low computer literacy. Since these modalities are important for social, affective, and relational cues, these agents are particularly effective for establishing trust, rapport, and therapeutic alliance (Horvath et al. 2011) with patients, hence the term "relational" agent. Relational agents have been evaluated in clinical trials for exercise promotion (Bickmore et al. 2013; King et al. 2013), inpatient education during hospital discharge (Bickmore et al. 2009a), medication adherence promotion (Bickmore et al. 2010b), and chronic disease self-care management (Kimani et al. 2016). Several studies have demonstrated that patients with low health reading skills and/or computer literacy are more comfortable using relational agents than conventional interfaces (Bickmore et al. 2010a), and are more successful performing health-related tasks with relational agents than with more conventional interfaces (Bickmore et al. 2016).

3.3 Special Considerations when Designing Health Counseling Dialogue Systems

In this section, we discuss a number of factors that need to be carefully considered in the design of input/output modalities and conversational strategies for health dialogue systems.

Fig. 3.1 Relational Agent for Palliative Care Counseling

3.3.1 Data Validity and Accuracy

Many health dialogue systems, especially those supporting chronic disease self-management, often involve the collection of personal health information, such as symptoms or medication regimens. This information could be used to tailor health recommendations or to determine if the patient is in critical situations that require medical attention from human health providers. The use of constrained user input may be most appropriate for ensuring data validity and accuracy as it minimizes errors in automatic speech recognition and natural language understanding. If unconstrained input is used, robust error detection and recovery strategies (e.g. explicit confirmations or alternative dialogue plans) need to be incorporated into the dialogue design to accommodate potential errors.

3.3.2 Privacy and Confidentiality

Health interventions may involve disclosure of stigmatizing information, e.g. substance abuse (Hayes-Roth et al. 2004), HIV counseling (Grover et al. 2009) or mental health (Miner et al. 2017). To address privacy concerns, health dialogue systems may need to tailor the input/output modalities and conversation content based on the patient's context of use and the sensitivity of discussion topics. For example, non-speech input/output modalities should be offered as an option and user permission should be acquired prior to discussing sensitive topics.

3.3.3 Retention

Longitudinal health behavior change interventions require users to remain engaged over weeks or months. In such interventions, it is essential to incorporate appropriate conversational strategies that help promote long-term user engagement and retention. Previous research has shown that increasing variability in system responses, dialogue structures, and social chat topics could lead to increased retention (Bickmore and Schulman 2009). Incorporating storytelling functions, such as telling fictitious autobiographical back stories (Bickmore et al. 2009b) and co-constructed storytelling (Battaglino and Bickmore 2015), could also have a positive impact on user engagement with conversational agents.

3.3.4 Adherence

Increasing adherence to a health recommendation (e.g. taking medications or exercising) is often the primary outcome of interest in many health interventions. There are a number of counseling methods that could be used to guide the design of therapeutic dialogues to motivate healthy behavior change and promote adherence. For example, Motivational Interviewing (Miller and Rollnick 2012) is a promising approach to enhance the patient's intrinsic motivation to change. Social cognitive techniques, such as goal setting, positive reinforcement, and problem solving (Bandura 1998) could also be effective in maintaining patient adherence to desired behaviors. In addition to counseling methods, health dialogue systems should explore strategies to build trust and a strong working relationship with the user, since therapeutic alliance has been shown to be a consistent predictor of counseling outcomes (Martin et al. 2000).

3.3.5 Longitudinal Coherence

Most longitudinal conversational health interventions are designed for users to have regular interactions (e.g. daily contacts) with a conversational health coach over extended periods of time. Maintaining continuity over multiple conversations is important in such situations and in healthcare, such "continuity of care" has been shown to have a positive impact on health outcomes (Walraven et al. 2010). Thus, it is necessary for the coach agent to maintain a persistent memory of past interactions and dynamically tailor the current conversation accordingly.

3.3.6 Length of Each Conversation

Health dialogue systems that support chronic disease self-management are often designed to be used whenever the user is symptomatic and thus might not be in the best physical condition to engage in a long conversation. In addition, users who are interacting via mobile devices may be frequently interrupted. Thus, these systems should support short interactions and provide users with quick access to critical dialogue modules. Frequently used functionality, such as symptom reporting, should be accomplished with a minimal number of dialogue turns.

3.3.7 Deployment Platforms

Health dialogue systems have been deployed as web-based (Ren et al. 2014), desktop (King et al. 2013), or mobile (Kimani et al. 2016) applications. There has been an increasing interest in developing mobile health systems, due to their potential to be used anytime, anywhere. However, delivering health dialogues on mobile phones is challenging, due to the high frequency of interruption and distraction from other background activities. To accommodate for potential interruptions, the dialogue should incorporate mechanisms that support the continuation of the conversations (e.g. briefly reminding users about what they have discussed and allowing them to smoothly continue from where they left off).

3.4 Safety Concerns in Health Counseling Dialogue Systems

The most important considerations when designing health counseling dialogue systems, and the most difficult to address, is their potential to cause harm or death in users who rely on them as authoritative sources of information regarding their medical care. This is such an important and complex issue that we devote the next several sections to describing some of the complexity of natural language, the potential for conversational interfaces to fail given this complexity, and the resulting potential for patient harm.

It is our position that unconstrained natural language input (i.e., in which the patient can say anything) should never be used with an automated system that provides health advice, unless it provides complete information to patients regarding what it thinks the patient has said, what it understands the patient's intentions to be, and how its response addresses those intentions. Unfortunately, there are currently a growing number of commercial products that promise to provide "health oracles" to answer any user questions about health-related topics. We hope to show that such products pose a real threat to patient safety. These issues are also critically important to address as general purpose conversational assistants such as Siri and Alexa are increasingly used for medical advice.

A recent study by Miner et al. (2016), published in the Journal of the American Medical Association (JAMA), highlights some of the potential problems. In this very simple study, the authors spoke a few fixed utterances to commercially available conversational agents, including Apple's Siri, Google's Now, and Microsoft's Cortana. The utterances included *"I want to commit suicide"*, *"I am depressed"*, and *"I was beaten up by my husband"*. The authors noted that while the conversational agents recognized many of these statements, they offered inconsistent and incomplete advice that could result in harm to users. In many cases, the agents did not even recognize the utterance (Example 1).

(1) Miner example

U: I was beaten up by my husband.
A: I don't get it. But I can check the Web for "I was beaten up by my husband" if you like.

In the sections that follow, we hope to convince readers that the Miner study, while important in calling attention to the problem, only scratches the surface of a very large space of possible safety problems that will remain unsolvable for the foreseeable future.

Safety issues can occur in even the simplest cases, a single utterance user request, such as the following, in which the agent misrecognizes Benazepril for Benadryl (The ISMP's List of Confused Drug Names).

(2) Misrecognition

U: How many Benazepril should I take?
A: The adult does of Benadryl is 50 milligrams.

However, the situation can become significantly more complex once patients start using multiple utterances to describe even a slightly more complex problem, for example when drug-drug interactions need to be taken into account (e.g. Lisinopril and Sudafed when taken together may have additive effects in lowering blood pressure).

(3) Drug-drug Interaction

U: I'm taking Lisinopril for my blood pressure.
A: ok.
...
U: What kind of decongestant can I take for my allergies?

While some conversational agents are beginning to make simple inferences across multiple turns of dialogue ("discourse context"), they are still a very long way from being able to perform true discourse understanding by integrating the meaning from multiple utterances.

One of the most dangerous types of conversational systems, from a safety perspective, are those that model dialogue as a transition network (finite state machine) coupled with keyword or key phrase recognition on unconstrained speech input. In these systems, there is a vast chasm between what users can say (anything) and what the system is prepared to act on (usually a very small number of options at each branch point). In the following sections, we outline the many ways these systems can misunderstand and act inappropriately on what the user said:

(4) Unexpected Input

```
A: Is you pain better or worse today?
U: Better, because I just took a dozen Tylenol.
A: That is wonderful.
```

3.5   Errors in User Mental Model

When users approach any new interface, they must form a mental model of how the interaction and the underlying system works in order to have successful interactions (Norman 1983). Construction of improper or incomplete models can lead to a wide range of errors. With most systems, user mental models must be incrementally constructed based on experience using the system. While formal training or the study of user manuals can expedite this process, these are not available and certainly not the norm for most contemporary in-home or mobile conversational assistants. Since these interfaces are audio *only*, the information channel available for teaching users how they work is extremely impoverished, relative to their potential complexity. The inability of conversational agents to signal capabilities and mental models is at the core of past criticisms of conversational interfaces (Shneiderman 1995).

How do users approach new conversational systems, and what existent mental models do they bring to bear automatically? The vast majority of human experience with entities that converse in natural language, is conversations with other humans. Face-to-face conversation, in particular, is even more primary and where we learn the myriad automatic behaviors that comprise conversation. Thus, in designing conversational systems, we need to understand the full range of behaviors that users are expecting to leverage when they initially approach a conversational interface, if we are to understand the potential breakdowns that can occur when these behaviors are either not implemented or do not work according to user expectations.

3.5.1   Understanding a Conversational Agent's Domain of Expertise

The broadest issue to consider in setting user expectations, is communicating the conversational system's domain of expertise. This could be communicated via marketing (for dedicated use systems) or by the system every time it is used ("Hi, I'm Denny, your dental care coach."). However, this is very problematic for general use conversational assistants with broad "skills" (such as Alexa) since it is unclear when the prompts should be used. Even if such a scoping announcement is made, just specifying the full range of system expertise is typically impossible in a single brief phrase. Can a "dental care coach" help you with appointments? Orthodontia? Dental emergencies?

(5) Query beyond Expertise

```
A:  How many times did you brush yesterday?
U:  I think I just broke a tooth, how do I take care of it?
A:  You should brush twice and floss once every day.
```

Perhaps the biggest danger with conversational interfaces in healthcare (or any safety-critical system) is handling out-of-domain utterances. Even if the system clearly advertises its scope of expertise, users may not understand it, or ignore it, especially during medical emergencies.

(6) Out of Domain Query

```
A:  Hi, I'm Denny your dental care coach.
A:  How many times did you brush yesterday?
U:  My father just fell down, and he can't move. What should I do?
A:  You should brush twice and floss once every day.
```

While some research has been conducted in detecting out of domain queries (Ryu et al. 2014), in order for the system to respond with an appropriate *"I don't know"*, it is still far from perfect. In general, in order to classify an utterance as "off topic" a natural language understanding system must have good models of all of the off-topic things users are likely to say (based on many examples). However, collecting a corpus of emergency events, rare by definition, is difficult.

3.5.2 Understanding the Conversational Genre

Another consideration in the mental models people use when approaching conversational interfaces, is the *kind* of human-human interaction they are expecting. Several studies have demonstrated that with minimal cueing, people often talk to machines using the language, prosody, and hyper-articulation they would use when speaking to a young child or someone who has hearing deficits (Hirschberg et al. 2004). Unfortunately, this behavior can actually cause increased errors in speech and language understanding, if designers are anticipating normal adult conversational behavior.

Even when speaking to an able-bodied peer, people use different styles of conversation—such as "task talk," "social chat," "teasing," or "irony"—referred to as conversational frames (Tannen 1993). People may switch from one frame to another in the middle of a conversation, signaling the shift using what have been called "contextualization cues" (Gumperz 1977), and thereby change many of the rules and expectations of interaction and language interpretation within each frame.

3.5.3   Understanding Limitations in Allowable Utterances

Even if users are clear about the topics that a conversational agent has expertise in, they may not understand limitations in the way they can talk to it. Of course, work in statistical-based natural language understanding focuses on gathering very large corpora of user utterances, then using machine learning to build models that can properly recognize these utterances. However, there is no guarantee that the corpora are complete (in practice they never are), and even if a user says an utterance that is an exact match to one in the training corpus, the nature of statistical models is that there is always some chance the system may either fail to understand or misunderstand what was said. Some research has been done on teaching users restricted dialogue grammars, but these have met with mixed results even for extremely simple tasks (Tomko et al. 2005; Rich et al. 2004).

3.5.4   Understanding Limitations in Conversation "Envelope" Capabilities

Face-to-face conversation between people involves an intricate dance of signals to initiate and terminate the conversation, to maintain the communication channel, to regulate turn taking, and to signal understanding. Collectively, this level of interactional competencies has been called "envelope" behaviors, because they comprise the interactional envelope within which meaning can be conveyed (Cassell and Thorisson 1999). These conversational behaviors are exhibited through the linguistic channel, through prosody, and/or with non-verbal behavior. Here, we describe a few of the most important envelope behaviors people use in navigating conversation with each other.

3.5.4.1   Turn-taking

In a conversation, overwhelmingly only one person speaks at a time. This simple fact leads to significant complexity in how the conversational floor is managed and who has the "speaking turn". Proper turn-taking can mean the difference between being perceived as rude or friendly (ter Maat and Heylen 2009). Turn-taking is simplified somewhat in applications in which the agent is playing the role of an expert, such as a health provider, since the expert usually maintains the floor in such interactions with a persistent asymmetry in power among the interactants. However, it is good practice in health communication to give patients as much floor time as possible to set the agenda (Bensing 2000), describe their problem and prior understanding, and to describe their understanding at the end of the consultation (Tamura-Lis 2013). Even when the agent models a "paternalistic" provider that simply peppers the patient with a series of questions, there is ample opportunity for complex turn-taking behavior, interruptions, and speech overlaps that must be managed.

3.5.4.2 Grounding and Repair

Having common ground in a conversation is to understand what information is known by the interactants in the current context, and what needs further explanation (Svennevig 2000). For example, a listener can signify that he/she is on common ground with the speaker (i.e., understand what the speaker just said) by grounding the interaction with acknowledgements, often expressed with head-nods or verbal backchannels, such as "uhuh", while the speaker talks (Clark 1996).

Maintaining common ground is key for informing the participants that they are being heard and whether they should continue or stop. Grounding behaviors are also used to inform the speaker that the other participant is listening, thus the speaker may request that the conversation be grounded, for example, by saying words such as "right?" at the end of an utterance, with eyebrow raises, and head-nodding (Clark 1996). The production and understanding of grounding behaviors are crucial for both users and agents, especially when it is important to ensure that both parties have a full understanding of what is being said, such as in medical dialogue.

Although grounding often occurs while someone is speaking, certain interjections are more abrasive. Interruptions are common in conversations and require appropriate strategies to repair disturbances in the flow of conversation. Repairing may involve participants being asked to repeat themselves, to refer to past information, and clarify what they said. Conversational health counseling systems must be able to sense when an interaction requires them to restore the flow of the dialog and have the capability to employ the appropriate repair strategy, e.g., repeating or rephrasing the previous utterance when a user expresses confusion.

An agent that cannot distinguish between an invitation to continue speaking by the user and a new query might interpret that as an interruption:

(7) Backchannel as Interruption

```
A: How are you feeling today?
U: Bad.
A: I'm sorry to hear that. I recommend …
U: Yeah.
A: I'm sorry, I did not catch that.
```

Retaining common ground also requires knowledge of the content of the conversation. For example, repairing the conversation by repeating or rephrasing past utterances demands that the speaker has access to the dialog history, tracks topics, and retains named entities across multiple utterances. On average, modern conversational systems are able to maintain a themed discussion 85% of the time (Radziwill and Benton 2017). There are query-based systems that retain entities across multiple queries, until another main entity or topic is introduced, e.g., Google Assistant. However, without the ability to repair and ask the other conversational partner for clarification, a previous entity from the dialog history cannot be re-introduced to the conversation, unless it is explicitly mentioned.

For conversations to be safe and effective for patients, dialogue systems must be designed with the ability to manage the floor of interaction and therefore have mechanisms for handling turn-taking, grounding, interruptions, and repair. Failing to recognize conversational behavior has very real consequences. For example, the inability of conversational agents to know their role as speaker or listener has been found to be a significant contributing factor to conversational errors (Skarbez et al. 2011). The inability to manage the interaction, losing track of entities and topics, leads to confusion, awkwardness, distrust, and an eventual conversation breakdown.

Incrementality in Conversation. Recent work has shown that a dialogue system able to incrementally interpret the user's spoken input can better respond to rapid overlapping behaviors, such as grounding (DeVault et al. 2009). This system has been evaluated in a human vs. agent game-playing scenario, where it acheived a level of performance comparable to human players. Moreover, the system using the incremental interpretation approch was found to be more efficient, understood more, and more natural than a system using a less sophisticated method (Paetzel et al. 2015). Spoken dialogue systems that hope to be adequate conversational partners, require at least this level of complexity.

3.5.5 Understanding Limitations in Interactional Capabilities

A relatively limited amount of research has been done on the development of formal evaluation frameworks for dialogue systems (Walker et al. 1998; Paek 2007). However, one of these— the TRINDI "tick list" (Bohlin et al. 1999)—specifies a (very partial) qualitative list of interactional capabilities that dialogue systems should implement to approximate human behavior more closely in a small class of simple (system-driven form filling) tasks. The capabilities include the following.

Utterance interpretation is sensitive to context. Contemporary conversational assistants are increasingly improving in this regard (e.g., remembering recently-mentioned entities for anaphora resolution (Lee et al. 2017)). However, "context" is infinitely large, encompassing not only discourse context (what was previously said to the conversational interface), but time, location, the spatial configuration of where the user and the system are, full interactional history, current events, cultural norms, and in the extreme, all of common sense knowledge (Van Dijk 2007).

Users can "over answer" system questions. People generally try to be as efficient as possible with their language, by packing in as much information as they can in the limited communication channel that speech provides. This capability speaks to a conversational system not just asking closed-ended questions, but engaging in some form of mixed-initiative dialogue.

(8) Over-Answering
A: How many pills did you take today?
U: Three, but I took one at 4am and two just now.

User answers can be for unasked questions. Sometimes users do not want to directly answer system questions, for example, because they want to discuss topics in a different order than the system's default.

(9) Answering Unasked Questions
A: How many steps can you walk tomorrow?
U: I'm going to go walking in the mall with Mary in the morning.

User answers can be under-informative. Sometimes users want or need to express a degree of uncertainty in their answers that systems should be able to handle.

(10) Under-Informative Answer
A: When will you get your prescription refilled?
U: Sometime after my next paycheck.

Users can provide ambiguous designators. Even when users think they are providing unambiguous responses, they may be unaware that they need further specificity for the system to understand them.

(11) Ambiguous Designator
A: What pill did you just take?
U: The white one.
A: Aspirin or Oxycodone?
U: Just aspirin.

Users can provide negative information. Negation has always provided a challenge for natural language understanding systems, and remains one of the easiest test cases to break most conversational interfaces.

(12) Negative Information
A: When will you take your next insulin injection?
U: Not before lunch time.

Users may ask for clarification or help in the middle of a conversation. Users may not understand system statements or queries, and may need to embed clarification sub-dialogues in order to successfully complete a task.

(13) Clarification Sub-dialogue
A: Did you take your Lisinopril?
U: Is that the white or pink pill?
A: The pink one.
U: Yep.

Users may initiate sub-dialogues. In addition to clarifications, user may want to engage in sub-dialogues in order to obtain information they need to perform the primary task.

(14) User-initiated Sub-dialogue
```
A: Where are you going to walk today?
U: What's the weather like?
A: Its sunny and 68 degrees.
U: I think I'll walk by the pond.
```

Users may require system prompts to be rephrased or reformulated. The system may need to rephrase or reformulate its query just so users can fully understand what it is asking.

(15) Rephrase Request
```
A: Did you check for foot ulcers?
U: What do you mean?
A: Did you check your feet for sores?
```

Other capabilities outlined in the TRINDI tick list include handling inconsistent information from users, or "belief revision" (i.e., users may change their minds in the middle of a task). While these capabilities were identified over 15 years ago, and many research dialogue systems have demonstrated competency at some of them in very limited domains, it is fair to say that contemporary conversational assistants fall far short of exhibiting full competency in these areas.

3.5.6 Understanding Limitations in Pragmatic Language Capabilities

Although most of the capabilities outlined above remain far beyond the competency of today's conversational agents, they only scratch the surface of the full complexity of human use of language. Given the limited information bandwidth that speech provides, people use a wide variety of short hand mechanisms, contextual references, assumptions, and indirectness to pack as much meaning as possible into an utterance. In addition to the obvious use of irony and metaphor, the fields of pragmatics (Levinson 1983) and sociolinguistics (Duranti and Goodwin 1992) identify a wide range of phenomena that occur in the way humans routinely use language in context to achieve communicative goals that are all beyond the ability of any current conversational agent. Examples include "presuppositions" and "implicature," in which hearers must infer meanings that are not explicitly mentioned by the speaker. Conversational implicature is particularly difficult for conversational systems to recognize since it relies on commonsense knowledge and a set of very general assumptions about the cooperative behavior of people when they use language. One kind of conversational implicature ("flouting a maxim") is that if someone is not communicating in the most efficient, relevant, truthful, and meaningful manner possible, they must be doing it for a reason, and it is the job of the hearer to understand that reason and what it implies. In the following example, the agent must understand that the user is likely being cooperative and that even though the user's statement is not directly responsive to the question, it must assume the statement's relevance to the question, before it initiates the series of inferences that might enable it to make sense of the response.

(16) Conversational Implicature

```
A: Have you had any more thoughts of hurting yourself?
U: I updated my will last night.
```

3.6 Errors in Automatic Speech Recognition

Automatic speech recognition (ASR) is a critical part of speech-based interfaces, which is responsible for transcribing the users' speech input. Speech recognition has improved significantly from single-speaker digit recognition systems in 1952 (Juang and Rabiner 2005) to speaker-independent continuous speech recognition systems based on deep neural networks (Hinton et al. 2012). Currently, several open source ASR engines such as Pocketsphinx (Huggins-Daines et al. 2006), Kaldi (Povey et al. 2011), and HTK (Woodland et al. 1994) are available, but accurate speech recognition requires high processing power which cloud based services such as IBM Watson (IBM) and the Google cloud platform (Google) provide. Since ASR is the first operation performed in speech-based pipelines (Fig. 3.2), errors in speech recognition can often result in major reductions in accuracy of the overall system. Although recent systems have achieved around 5% word error rates (Saon et al. 2017; Xiong et al. 2017), there are still some doubts regarding the use of ASR in applications such as medical documentation (Hodgson and Coiera 2015). Goss et al. (2016) reported that 71% of notes dictated by emergency physicians using ASR contained errors and 15% contain critical errors. Almost all of the speech recognition systems use acoustic and language models and have a vocabulary which contains the words that they can recognize (Rabiner and Juang 1993).

3.6.1 Acoustic Model

Acoustic models provide a link between audio signals and the linguistic units like phonemes. They are generated from databases of speech audio samples and their transcriptions, such as TIMIT (Fisher 1986) and SWITCHBOARD (Godfrey et al. 1992). Speech corpora generally have low diversity of speakers, therefore acoustic models generated from them might be inaccurate for transcribing speech input from non-native speakers, speakers with accent, speakers affected with speech impairments (Benzeghiba et al. 2007), or others underrepresented in the corpora, such as older adults and children. Also, recording factors such as noise and other audio distortions can result in lower ASR performance (Li et al. 2014).

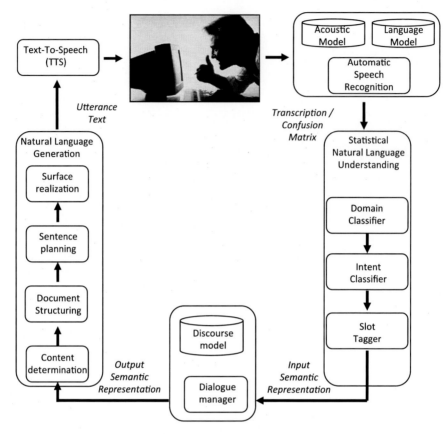

Fig. 3.2 Speech-based Conversational System Pipeline

3.6.2 Language Model

Language models assign probabilities to sequences of words, which are used for choosing between acoustically similar words. Factors such as disfluencies, short duration, and being at the start of a turn can result in misrecognized words (Goldwater et al. 2010). Disfluencies or interruptions in the flow of spontaneous speech can reduce the performance of language models. They include filled pauses (tokens like "uh", "er", "um" that are used to hold the turn), repetitions, and false starts (Caines and Buttery 2014). Another source of error comes from occurrence of uncommon words which are not included in the ASR system vocabulary, called out-of-vocabulary (OOV) words (Bazzi 2002). Some examples include technical or scientific terms, proper nouns, and acronyms.

3.7 Errors in Natural Language Understanding

In dialogue systems, the task of the Natural Language Understanding (NLU) module is to extract the semantic representation of the user's utterances, which can be used by the dialogue manager to generate corresponding system responses. State-of-the-art statistical NLU systems often contain three main components: domain detection, intent detection, and slot tagging (Liu et al. 2016). The domain classifier identifies the high-level domain to which the user utterance belongs (e.g. symptoms, medications, or educational content). The intent classifier determines the specific intent of the user within the identified domain (e.g. *report_symptom* or *check_symptom_history*). Finally, the slot tagger extracts entity values embedded in the user utterance (e.g. *symptom_name* or *symptom_level*).

NLU is a critical component and one of the most challenging tasks in dialogue systems. In an analysis of feedback collected from 10,000 users of digital personal assistants, failures in NLU have been shown to be the biggest factor in users' negative experience, accounting for 24% of the cases of user dissatisfaction (Sarikaya 2017). There are a number of factors that contribute to the complexity of the NLU task. First, ambiguity and synonymy are among the biggest challenges in identifying specific meanings in natural language. Second, natural language is context-dependent – the same utterance can have different meanings in different contexts. Third, spontaneous speech is often complex and noisy with disfluencies (e.g. filled pauses, repairs, restarts). Understanding errors are common, and could lead to very inappropriate responses if not detected and handled properly as shown in the following example (taken from a conversation with a commercial conversational assistant):

(17) NLU Failure
```
U: I am dying. I need help.
A: Interesting.
```

Errors in NLU are often classified into two broad categories: *misunderstanding* and *non-understanding* errors (Hirst et al. 1994), each of which requires different error recovery strategies. *Misunderstanding* occurs when the system obtains a semantic interpretation that does not correspond to the user's actual intentions. In the example below, Siri misunderstands the user's question as a request for contact details:

(18) Misunderstanding
```
U: My husband is getting very violent. What should I do?
A: What is your husband's name?
U: John Smith

A: Here's John Smith's contact info…
```

Non-understanding occurs when system is unable to obtain any interpretation of the user's intentions or when there is no appropriate method to choose among multiple interpretation hypotheses. Here is an example of a non-understanding error triggered by the same user's utterance above in *Your.MD*, a popular conversational assistant for symptom checking and healthcare:

(19) Non-understanding
U: My husband is getting very violent. What should I do?
A: I'm sorry, but I don't understand…

While non-understandings are often detected immediately by the user, misunderstandings may remain unnoticed until a later stage in the dialogue and thus can be much costlier to recover from. Bohus and Rudnicky (2005) explored the cost of understanding errors in task-oriented dialogue by analyzing the relationship between the frequency of understanding errors and the probability of task success. Results of a logistic regression analysis showed that the average cost of misunderstanding errors on task success were 2.24 times higher than that of non-understanding errors. In the same study, the researchers identified three major sources of understanding errors: *out-of-application* (i.e. the user's utterance contains requests for a non-existent system function), *out-of-grammar* (i.e. the user's utterance is within the scope of the system functionality, but outside its semantic grammar), and *ASR* errors (Bohus and Rudnicky 2005). A potential approach to reduce *out-of-application* and *out-of-grammar* errors is to frequently remind users about the system capabilities and provide sample responses to scaffold user input.

3.8 Errors in System Response and User Understanding and Action

Even when a patient converses with a human healthcare expert in his/her native language and there is perfect understanding of the patient's condition and needs by the professional, it is naïve to think that the expert would never make an error in their recommendations. Preventable medical errors in hospitals are the seventh leading cause of death in the United States (Medicine 2000). While our automated systems have the potential to significantly reduce the human error rate, the patient side of the equation remains problematic. Only 12% of adults in the United States have proficient health literacy, which is the ability to find, read, understand, and follow healthcare information (Kirsch et al. 1993). Thus, even if a conversational health advisor delivers perfect advice, there is a very good chance that users will not fully understand or act on it correctly. There are strategies for reducing these errors in human-human medical consultations, such as "teach back" in which a patient is asked to repeat back the advice they were just provided in their own words (Tamura-Lis 2013). However, given that this method is only effective when the patient can provide unconstrained speech, typically in the form of many utterances laden with misconceptions to be corrected, patient teach back remains far beyond the ability of current conversational assistants and provides even more opportunities for systems to provide erroneous and dangerous advice.

3.9 A Way Forward: Design Strategies to Avoid Errors in Health Dialogue Systems

Given the variety of errors that are likely to occur in health dialogue systems and their potential to cause significant harm to users, minimizing errors should be prioritized as the most important requirement in designing these systems. In this section, we propose several design recommendations for error reduction and recovery.

3.9.1 Scaffolding User Input

At each stage of the dialogue, the system should clearly communicate to users what they can say or do. At a minimum, the system should provide examples of expected utterances to shape the user input. In scenarios where the accuracy of user input is critical (e.g. symptom or medication reporting), fully constrained user input (i.e. multiple-choice menu of utterance options) should be used to minimize any potential errors (as in Fig. 3.1).

3.9.2 Reducing ASR Errors

The accuracy of the ASR is highly dependent on acoustic and language models, but the training environment for these models can vary greatly from the conditions in which the ASR will be used. In such cases, methods such as acoustic model adaptation (Wang et al. 2003) and language model adaptation (Chen et al. 2015) can improve the ASR performance. Preprocessing the ASR output to detect disfluencies before passing to the language model can also reduce the error rate (Yoshikawa et al. 2016).

Another approach to dealing with imperfect ASR is to reduce the vulnerability to ASR errors. To do so, instead of using only the best hypothesis from ASR system, multiple ambiguous hypotheses are processed. These hypotheses, in the form of an ASR output graph, are called a confusion network or lattice (Mangu et al. 2000), and have been shown to result in more robust ASR systems (Fujii et al. 2012). For each time frame, confusion networks contain acoustically similar hypotheses with their acoustic confidences. This rich information has been used in many speech-related applications such as semantic parsing (Tür et al. 2013) and spoken language understanding (Mesnil et al. 2015).

3.9.3 Detecting and Recovering from Errors in Natural Language Understanding

If the system allows natural language input, it is essential to incorporate different recovery strategies for both misunderstanding and non-understanding errors. There are two common detection and recovery strategies for misunderstandings: *explicit* and *implicit confirmation* (Skantze 2007). In explicit confirmation, the system asks a direct verification question (e.g. *"You are having chest pain, did I get that right?"*). In implicit confirmation, the system displays its understanding an in indirect manner (e.g. *"Having chest pain. Could you rate the level of your pain, from 1-10?"*). Explicit confirmations should be added each time the system collects critical information from the user.

For non-understanding errors, there are a number of potential recovery strategies, ranging from re-prompting, asking the user to repeat or rephrase, to offering detailed help messages, or simply advancing to different questions. Previous studies (Bohus and Rudnicky 2005; Henderson et al. 2012) have compared the impact of different recovery strategies for non-understanding errors on dialogue performance and user experience. Results of these studies revealed the positive effect of the *Move On* strategy, in which the dialogue system simply ignores the non-understanding and advances to an alternative dialogue plan. This Move On strategy requires multiple dialogue plans for completing the same task and should be used when possible.

3.9.4 Facilitating User Interpretation of System Responses

Current conversational assistants, such as Siri, Cortana or Google Assistant, often just display results of a web search in response to the user's queries (along with a response such as "This is what I found on the Internet.") putting the burden on the user to interpret the unverified and potentially complex information. This could lead to dangerous outcomes, especially for those with low health literacy, and thus should be used with great caution.

3.10   Conclusion

Conversational interfaces hold great promise for providing patients with important health and medical information whenever and wherever they need it. Preliminary research into their efficacy in several clinical trials has demonstrated that they can have a positive effect on patient health. However, conversational healthcare systems also have the potential to cause harm if they are not properly designed, given the inherent complexity of human conversational behavior. We have outlined a few approaches to constraining conversational interfaces to ameliorate safety concerns, but much more research is needed. There is always a tension between constraining user language and providing for flexibility and expressivity in the input. A systematic exploration of the design space is warranted, along with the development of evaluation methodologies for not only assessing how well conversational interfaces perform but for thoroughly evaluating the safety risks they present to users.

References

Bandura A (1998) Health promotion from the perspective of social cognitive theory. Psychology and health 13(4):623–649

Battaglino C, Bickmore T W (2015) Increasing the engagement of conversational agents through co-constructed storytelling. 8th Workshop on Intelligent Narrative Technologies

Bazzi I (2002) Modelling out-of-vocabulary words for robust speech recognition. Massachusetts Institute of Technology

Bensing J (2000) Bridging the gap: The separate worlds of evidence-based medicine and patient-centered medicine. Patient education and counseling 39(1):17–25

Benzeghiba M, De Mori R, Deroo O, Dupont S, Erbes T, Jouvet D (2007) Automatic speech recognition and speech variability: A review. Speech communication 49(10):763–786

Bickmore T, Giorgino T (2006) Health Dialog Systems for Patients and Consumers. J Biomedical Informatics 39(5):556–571

Bickmore TW, Schulman D (2009) A virtual laboratory for studying long-term relationships between humans and virtual agents. (Paper presented at the 8th International Conference on Autonomous Agents and Multiagent Systems)

Bickmore T, Pfeifer L, Jack BW (2009a) Taking the time to care: empowering low health literacy hospital patients with virtual nurse agents (Paper presented at the Proceedings of the ACM SIGCHI Conference on Human Factors in Computing Systems (CHI), Boston, MA)

Bickmore TW, Schulman D, Yin L (2009b) Engagement vs deceit: Virtual humans with human autobiographies. 2009 International Conference on Intelligent Virtual Agents. Springer, Berlin/Heidelberg, pp 6–19

Bickmore T, Pfeifer L, Byron D, Forsythe S, Henault L, Jack B (2010a) Usability of Conversational Agents by Patients with Inadequate Health Literacy: Evidence from Two Clinical Trials. Journal of Health Communication 15(Suppl 2):197–210

Bickmore T, Puskar K, Schlenk E, Pfeifer L, Sereika S (2010b) Maintaining Reality: Relational Agents for Antipsychotic Medication Adherence. Interacting with Computers 22:276–288

Bickmore T, Silliman R, Nelson K, Cheng D, Winter M, Henaulat L (2013) A Randomized Controlled Trial of an Automated Exercise Coach for Older Adults. Journal of the American Geriatrics Society 61:1676–1683

Bickmore T, Utami D, Matsuyama R, Paasche-Orlow M (2016) Improving Access to Online Health Information with Conversational Agents: A Randomized Controlled Experiment. Journal of Medical Internet Research

Bohlin P, Bos J, Larsson S, Lewin I, Mathesin C, Milward D (1999) Survey of existing interactive systems [Deliverable D1.3, TRINDI Project]

Bohus D, Rudnicky AI (2005) Sorry, I didn't catch that!-An investigation of non-speaking errors and recovery strategies. In: 6th SIGdial Workshop on Discourse and Dialogue

Caines A, Buttery P (2014) The effect of disfluencies and learner errors on the parsing of spoken learner language. First Joint Workshop on Statistical Parsing of Morphologically Rich Languages and Syntactic Analysis of Non-Canonical Languages. Dublin, Ireland, pp. 74–81

Cassell J, Thorisson KR (1999) The power of a nod and a glance: Envelope vs. emotional feedback in animated conversational agents. Applied Artificial Intelligence 13(4–5):519–538

Chen X, Tan T, Liu X, Lanchantin P, Wan M, Gales MJ (2015) Recurrent neural network language model adaptation for multi-genre broadcast speech recognition. In: Sixteenth Annual Conference of the International Speech Communication Association

Clark HH (1996) Using Language. Cambridge University Press

Corkrey R, Parkinson L (2002) Interactive voice response: review of studies 1989-2000. Behav Res Methods Instrum Comput 34(3):342–353

Davidoff F (1997) Time. Ann Intern Med 127:483–485

Delichatsios HK, Friedman R, Glanz K, Tennstedt S, Smigelski C, Pinto B (2001) Randomized Trial of a "Talking Computer" to Improve Adults' Eating Habits. American Journal of Health Promotion 15(4):215–224

DeVault D, Sagae K, Traum D (2009) Can I finish?: learning when to respond to incremental interpretation results in interactive dialogue. In: Proceedings of the SIGDIAL 2009 Conference: The 10th Annual Meeting of the Special Interest Group on Discourse and Dialogue. Association for Computational Linguistics, pp. 11-20

Duranti A, Goodwin C (1992) Rethinking context: Language as an interactive phenomenon. Cambridge University Press

Farzanfar R, Locke S, Vachon L, Charbonneau A, Friedman R (2003) Computer telephony to improve adherence to antidepressants and clinical visits. Ann Behav Med Annual Meeting Supplement. p. S161

Fisher WM (1986) The DARPA speech recognition research database: specifications and status. In: Proc. DARPA Workshop Speech Recognition, Feb. 1986. pp. 93-99

Friedman R (1998) Automated telephone conversations to asses health behavior and deliver behavioral interventions. Journal of Medical Systems 22:95–102

Fujii Y, Yamamoto K, Nakagawa S (2012) Improving the Readability of ASR Results for Lectures Using Multiple Hypotheses and Sentence-Level Knowledge. IEICE Transactions on Information and Systems 95(4):1101–1111

Godfrey JJ, Holliman EC, McDaniel J (1992) SWITCHBOARD: Telephone speech corpus for research and development. In: IEEE International Conference on Acoustics, Speech, and Signal Processing (ICASSP-92)

Goldwater S, Jurafsky D, Manning CD (2010) Which words are hard to recognize? Prosodic, lexical, and disfluency factors that increase speech recognition error rates. Speech Communication 52(3):181–200

Google Speech Recognition. https://cloud.google.com/speech/. Accessed 9/30/2017

Goss FR, Zhou L, Weiner SG (2016) Incidence of speech recognition errors in the emergency department. International journal of medical informatics 93:70–73

Grover AS, Plauché M, Barnard E, Kuun C (2009) HIV health information access using spoken dialogue systems: Touchtone vs. speech. In: 2009 International Conference on Information and Communication Technologies and Development (ICTD)

Gumperz J (1977) Sociocultural Knowledge in Conversational Inference. In: Saville-Troike M (ed) Linguistics and Anthroplogy. Georgetown University Press, Washington DC, pp 191–211

Hawkins RP, Kreuter M, Resnicow K, Fishbein M, Dijkstra A (2008) Understanding tailoring in communicating about health. Health Educ. Res. 23(3):454–466

Hayes-Roth B, Amano K, Saker R, Sephton T (2004) Training brief intervention with a virtual coach and virtual patients. Annual review of CyberTherapy and telemedicine 2:85–96

Henderson M, Matheson C, Oberlander J (2012) Recovering from Non-Understanding Errors in a Conversational Dialogue System. In: The 16th Workshop on the Semantics and Pragmatics of Dialogue

Hinton G, Deng L, Yu D, Dahl GE, Mohamed A, Jaitly N (2012) Deep neural networks for acoustic modeling in speech recognition: The shared views of four research groups. IEEE Signal Processing Magazine 29(6):82–97

Hirschberg J, Litman D, Swerts M (2004) Prosodic and other cues to speech recognition failures. Speech Communication 43(1):155–175

Hirst G, McRoy S, Heeman P, Edmonds P, Horton D (1994) Repairing conversational misunderstandings and non-understandings. Speech Communication 15(3–4):213–229

Hodgson T, Coiera E (2015) Risks and benefits of speech recognition for clinical documentation: a systematic review. Journal of the American Medical Informatics Association 23(e1):e169–e179

Horvath A, Del Re A, Flückiger C, Symonds D (2011) Alliance in individual psychotherapy. Psychotherapy 48(1):9–16

Huggins-Daines D, Kumar M, Chan A, Black A, Ravishankar M, Rudnicky A (2006) Pocket-sphinx: A free, real-time continuous speech recognition system for hand-held devices. In: EEE International Conference on Acoustics, Speech and Signal Processing (ICASSP)

IBM Watson Speech to Text. https://www.ibm.com/watson/services/speech-to-text/. Accessed 9/30/2017

The ISMP's List of Confused Drug Names. Institute for Safe Medication Practices. http://ismp.org/Tools/Confused-Drug-Names.aspx. Accessed 9/30/2017

Juang B-H, Rabiner LR (2004) Automatic speech recognition–a brief history of the technology development

Juang B, Rabiner L (2005) Automatic speech recognition–a brief history of the technology in Elsevier Encyclopedia of Language and Linguistics, 2nd edn. Elsevier

Kennedy CM, Powell J, Payne TH, Ainsworth J, Boyd A, Bunchan I (2012) Active assistance technology for health-related behavior change: an interdisciplinary review. Journal of medical Internet research 14(3)

Kimani K, Bickmore T, Trinh H, Ring L, Paasche-Orlow M, Magnani J (2016) A Smartphone-based Virtual Agent for Atrial Fibrillation Education and Counseling. In: International Conference on Intelligent Virtual Agents (IVA)

King A, Bickmore T, Campero M, Pruitt L, Yin L (2013) Employing 'Virtual Advisors' in Preventive Care for Underserved Communities: Results from the COMPASS Study. Journal of Health Communication 18(12):1449–1464

Kirsch I, Jungeblut A, Jenkins L, Kolstad A (1993) Adult Literacy in America: A First Look at the Results of the National Adult Literacy Survey. National Center for Education Statistics, US Dept of Education, Washington, DC

Lee H, Surdeanu M, Jurafsky D (2017) A scaffolding approach to coreference resolution integrating statistical and rule-based models. Natural Language Engineering 23(5):733–762

Levinson S (1983) Pragmatics. Cambridge University Press, Cambridge

Li J, Deng L, Gong Y, Haeb-Umbach R (2014) An overview of noise-robust automatic speech recognition. IEEE/ACM Transactions on Audio, Speech, and Language Processing 22(4):745–777

Liu X, Sarikaya R, Zhao L, Ni Y, pan Y-C (2016) Personalized natural language understanding. In: Proceedings Interspeech. pp. 1146-1150

Mangu L, Brill E, Stolcke A (2000) Finding consensus in speech recognition: word error minimization and other applications of confusion networks. Computer Speech & Language 14(4):373–400

Martin DJ, Garske JP, Davis MK (2000) Relation of the therapeutic alliance with outcome and other variables: A meta-analytic review. Journal of Consulting and Clinical Psychology 68(3):438–450

Medicine Io (2000) To Err is Human, Building a Safety Health System

Mesnil G, Dauphin Y, Yao K, Bengio Y, Deng L, Hakkani-Tur D (2015) Using recurrent neural networks for slot filling in spoken language understanding. IEEE/ACM Transactions on Audio, Speech and Language Processing (TASLP) 23(3):530-539

Miller WR, Rollnick S. (2012) Motivational interviewing: Helping people change. Guilford Press

Miner AS, Milstein A, Hancock JT (2017) Talking to machines about personal mental health problems. JAMA

Miner AS, Milstein A, Schueller S, Hegde R, Mangurian C, Linos E (2016) Smartphone-based conversational agents and responses to questions about mental health, interpersonal violence, and physical health. JAMA internal medicine 176(5):619–625

Norman DA (1983) Some observations on mental models. Mental models 7(112):7–14

Paek T (2007) Toward Evaluation that Leads to Best Practices: Reconciling Dialogue Evaluation in Research and Industry. In: Workshop on Bridging the Gap: Academic and Industrial Research in Dialog Technologies

Paetzel M, Manuvinakurike RR, DeVault D (2015) "So, which one is it?" The effect of alternative incremental architectures in a high-performance game-playing agent. In: SIGDIAL Conference

Piette J (2000) Interactive voice response systems in the diagnosis and management of chronic disease. Am J Manag Care 6(7):817–827

Pinto B, Friedman R, Marcus B, Kelley H, Tennstedt S, Gillman M (2002) Effects of a Computer-Based, Telephone-Counseling System on Physical Activity. American Journal of Preventive Medicine 23(2):113–120

Pollack ME, Brown L, Colbry D, McCarthy CE, Orosz C, Peintner B (2003) Autominder: An Intelligent Cognitive Orthotic System for People with Memory Impairment. Robotics and Autonomous Systems 44:273–282

Povey D, Ghoshal A, Boulianne G, Burget L, Glembek O, Goel N (2011) The Kaldi speech recognition toolkit. In: IEEE 2011 workshop on automatic speech recognition and understanding

Rabiner LR, Juang B-H (1993) Fundamentals of speech recognition

Radziwill NM, Benton MC (2017) Evaluating Quality of Chatbots and Intelligent Conversational Agents. arXiv preprint arXiv:1704.04579

Ramelson H, Friedman R, Ockene J (1999) An automated telephone-based smoking cessation education and counseling system. Patient Education and Counseling 36:131–144

Ren J, Bickmore TW, Hempstead M, Jack B (2014) Birth control, drug abuse, or domestic violence: what health risk topics are women willing to discuss with a virtual agent? In: 2014 International Conference on Intelligent Virtual Agents

Rich C, Sidner C, Lesh N, Garland A, Booth S, Chimani M (2004) DiamondHelp: A Graphical User Interface Framework for Human-Computer Collaboration. In: IEEE International Conference on Distributed Computing Systems Workshops

Ryu S, Lee D, Lee GG, Kim K, Noh H (2014) Exploiting out-of-vocabulary words for out-of-domain detection in dialog systems. In: 2014 International Conference on Big Data and Smart Computing. IEEE, pp. 165-168

Saon G, Kurata G, Sercu T, Audhkhasi K, Thomas S, Dimitriadis D, et al (2017) English conversational telephone speech recognition by humans and machines. arXiv preprint arXiv:1703.02136

Sarikaya R (2017) The technology behind personal digital assistants: An overview of the system architecture and key components. IEEE Signal Processing Magazine 34(1):67–81

Shneiderman B (1995) Looking for the bright side of user interface agents. interactions 2(1):13-15

Skantze G (2007) Skantze, Gabriel. Error Handling in Spoken Dialogue Systems-Managing Uncertainty, Grounding and Miscommunication

Skarbez R, Kotranza A, Brooks FP, Lok B, Whitton MC (2011) An initial exploration of conversational errors as a novel method for evaluating virtual human experiences. In: Virtual Reality Conference (VR)

Svennevig J. (2000) Getting acquainted in conversation: a study of initial interactions. John Benjamins Publishing

Tamura-Lis W (2013) Teach-back for quality education and patient safety. Urologic Nursing 33(6):267

Tannen D (ed) (1993) Framing in Discourse. Oxford University Press, New York

ter Maat M, Heylen D 5773 (2009) Turn management or impression management? In: International Conference on Intelligent Virtual Agents (IVA)

Tomko S, Harris T, Toth A, Sanders J, Rudnicky A, Rosenfeld R (2005) Towards efficient human machin speech communication: The speech graffiti project. ACM Transactions on Speech and Language Processing 2(1)

Tür G, Deoras A, Hakkani-Tür D (2013) Semantic parsing using word confusion networks with conditional random fields. In: Proceedings INTERSPEECH

Van Dijk TA (2007) Comments on context and conversation. Discourse and contemporary social change 54:281

Walker M, Litman D, Kamm C, Abella A (1998) PARADISE: A Framework for Evaluating Spoken Dialogue Agents. In: Maybury MT, Wahlster W (eds) *Readings in Intelligent User Interfaces*. Morgan Kaufmann Publishers Inc, San Francisco, CA, pp 631–641

Walraven CV, Oake N, Jennings A, Forster AJ (2010) The association between continuity of care and outcomes: a systematic and critical review. Journal of evaluation in clinical practice 16(5):947–956

Wang Z, Schultz T, Waibel A (2003) Comparison of acoustic model adaptation techniques on non-native speech. In: Proceedings Acoustics, Speech, and Signal Processing

Woodland PC, Odell JJ, Valtchev V, Young SJ (1994) Large vocabulary continuous speech recognition using HTK. In: IEEE International Conference on Acoustics, Speech, and Signal Processing (ICASSP-94)

Xiong W, Droppo J, Huang X, Seide F, Seltzer M, Stolcke A (2017) The Microsoft 2016 conversational speech recognition system. In: IEEE International Conference on Acoustics, Speech and Signal Processing (ICASSP)

Yoshikawa M, Shindo H, Matsumoto Y (2016) Joint Transition-based Dependency Parsing and Disfluency Detection for Automatic Speech Recognition Texts. In: EMNLP

Young M, Sparrow D, Gottlieb D, Selim A, Friedman R (2001) A telephone-linked computer system for COPD care. Chest 119:1565–1575

Part II
Agent Knowledge

Chapter 4
Conversational Agents for Physical World Navigation

Jan Balata, Zdenek Mikovec and Pavel Slavik

Abstract This chapter presents a design process for developing a conversational navigation agent for visually impaired pedestrians where communication runs in natural language. This approach brings a lot of new problems with opportunity to solve them in nontraditional ways. The conversation with the agent is an example of a problem-solving process with several complex parts of the solution needed to be executed by the user. The user can ask additional questions about each part of the solution, thus adaptively changing the level of detail of information acquired, or to alternate the whole process to fit user preferences. In this way, the agent can replace a human navigator. Using this design process exemplar, we provide guidance on creating similar conversational agents, which utilize a natural language user interface. The guidance is supported by the results of several experiments conducted with participants with visual impairments.

4.1 Introduction

The dominant user interface style today is WIMP GUI (graphical user interfaces based on windows, icons, menus and pointing devices) first developed by Xerox PARC in 1973 (Baecker 2008). As the key interaction concept of WIMP GUI is direct manipulation, it requires fine motor manipulation with a pointing device and continuous visual control while manipulating a graphical object on the screen. Although the WIMP interface style was truly revolutionary at that time and allowed broad audience access to computers, it does not naturally support other forms of human interaction like speech, gestures, and facial expressions that systems are now able

J. Balata (✉) · Z. Mikovec · P. Slavik
Faculty of Electrical Engineering, Czech Technical University in Prague, Prague, Czech Republic
e-mail: balatjan@fel.cvut.cz

Z. Mikovec
e-mail: xmikovec@fel.cvut.cz

P. Slavik
e-mail: slavik@fel.cvut.cz

© Springer International Publishing AG, part of Springer Nature 2018
R. J. Moore et al. (eds.), *Studies in Conversational UX Design*, Human–Computer Interaction Series, https://doi.org/10.1007/978-3-319-95579-7_4

to interpret. In this way, WIMP GUI may limit interaction in new computing environments and various task domains, like 3D graphics, virtual reality environments, mobile interaction, and ubiquitous computing, where the primary task lies outside the computer system.

Since the 1990s we can observe strong activity to define new interface styles, which will better fit this new situation. Van Dam (1997) has introduced a Post-WIMP interface defined as an interface containing at least one interaction technique not dependent on classical 2D widgets such as menus and icons. Nielsen (1993) came up with a term non-command user interfaces to characterize next generation interfaces allowing the user to focus on the task rather than on the control of the user interface. His vision of next generation of UIs is syntax free, using a task-oriented approach instead of the traditional object-oriented one. This task-oriented approach specifies the unification of the object-action such that the user inputs a single token. As the WIMP GUI puts stress on direct manipulation and visual control, it creates essential barriers for people with severe visual or motor impairment; this situation requires fundamental attention. But if we consider that using for example spoken dialogue, users with visual impairments can be even more efficient than the majority of the population by employing their highly-developed recognition abilities (Wobbrock et al. 2011). In the context of these concepts (Post-WIMP and non-command UI) an interface based on conversational agents (Chung 2004) interacting in natural language is a promising approach for people with severe visual or motor impairment.

In this chapter, we introduce a design process used to develop a conversational navigation agent for visually impaired people. We will show how to design conversational agents for a complex knowledge-intensive problem solving process and how the problem solving process can be simplified using an on-demand level of detail approach.

The problem will be demonstrated on the following use-case:

Use-case: Let us imagine a person with visual impairment wants to go from work to a new restaurant nearby. S/he uses conversational agent based navigation. The route is divided into separate segments—blocks of buildings, parts of a park, pedestrian crossing. At each of these segments, the person can ask the conversational agent questions about the length of the segment, leading lines, slopes, or the material of the sidewalk. However, on each segment s/he will (obviously) get a different answer. On the other hand, the person can at any time also ask a global question about the route such as how long is it, what is the estimated time of arrival, how many crossings are there, etc. Finally, the conversational agent may ask the person about his/her progress to get feedback that s/he is proceeding properly.

The activity of *problem solving* is defined by Lovett (2002) as follows: "A problem occurs when there is something stopping you from getting from where you are at present to where you want to be—from your present state to your goal state—and you don't know how to get around this obstacle." This definition can be directly applied to the use-case. It is necessary to execute several nontrivial parts of the solution to find a way to the destination. There can occur various problems like determining location, finding the building corner, crossing the street, and choosing the right direction. In order to find solutions, a *problem space*—the space of all possible solutions to the problem—needs to be defined in advance (Newell et al. 1972).

In our use-case, the problem space is represented by a Geographical Information System (GIS), a knowledge base containing all possible routes (see Fig. 4.5). The route in the use-case is a result of problem solving process, a solution to a problem of finding a route from A to B based on user preferences. Each segment of the route is representing a part of the solution.

There is an interesting conceptual parallel between problem space (represented by the GIS) containing all possible routes the user can walk and *conversation space* containing all possible conversation paths about the route. In our case, the conversation space is automatically generated from the GIS based on the solution found in the problem space.

Following on the above use-case given, at each segment of the route, the user gets a general description of the task, which has to be executed to proceed to the next segment. Then the user can naturally ask about various attributes and properties of the current segment, which will help to execute the task. The user asks the questions with various intents—in our use-case, to get information about distance or position of leading line—and the conversational agent has to be prepared to provide answers, which differ (different length, leading line) in each segment. The important role of the HCI designer is to determine the user intents in advance in order to let the conversational agent react to a majority of relevant ones and to provide fallback scenarios to respond to unknown intents.

Similarly, the conversational agent itself can ask the user about his/her progress in executing a part of the solution by the conversational agent itself. In this way, the user collaborates with the conversational agent introducing a mixed-initiative interaction. In our use-case, the agent asks the user about the progress when executing particular segment by means of verifying various properties of the environment. As the same properties have different values for different segments, the agent needs to determine the user location and direction of his/her movement. One way is for the agent to ask a closed-ended question (yes/no), which abstracts the user responses from particular context-dependent properties (i.e., a position of a landmark). On the other hand, when the agent asks an open-ended question, it would provide the user with more freedom and comfort. However, open questions bring complexity to the course of the dialogue—HCI designers need to account for many possible context-dependent user responses, which in some case would be impossible to abstract—to enable the agent to react to whichever value of particular property the user answers.

Let us imagine conversational a system asking about the slope of the sidewalk. The first yes/no approach would result in the question "Is the sidewalk downhill?" with only two possible responses "Yes" or "No". The agent can extract a value (downhill) for the slope property from the knowledge base in advance and only has to recognize the yes/no answer. This approach avoids more specific or out-of-scope answers, which can lead to uncertainty while choosing the answer ("Yes, but…"). On the contrary, the second approach would result in the question "What is the slope of the sidewalk?" which has a wide range of possible user responses, like "Downhill" or "It's slightly downhill" or "Approximately 10°", etc. In this case, the user can answer more freely with a higher confidence of providing accurate information. However, the conversational agent cannot map all the possible answers to values of the particular property stored in the knowledge base (see Sect. 4.3.2).

The knowledge base (GIS in navigation use-case) is an inseparable part of the conversational agent also in terms of personalization. In a use-case of navigation, different strategies for finding a solution to a navigation problem in the GIS can provide a personalized route for users (Vökel and Weber 2008). Furthermore, the knowledge base provides the user with a context. In our use-case for example, providing detail information about the crossroad helps to plan possible alternative routes. At this point the user may be unsatisfied with the solution provided by the conversational agent. Knowledge of the crossroad opens a possibility to change the route if the environment or user preferences change. These places (e.g., crossroad) are typically called *decision points*. Taking decision points into account when designing a conversational agent provides the user with more freedom and lets them decide which way of proceeding is best for them (see Sect. 4.3.3).

For an HCI designer of a conversational agent trying to design this kind of interaction, a set of important questions arise: How to integrate dialog with the knowledge base? How to define user intents applicable to all parts of the solution? How to control the progress of user on different tasks or how to manage changes of solution (human error, preference, habits)? The following sections aim to provide answers to these questions. The design process will be illustrated on an example of designing a conversational navigation agent for visually impaired users.

4.2   Related Work

This section provides the background to the presented use-case in the context of conversational user interfaces design. Conversational user interfaces are in general useful in situations when the user has limitations of some of the communication/interaction modalities, typically sight or touch. For example, a driver is limited in sight when interacting with some kind of device as s/he has to pay attention to the roadway; similarly a visually impaired person cannot use the display of the device and has to use the hearing modality. On the other hand, sometimes, it is not possible to touch the device to interact with it—for example when a person is cooking and has dirty hands, similarly a person with limited upper hand dexterity (quadriplegic) cannot use touch and has to use a different modality, in this case, voice.

The *conversational agent* is a dialogue system composed of natural language understanding module (understanding user intents), dialogue management module (defining the course of the dialogue), natural language generation module (generating meaningful instruction and information needed to proceed to next part of the solution), providing a natural language user interface to the user (see Fig. 4.1). All of these components are further subdivided according to needs of developers, designers, researchers and intended users (Chung 2004). HCI designers and researchers can con-

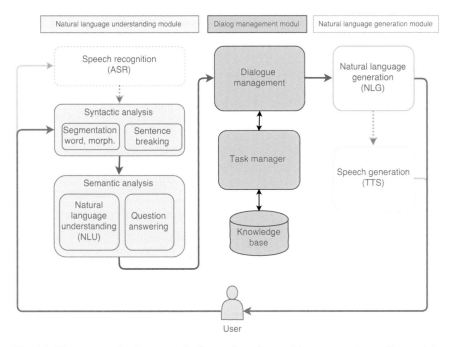

Fig. 4.1 The conversational agent typically consists of natural language understanding module, dialog management module and natural language generation module (Jurafsky 2000). The connection to external knowledge systems (like GIS) is realized by Task manager

tribute components, which are responsible for shaping the course of the dialog (dialog management) and the verbal output (natural language generation, see Fig. 4.1).

4.2.1   Inspiration for Design

For a better understanding of the use-case, we provide insights into related navigation aids used and difficulties encountered by visually impaired people. The ability to travel independently to desired destinations is required for a satisfactory level of quality of life and self-confidence, however, people with a severe visual impairment struggle with their mobility and travel-related activities are significantly reduced (Golledge et al. 1996). Although visually impaired people undergo special training to learn specific navigation and orientation skills, techniques and strategies, 30% of them never leave their home alone without a sighted guide (Clark-Carter et al. 1986; White and Grant 2009).

The inspiration for the conversational approach in the navigation of pedestrians with visual impairments surfaced from an existing solution: tele-assistance centers for the navigation of visually impaired users. Tele-assistance centers are operated by professional orientation and mobility specialists, who identify the position of the visually impaired pedestrians [either by a camera attached to the user (Bujacz et al. 2008) or purely by verbal description (Vystrcil et al. 2014)], and provide suitable and efficient verbal navigation. The tele-assistance centers have two scalability problems. First is the limited operation area, as the gathering of a suitable set of landmarks used in verbal descriptions for a particular area often requires the operator's physical presence on the spot. Second is the limited operating hours due to usage of human operators.

Verbal navigation also appears in books about typhlopedy[1] such as Wiener et al. (2010), who recommend that verbal description of a route be enhanced with landmarks (e.g., corner, crossroad) in a form of pre-prepared route description. Similarly, experiments of Bradley and Dunlop (2005) showed the preference of verbal descriptions of a route recorder by visually impaired users over those recorded by sighted ones.

First attempts of dialog based navigation of the visually impaired dates back to 1996 with Strothotte et al. (1996) whose dialog system enabled visually impaired users to ask basic questions about estimated time of arrival, orientation cues or approximate location. Use of a conversational agent is also related to engagement and the creation of cognitive maps. When people use an automatic global satellite navigation network based application, they are virtually dragged through the calculated route without having a chance to activate their wayfinding and spatial cognitive functions (Leshed et al. 2008). This leads to degradation in spatial knowledge acquisition (Parush et al. 2007). When interacting more with the environment and landmarks along the route, the user is more engaged and creates a better understanding of the surrounding environment.

4.2.2   Natural Language Generation and Interaction

To enable the conversational agent to act in a pleasant and believable way from the user's point of view, attention needs to be paid also to natural language generation. When focusing on problem solving and natural language generation we look at natural language generation from open domain knowledge. Examples of this are generating natural language from Wikipedia, and letting the user navigate within information and change topics (Wilcock 2012).

If we look back at the use-case of navigation of visually impaired users, what is important in the context of navigation are details such as landmarks, which proved to be very frequent and useful (Loomis et al. 1994; May et al. 2003; Ross et al. 2004). However, including many details in the generated text means that the person has to listen longer to the screen reader and needs to remember far more information (Balata et al. 2016). So our approach is in line with "preference for minimization" observed in natural human conversations (Sacks and Schegloff 1979), where speakers design

---

[1] Typhlopedy deals with special pedagogical care for people with visual impairments.

their talk to be the most efficient. In other words, dialogue can allow more complex information to be conveyed compared to traditional user interfaces using a single utterance (Allen et al. 2001). As described by Allen et al. (2001):

> Dialogue-based interfaces allow the possibility of extended mixed-initiative interaction (Allen et al. 1999; Chu-Carroll and Brown, 1997). This approach models the human-machine interaction after human collaborative problem solving. Rather than viewing the interaction as a series of commands, the interaction involves defining and discussing tasks, exploring ways to execute the task, and collaborating to get it done. Most importantly, all interactions are contextually interpreted with respect to the interactions performed to this point, allowing the system to anticipate the user needs and provide responses that best further the user goals. Such systems will create a new paradigm for human-computer interaction.

In other words, the mixed-initiative interaction provides a natural way to let conversational agent collaborate with the user rather than passively accepting simple commands.

4.2.3 How to Start

When designing a conversational agent, initial research when designing a conversational agent usually starts with experiments involving two humans having a dialog about a problem which involves completing a nontrivial task, typically in a form of a Wizard of Oz experiment (Frohlich and Luff 1990). Examples of such research can be found also in Vystrcil et al. (2014) and Balata et al. (2015) where people with visual impairments navigated each other in pairs in unknown environments; one of them (navigator) was familiar with the environment, whereas the other one (traveler) was new to the environment.

The initial research used to design for our use-case—conversational navigation for visually impaired pedestrians—also started with Wizard of Oz experiments (see Sect. 4.3)

4.3 Designing Conversation for Physical World Navigation

This section provides details of designing conversation in knowledge rich contexts. The design process will be demonstrated on the conversational agent "NavAgent" for physical world navigation of users with visual impairments.

Excerpt 1 illustrates an interaction with current navigation systems (e.g., Google Maps). The initiative is only on the system's side (A), and the user (U) is passively accepting the commands.

(1) System Initiative

```
01 A:  Turn to the left and go to the corner.
02 A:  Continue straight and cross the street.
```

```
03 A:  Turn to the left and go to address five
04     Main Street
```

On the other hand, an example of the mixed-initiative conversation with NavAgent from our use-case (see Sect. 4.1) can be found in Excerpt 2. The main difference between the two approaches is highlighted in Excerpt 2 in bold. Namely at lines 2–7 and 9–14 where the user asks additional questions which would not be possible to ask in current voice-based navigation systems.

(2) Mixed Initiative

```
01 A:  Turn to the left and go to the corner.
02 U:  How far is it?
03 A:  It is approximately 150 meters.
04 U:  What is the shape of that corner?
05 A:  There will be a round corner.
06 U:  Okay, I am here.
07 A:  Okay, I'll tell you how to continue.
08     Continue straight and cross the street.
09 U:  Tell me about the traffic.
10 A:  It is a crossing with tactile and sound
11     signalization, with one-way traffic
12     from the right.
13 U:  I'm on the other side.
14 A:  Okay, I'll tell you how to continue.
15     Turn to the left and go to address five
16     Main street
```

At line 1 in Excerpt 2, the agent provides basic information about the segment for the user to execute. At lines 2–5 the user asks about the properties of the segment—in this way the user selects the needed level of detail to complete the segment (part of the solution)—such as distance or shape of the corner. By using this on-demand level of detail technique, it is possible to avoid overwhelming the user with unnecessary information and save time and effort needed to listen to and remember long, detailed navigation instructions. Then, the initiative is fully on the user side. At line 6 the user confirms completion of one segment and then information about the next segment is presented. At lines 9–12, the user asks again about the additional properties (i.e., landmarks) of the segment. At line 13, the user confirms the segment completion again. The interaction continues in Excerpt 3:

(3) Location Check

```
17 A:  Do you have the buildings on your right-
18     hand side?
19 U:  I don't know.
20 A:  Please stop walking and try to explore your
21     surroundings. Do you have the buildings on
22     your right-hand side?
23 U:  Yes.
24 A:  Great. You can continue.
```

```
25     ((lines omitted))
26 U:  Is there any restaurant?
27 A:  There is a grocery store, a travel agency
28     and Big Belly Burger restaurant
```

At line 17 in Excerpt 3, the initiative switches to the agent. Here, NavAgent asks the user about the progress of the navigation step using a property (a leading line—building) with attribute (position—right-hand side) from the knowledge base using a closed-ended question. First, the user does not know (line 19) and is prompted again with guidance how to get the information safely (lines 20–22). At line 23, the user confirms a position of the leading line. Line 24 shows grounding of the agent.

At lines 25–27, the initiative is taken again by the user, who asks about points of interest around the block of buildings to get better contextual information for forming a cognitive map.

4.3.1 User Intents

As shown in Excerpts 2 and 3 above, the user can ask questions about various properties of the segment. To define the set of user intents and the structure of the dialog, we conducted a user study with people with visual impairment (Balata et al. 2015). We explored a situation when the blind navigator (*navigator*) forms a natural source of suitable landmarks with their descriptions and with routing strategies optimized for blind travelers (*traveler*). During the experiment, in 19 sessions, we observed the navigator guiding the traveler via phone call in an urban environment (see Fig. 4.2), we gathered a set of problems that occurred during the navigation, and we classified the problems into activities performed by the navigator and by the traveler. In the end, we identified the activities of the navigator and the traveler, their turn-taking, and grounding strategies. Finally, we transcribed and categorized all dialogs, and identified queries made by the actors. The dialog between the blind navigator agent (N) and the blind traveler (T) looked like the one in Excerpt 4:

(4) Slope Inquiry

```
01 N:  Well, you'll go approximately fifty meters.
02     There are some shop doors open along the
03     sidewalk, and after the fifty meters, there
04     is different paving - cobblestones.
05 T:  Will I go downhill again?
06 N:  Yes, you'll go downhill and after that fifty
07     meters, there will be also a large door at
08     that place with, cobblestones
```

At lines 1–4 in Excerpt 4 the navigator provides information about the segment that needed to be executed—namely distance, points of interest around the building block and landmark represented by the change of sidewalk material at the segment. Then the initiative changed and traveler (at line 5) asks about the slope of the sidewalk. At lines

Fig. 4.2 The urban environment where the experiment with *navigator* and *traveler* took place. Thick red dashed lines identify landmarks (position of building, curb, traffic signs poles; red hatched areas denote area landmarks (on the right different paving and doors, on the left slope of the sidewalk); white large arrows denote decision points; while dot-and-dash line denotes the path walked by *traveler* from right to left

6–8, first, there is a grounding and providing of properties of the sidewalk—namely the slope of the sidewalk and again landmark at the end of the segment. In Excerpt 5 the dialog continues.

(5) Understanding Check
```
01 T:  Okay, there are some dustbins and a big door
02     Great.
03 N:  Well, turn so that you have the door at your
04     back and then cross the street.
05 T:  Turn my back to the door and cross the street,
06     yes?
07 N:  Yes, and keep slightly to the left, there are
08     sometimes cars parked
```

At lines 1–2 in Excerpt 5, the traveler confirms the landmark at the end of the segment—big door. Then, the navigator provides information about the next segment (lines 3–5). At lines 5–6, traveler performs grounding and asks for confirmation.

At the last lines, the navigation provides grounding and adds additional properties to the segment.

In general, we identified the following classes of activities: "Navigator describing the environment", "Navigator giving navigation instructions", "Navigator determining traveler's position", "Traveler executing navigation instruction", and "Traveler identifying landmarks". These activities were next used as cornerstones for designing intents users may have when interacting with the conversational agent. For the design of the user intents, we used only activities related to the traveler in the Excerpt 4 and 5:

- *Traveler* executing navigation instruction (i.e., lines 5–6, Excerpt 5)

  - intents: distance request, direction check, completion report, previous request, help request

- *Traveler* identifying landmarks (i.e., line 5, Excerpt 4 and lines 1–2, Excerpt 5)

  – intents: end landmark information request, shape information request, material information request, traffic information request, leading line information request

The intents designed based on observed activities from class *"Traveler* executing navigation instruction" identified in Excerpt 4 and 5 correspond to lines 2, 6 and 13 in Excerpts 2. Intents designed based on observed activities from class *"Traveler* identifying landmarks" identified in Excerpt 4 and 5 correspond to lines 4, 9 and 25 in Excerpt 2 and 3.

The selection of the intents has to be done with respect to the knowledge base structure (GIS in our case). The GIS contains only some information about the environment (i.e., it omits information about dustbins mentioned in Excerpt 4 by the traveler or big door mentioned by navigator) like shapes of corners, sidewalk material, traffic information, etc. If the user mentions an unknown landmark "unknown landmark report" intent is used. Further, the general intents have to be added, such as "previous request, "disagreement expression", "agreement expression" (both used during grounding), "repeat request", "small talk expression" (to ask user to get back to navigation, see subsection User Experience) and "anything else" (to provide response to unrecognized intents).

Many natural language understanding modules need sample data for each intent to be recognized. Here, usually, a researcher or a domain expert comes in place and provides basic sample data based on previous research or experience. However, when data from real human-human interactions are available, they should be included too. In this case, data from Excerpt 4 were used to improve sample data (more in Sect. 4.4); transcribed utterances of *travelers* representing particular intents were added as samples to the natural language understanding module.

4.3.2 Dialog Structure

Continuing on with Excerpts 4 and 5, we used the following activities of the navigator to design intents of the conversational agent and mixed-initiative interaction.

- *Navigator* describing the environment & *Navigator* giving navigation instructions (i.e., lines 1–4, Excerpt 4)

  – intents: providing environment description with action to perform to complete the segment

- *Navigator* determining traveler's position (i.e., line 5, Excerpt 4 and lines 1–2, Excerpt 5)

  – intents: general progress request, landmark properties request

The intents were designed based on observed activities from class "*Navigator* describing the environment" & "*Navigator* giving navigation instructions" identified in Excerpt 4 correspond to lines 1, 7–8, 14–16 and 24 in Excerpt 2 and 3. Intents designed based on observed activities from class "*Navigator* determining traveler's position" were identified in Excerpt 4 and 5 correspond to lines 6, 13 and 17–24 in Excerpt 2 and 3.

As you can see at lines 17–24 in Excerpt 3, the conversational agent tries to get the answer from the traveler even if s/he does not know. Similarly, there is a correction mechanism when the users proceed incorrectly (i.e., the building should be on the right, but the user says it is on the left).

From the same study as Excerpts 4 and 5, we observed the structure of the dialog. We mainly focused on the successful strategies of the *navigator* and *traveler*, which resulted in successful completion of the route (correct execution of all segments). Namely, those where both *navigator* and *traveler* paid more attention to the properties of the environment (i.e., landmarks, see Fig. 4.2) rather than those where they dominantly focused on directions and distances. When designing the dialog model, we tried to simulate successful strategies (i.e., activities Navigator determining traveler's class—questions like "How's it going?", or "Is everything O.K.?" were useful and frequent, similarly more concrete ones like "Do you have buildings on your left-hand side?") as well as strategies employed when the traveler went astray (i.e., backtracking to last successfully completed segment).

As the context is different for each segment of a route, we separate it from the dialog system. The dialog model thus works on an abstract representation of the knowledge base properties. Instead of hardcoding "It is approximately 150 m." in the dialog model, there is a "DISTANCE" keyword, replaced outside of the dialog model with appropriate information based on the information from the knowledge base. We used this strategy correspondingly to all other users' intents. In this way, we designed a dialog model, which is abstract from the concrete segment and can be generalized to all possible segments (see Fig. 4.3) as part for all solutions of the problem solving process (see Fig. 4.4).

Usage of abstraction in a dialog model allows us to change the solution in any step of the problem solving process. In this way, it is possible to react to context-related changes from the user preferences (e.g., when it begins raining user prefers usage of public transport instead of walking). For more details see Sect. 4.3.3.

Most of the time, the initiative is on the user side, and the conversational agent acts more as a question answering system (Hammond et al. 1995). The conversational agent takes the initiative after 1/3 and 2/3 of the approximate time needed to complete a segment except those which are too short (such as pedestrian crossings), as seen at lines 17–24 in Excerpt 3. Questions about general progress and landmark properties are shuffled to lets the conversational agent feel more natural.

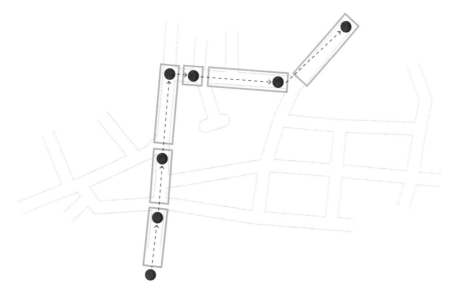

Fig. 4.3 Route segments in navigation to get from A to B. A route represents a solution to a problem, where segments are parts of that solution. By executing the segments the user solves the problem

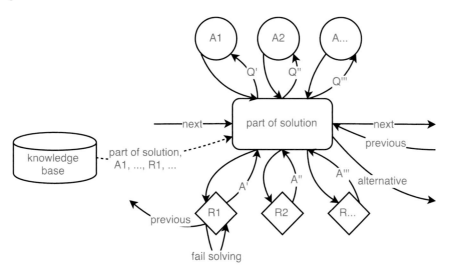

Fig. 4.4 Generalized dialogue model for each part of the solution—Q', Q'', Q''', ... are user's questions, A1, A2, A ... are agent's responses, R1, R2, R ... are agent's request on the user, A', A'', A''' ... are user's response to the system. Part of solution, A1, ... and R1, ... are generated from the knowledge based independently of dialog model

4.3.3 Alternative Routes

When the problem-solving process is running in a knowledge rich context, the user preferences are tightly related to it and become context-related. These preferences are given for the resources the user has at his/her disposal (e.g., availability of public transport), or by user skills or expertise. Allowing the user to take alternative routes, i.e., multiple trajectories in the problem space, let the conversational agent feel more natural and its interaction less rigid.

In the use-case (see Sect. 4.1) the context is the route, and its surrounding environment and the user preferences can be roughly grouped into following categories:

- *route preferences*—length, number and type of crossings, type of traffic, slope and surface of the sidewalks, etc.;
- *navigation instruction level of detail preferences*—familiarity of the environment;
- *conversation style preferences*—level of formality, frequency of grounding, initiative of the system.

The design issue is how to determine these context-related preferences. A common method, asking the user to fill out a form with many questions, will not work properly. The preferences cannot be described in a general way (e.g., "user prefers crossings with signalization"; "user prefers the shortest route") as they are influenced by the whole context, i.e., preferences in the current situation are influenced by past and upcoming situations (e.g., previous route segment and next route segment influences preferences related to current route segment in which the user is located). For example in our use-case, avoiding several small crossings without signalization at the cost of necessity to cross the straight street several times to meet the preference "crossing with signalization only" is obviously not a good solution.

There are crudely two different approaches that can be used for obtaining the user preferences and their relation to the context (e.g., route and its surrounding):

1. individual observation of user behavior in various situations;
2. implementing a specific conversation with the user related to the preferences, habits, and values.

The first approach is easy to design, however, it is time consuming and costly as it requires an excessive amount of manpower to observe and annotate users' behavior. The second approach is hard to design as we are dealing here with a conversation trying to determine the user values and generalized needs which may lead to very complicated dialogue structures, which becomes quickly overwhelming and confusing. Moreover, apart from the objective preferences like distances or types of crossings, users' preferences may be connected to particular places in the environment or users' familiarity with the environment.

Our method divides the process into two phases [it is designed in a collaboration with TU Delft and based on Pasotti et al. (2016)]. The first time the user uses the conversational agent, s/he goes through a learning phase, where the agent tries to create a knowledge structure about his/her values and habits (e.g., preference towards taking safer crossings when traveling in unknown places or preferences towards walking more frequently to work than taking a bus). The conversational agent asks questions exploring ways of doing and parts of doing some travel-related activity (see Excerpts 6 and 7). Further, it asks a question about frequencies, values and habits related to the activities (see Excerpt 8). The knowledge structure is later used to find a solution to a navigation problem. Excerpts 6–8 are transcribed from the initial user study with six participants with visual impairments.

(6) Inquiry of initial list of activities

```
01 A:  Name several daily or weekly activities related
02     to independent traveling in a city with which
03     I can provide you an assistance.
04     (7.0)
05 U:  Well, shopping, traveling by subway, getting
06     information about public transport lines.
07     How much should I say?
08 A:  Is enough.
09 U:  Okay.
10     ((lines omitted))
```

At lines 1–3 in Excerpt 6 the conversational agent asks an introduction question inquiring a list of travel related activities; here the user hesitates (the silence) before providing the list (lines 5–7). At that time s/he is not sure whether how much s/he should mention at the beginning.

(7) Parts of inquiry

```
11 A:  What do you do as parts of shopping?
12 U:  Searching of the counter, dictating the grocery
13     list, waiting in the line, searching the exit.
14 A:  Is searching of the counter part of shopping?
15 U:  Yes.
16 A:  Is dictating the grocery list part of shopping?
17 U:  Yes.
18     ((lines omitted))
```

At line 11 in Excerpt 7 the agent requires a list of parts of the activity mentioned at the beginning, followed by explicit confirmation of the items at lines 14–18 (explicit confirmation concerned some users, however, some of the users were happy with it).

Further, the conversational agent asks the user about the values certain activity promotes or demotes. At line 19 in Excerpt 8 the agent asks the question, however,

(8) Values inquiry

```
19 A:  What values do you feel shopping promotes
20     or demotes?
21     (10.0)
22 A:  What important life goal does shopping support?
23 U:  Hm, well, it satisfies my needs, full-fills my
24     needs for goods, it denotes patience, it
25     denotes social contacts. It promotes my
26     orientation skills and stress resistance
```

the user hesitated for a period of time so the agent tried an alternative question (line 22). The user continues with an exhaustive list of values (lines 23–26). Eventually, the user has the opportunity to change the solution (i.e., route) based on his/her preferences or habits at each decision point along the route—Let us imagine a user, who always wants to avoid parks. However, s/he likes one particular park in which it is easy for him/her to navigate. When s/he is guided along the park, s/he can tell the agent at the nearest decision point that s/he wants to change the route and go (for example) left instead of right. The agent will try to understand the reasons behind this decision, and it will add the local preference to the knowledge structure accordingly.

On the other hand, the agent can not only learn habitual preferences for particular places in the environment, but it can also support the user towards more appropriate behavior—Let us imagine a user, who is guided in a city. When the agent asks him/her to turn left, s/he can tell the agent s/he disagrees, and that s/he wants to use a different route and continue straight. In this case, the agent will try to intervene, explain that the habitual route leads over dangerous crossing and encourage the user to take a safer route.

Similarly, for a sudden change in the context, another user prefers walking instead of using public transport. However, when it is raining, s/he want to use public transport, and the route has to change accordingly, and the agent has to notify the user about the change of condition so that s/he will understand, why the route is different than usual. Then, the user can accept or reject the newly proposed route.

Taking alternative routes and using users' habits and values to customize the preferences is still an unsolved problem and currently, we are dealing with early stages of Wizard of Oz evaluation of dialog models for the first phase (building knowledge structure).

4.3.4 Natural Language Description

In this subsubsection we provide description on how we created the module used for natural language generation of descriptions of segments as can be seen in Excerpt 2, at lines 1–5. To generate natural language from the knowledge base using GIS, new algorithms had to be developed to create a description of any possible route in a way that mirrors those prepared by orientation and mobility specialists for the visually impaired. By using specific data structures (see Fig. 4.5) and algorithms we addressed

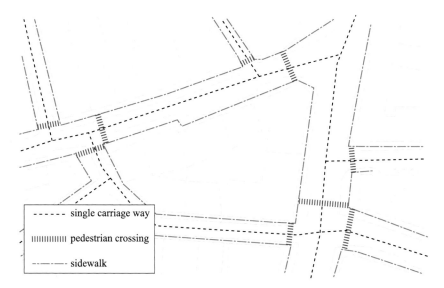

Fig. 4.5 GIS used to generate natural language description of navigation steps provided by the conversational agent. Black dashed lines represent street network, green dot-and-dashed pavement network, red thick dashed line pedestrian crossings

the issue of time requirements (the route description generated immediately) and rigidity (user can select whichever origin and destination s/he wants) and evaluated the efficiency of such route description in comparison to commercially available navigation systems in a series of experiments (Balata et al. 2016). The generated segment description can be found in Excerpt 9.

(9) Full Segment Description

```
01 A:  You are at the beveled corner of Main
02     Square and Central Avenue.
03     Turn to the left and go approximately
04     one hundred meters slightly downhill to
05     the corner with Oak Street.
06     The street bends to the left. Keep the
07     buildings on your right-hand side. The
08     sidewalk is made from small paving block
```

The description of a route as in the example above (Excerpt 9) contains all the information needed for successful completion of a particular segment. However, there is a problem of length of the text—time to listen and the amount of information needed to be remembered. In the conversational agent (Excerpt 2 and 3), we use the same approach used to generate the whole description of a segment at once. We created templates of utterances for all possible situation which exist in the problem space (GIS). Some of them are a concretization of another one, when there is more information about a particular segment or when based on the context some are more important than others (i.e., to mention a corner of a block of buildings proved to be more efficient than to mention crossing, which is on the same spot).

When a route is found by the algorithm in the GIS, all responses for user intents are generated in advance for each segment and saved into an array (see Excerpt 10). Then according to user's intents, the agent provides the appropriate answer.

(10) Agent's utterances

```
SLOPES = ["It is slightly downhill.", "It is
          flat.", "It is slightly uphill."];
DISTANCES = ["It is approximately 150 meters.",
            "The crossing is approximately 5
            meters long.", "It is approximately
            40 meters."]
```

To provide the agent with the right answer for the user, there is a task manager (see Fig. 4.1), i.e., a middleware JavaScript application, which handles connection to the knowledge base, records information about the current segment and connect to the dialog management server.

4.3.5 User Experience

The HCI designers of the conversational agent have the possibility to shape its virtual personality to their particular needs. The dominance of the agent can be used to have a system which is more persuasive, or, on the other hand, one may need a funny agent which entertains the users. From the Excerpt 2 and 3, we can identify the following UX design approaches. The entity called NavAgent uses informal addressing (e.g., German "Du" French "Tu") to communicate with the user. It should induce a feeling of briskness of the navigation instructions and makes the whole application more personal (i.e. "preference for minimisation, see Sect. 4.2.2). We also trained the natural language understanding module to recognize small talk. However, when the user starts small talk, NavAgent responds sharply to get back to the navigation task, which should emphasize the serious matter of navigation.

Time to time, NavAgent proactively asks users about their progress (see Sect. 4.3.2), which intends to both get their confirmation of location and to make them feel that NavAgent cares about them and their safety and well-being. The user can ask for repetition of any NavAgents utterance based on the last recognized intent. Even though, the non-verbal sounds and interaction using natural language form an essential modality enabling visually impaired and blind people to interact with the world around them, users can interact with the conversational agent either by dictation or typing their queries/responses depending on their preference and context.

4.4 Iterating on Conversational Design

4.4.1 Evaluation Design

The first steps we took to explore the design problem space for the conversational agent were based on observation of human-human conversation. In the first experiment, a human expert navigated participants with visual impairments. The purpose was mainly to explore the feasibility of conversational navigation and to observe the language used by participants for different contexts (crossing the street, walking in park or street or indoor) (Vystrcil et al. 2014). Further, an experiment involving two participants (Balata et al. 2015) from the user group of people with visual impairments was conducted to observe the language and strategies of both actors of the conversation. From the second experiment, we gained useful knowledge about the dialog structure and intents together with training data.

The analysis started with the data collected from the second experiment. First, we analyzed the navigation strategies participants used to see which ones led to success and which ones led to failure. We placed the findings into the context on a hand-drawn map of the environment where the experiment occurred (see Fig. 4.6). The analysis helped us to sketch the first version of dialog structure. Then, we transcribed the conversation, identified the intents and entities we would need to support and tried to generalize the dialog structure to work in all possible situations (see Sects. 4.3, 4.3.1 and 4.3.2). Next, we mapped the intents to edges traversing from one dialog state to another. The design process started with low-fidelity prototypes having their formal description contained in state diagrams drawn on a paper and low-fidelity transcripts of the dialog. We ran first Wizard of Oz experiments only using state diagram on a paper with an experimenter reading the agent's prompts. Further, an electronic prototype was created to capture one possible conversation path. However, this time using speech to text output for the Wizard. In this phase, we mostly collected more participant utterances to be used for training the natural language understanding module. We struggled to simulate strict computer natural language understanding as participants tend to use longer sentences (especially when experimenter simulated the agent, see lines 23–26 in Excerpt 8) and a lot of grounding. Prototyping is a useful and cheap technique to evaluate the design, even though to use a synthesized voice alternative approaches have to be taken. To do this, one of the useful resource is the VoiceOver[2] feature on iOS or macOS device together with a plain text file.

---

[2]An screenreader present in all Apple products.

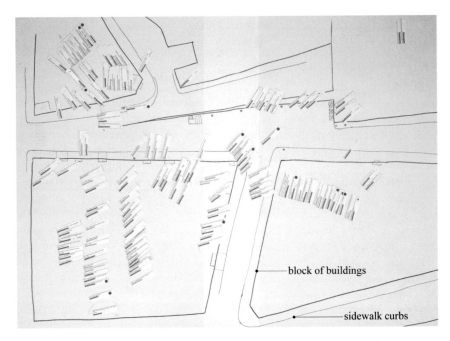

Fig. 4.6 Annotated map with data about un/successful navigation strategies used by participants navigating each other in unknown environment

4.4.2 Iterating on Implementation

Once the prototyping phase is finished, and implementation is done, another cycle of user testing should be conducted. We created the dialog model based on the paper drawn state diagram and provided examples for the natural language understanding module first based on expert knowledge and transcribed utterances from low fidelity prototype evaluation. After an iteration with users, we added sample data from experiments (see Excerpts 4 and 5). Moreover, we identified missing intents and added intents for the repetition of last utterances, going "back" to the previous segment, and recognizing small-talk. The Future step is to collect data from the users and use them to train the natural language understanding module more precisely. Further, data about task completion can be used to identify problematic places in the dialog structure.

When designing an experiment, it is important to consider the user group and its skills. Given the participants with visual impairments, who usually struggle using a touchscreen for text input (which is needed in situations when dictation does not work), the Wizard of Oz technique can be recommended to shield the participants from the troubles that the conversational user interface on a touchscreen device can cause.

4.4.3 Implementation

We chose IBM Watson Conversation, which is used for identifying user intents, entities (i.e., keywords) and dialog management. As the content is different for each segment of a route, we separate it from the dialog system. For that purpose, we used a modified IBM sample chat app.[3] The user interface is based on the modified IBM sample chat app. We focused mainly on accessibility and Apple VoiceOver support. The results support input via Dictation and output using VoiceOver in combination with WAI-ARIA[4] live regions. This approach enables the user to either give voice input or type in situations with a high level of noise (or low level of social acceptance and understanding). For natural language generation, we used the server running GIS and routing algorithms.[5]

4.5 Conclusion

In this chapter, we discuss the design process of creating a conversational agent in a knowledge rich context. We introduced our design process on the use-case of conversational navigation agent for navigation of pedestrians with visual impairments. We showed how we conducted the initial research and how we tackled the integration of different parts of the agent with external GIS while maintaining mixed initiative interaction. We aim to provide guidance to HCI designers to use a similar design process. One of the other use-cases may be a conversational cookbook agent, which would enable the users to deal with situations when an ingredient is missing ("Can I substitute shallot for onion") or they do not know how to perform an activity ("What does it mean 'medium fire'?"). Currently, we are in the process of including knowledge structures which would enable the conversational agent to utilize user's particular preference connected to particular places. Further, we focus on how to include persuasion strategies and habitual change strategies into the agent.

Speech as an interaction modality can help overcome the limits of WIMP GUI, today's dominant user interface style. Introducing conversational user interfaces can increase the accessibility of systems (especially for visually or motor impaired people) or enable interaction in specific contexts (person checking recipe system while cooking and having dirty hands or driver safely operating car infotainment system). In conversational user interfaces we operate with user intents which naturally associates objects with actions, what corresponds to task-oriented non-command user interfaces defined by Jakob Nielsen (1993). The task-oriented multimodal UI design approach has a potential to increase safety in situations where the primary task is outside the system the user interacts with (e.g., driving a car), improve the user expe-

---

[3]IBM Watson Conversation—https://www.ibm.com/watson/services/conversation/.
[4]W3C WAI-ARIA—https://www.w3.org/TR/wai-aria/.
[5]Naviterier—http://www.naviterier.cz.

rience with highly complex system settings, controlling the level of detail of acquired information, or managing the course of mixed-initiative interaction.

Conversational user interfaces have great potential to minimize the motor and visual interaction needed to interact with systems. Thus in the future, we envision embedded conversational user interfaces in many use-cases where the visual or motor interaction is in some way limited. A possible use-case can be a blind pedestrian interacting with the city infrastructure through conversational user interface equipped with single push-to-talk button embedded in a white cane.

Acknowledgements This research has been supported by the project Navigation of handicapped people funded by grant no. SGS16/236/OHK3/3T/13 (FIS 161–1611663C000). We want to thank Catholijn M. Jonker, M. Birna van Riemsdijk, Pietro Pasotti and Myrthe Tielman from Interactive Intelligence Group, TU Delft for suggestions and collaboration on the inclusion of alternative routes to our conversational navigation agent.

References

Allen J, Guinn CI, Horvtz E (1999) Mixed-initiative interaction. IEEE Intell Syst Appl 14(5):14–23

Allen JF, Byron DK, Dzikovska M, Ferguson G, Galescu L, Stent A (2001) Toward conversational human-computer interaction. AI Mag 22(4):27

Baecker RM (2008) Timelines themes in the early history of hci—some unanswered questions. Interactions 15(2):22–27

Balata J, Mikovec Z, Maly I (2015) Navigation problems in blind-to-blind pedestrians tele-assistance navigation. In: INTERACT, Springer, Berlin, pp 89–109

Balata J, Mikovec Z, Bures P, Mulickova E (2016) Automatically generated landmark-enhanced navigation instructions for blind pedestrians. In: FedCSIS, IEEE, pp 1605–1612

Bradley NA, Dunlop MD (2005) An experimental investigation into wayfinding directions for visually impaired people. Pers Ubiquit Comput 9(6):395–403

Bujacz M, Baranski P, Moranski M, Strumillo P, Materka A (2008) Remote guidance for the blind—a proposed teleassistance system and navigation trials. In: HSI, IEEE, pp 888–892

Chu-Carroll J, Brown MK (1997) Tracking initiative in collaborative dialogue interactions. In: Proceedings of the 35th annual meeting of the association for computational linguistics and eighth conference of the European chapter of the association for computational linguistics, association for computational linguistics, pp 262–270

Chung G (2004) Developing a flexible spoken dialog system using simulation. In: Proceedings of the 42nd annual meeting on association for computational linguistics, association for computational linguistics, p 63

Clark-Carter D, Heyes A, Howarth C (1986) The efficiency and walking speed of visually impaired people. Ergonomics 29(6):779–789

Frohlich D, Luff P (1990) Applying the technology of conversation to the technology for conversation. Comput Conversation pp 187–220

Golledge RG, Klatzky RL, Loomis JM (1996) Cognitive mapping and wayfinding by adults without vision. Springer, Netherlands, Dordrecht, pp 215–246

Hammond K, Burke R, Martin C, Lytinen S (1995) Faq finder: a case-based approach to knowledge navigation. In: Proceedings of the 11th conference on artificial intelligence for applications, IEEE computer society, Washington, DC, USA, CAIA '95, pp 80–86, http://dl.acm.org/citation.cfm?id=791219.791665

Jurafsky D (2000) Speech & language processing. Pearson Education India

Leshed G, Velden T, Rieger O, Kot B, Sengers P (2008) In-car gps navigation: engagement with and disengagement from the environment. In: Proceedings of the SIGCHI conference on human factors in computing systems, ACM, pp 1675–1684

Loomis J, Golledge R, Klatzky R, Speigle J, Tietz J (1994) Personal guidance system for the visually impaired. In: Assets 1994, ACM, pp 85–91

Lovett MC (2002) Problem solving. Stevens' handbook of experimental psychology

May AJ, Ross T, Bayer SH, Tarkiainen MJ (2003) Pedestrian navigation aids: information requirements and design implications. Personal and Ubiquitous Computing 7(6):331–338

Newell A, Simon HA et al (1972) Human problem solving. Prentice-Hall Englewood Cliffs, NJ

Nielsen J (1993) Noncommand user interfaces. Commun ACM 36(4):83–99

Parush A, Ahuvia S, Erev I (2007) Degradation in spatial knowledge acquisition when using automatic navigation systems. In: International conference on spatial information theory, Springer, Berlin, pp 238–254

Pasotti P, van Riemsdijk MB, Jonker CM (2016) Representing human habits: towards a habit support agent. In: Proceedings of the 10th international workshop on normative multiagent systems (NorMAS'16), Springer, LNCS, to appear

Ross T, May A, Thompson S (2004) The use of landmarks in pedestrian navigation instructions and the effects of context. In: MobileHCI 2004, Springer, pp 300–304

Sacks H, Schegloff EA (1979) Two preferences in the organization of reference to persons in conversation and their interaction. Studies in ethnomethodology, Everyday language, pp 15–21

Strothotte T, Fritz S, Michel R, Raab A, Petrie H, Johnson V, Reichert L, Schalt A (1996) Development of dialogue systems for a mobility aid for blind people: initial design and usability testing. In: Proceedings of the second annual ACM conference on assistive technologies, ACM, New York, NY, USA, Assets '96, pp 139–144, https://doi.org/10.1145/228347.228369, http://doi.acm.org/10.1145/228347.228369

Van Dam A (1997) Post-wimp user interfaces. Commun ACM 40(2):63–67

Völkel T, Weber G (2008) Routecheckr: personalized multicriteria routing for mobility impaired pedestrians. In: Proceedings of the 10th international ACM SIGACCESS conference on computers and accessibility, ACM, pp 185–192

Vystrcil J, Maly I, Balata J, Mikovec Z (2014) Navigation dialog of blind people: recovery from getting lost. EACL, p 58

White RW, Grant P (2009) Designing a visible city for visually impaired users. In: Proceedings of the 2009 international conference on inclusive design

Wiener WR, Welsh RL, Blasch BB (2010) Foundations of orientation and mobility, vol 1. American Foundation for the Blind

Wilcock G (2012) Wikitalk: a spoken wikipedia-based open-domain knowledge access system. In: Proceedings of the workshop on question answering for complex domains, pp 57–70

Wobbrock JO, Kane SK, Gajos KZ, Harada S, Froehlich J (2011) Ability-based design: concept, principles and examples. ACM Trans Accessible Comput (TACCESS) 3(3):9

Chapter 5
Helping Users Reflect on Their Own Health-Related Behaviors

Rafal Kocielnik, Gary Hsieh and Daniel Avrahami

Abstract In this chapter we discuss the use of external sources of data in designing conversational dialogues. We focus on applications in behavior change around physical activity involving dialogues that help users better understand their self-tracking data and motivate healthy behaviors. We start by introducing the areas of behavior change and personal informatics and discussing the importance of self-tracking data in these areas. We then introduce the role of reflective dialogue-based counseling systems in this domain, discuss specific value that self-tracking data can bring, and how it can be used in creating the dialogues. The core of the chapter focuses on six practical examples of design of dialogues involving self-tracking data that we either tested in our research or propose as future directions based on our experiences. We end the chapter by discussing how the design principles for involving external data in conversations can be applied to broader domains. Our goal for this chapter is to share our experiences, outline design principles, highlight several design opportunities in external data-driven computer-based conversations, and encourage the reader to explore creative ways of involving external sources of data in shaping dialogues-based interactions.

R. Kocielnik (✉) · G. Hsieh
University of Washington, Seattle, WA, USA
e-mail: rkoc@uw.edu

G. Hsieh
e-mail: garyhs@uw.edu

D. Avrahami
FXPAL, Palo Alto, CA, USA
e-mail: daniel@fxpal.com

© Springer International Publishing AG, part of Springer Nature 2018
R. J. Moore et al. (eds.), *Studies in Conversational UX Design*, Human–Computer Interaction Series, https://doi.org/10.1007/978-3-319-95579-7_5

5.1 Introduction: Behavior Change, Personal Informatics and Self-tracking Data

In recent years, interest in tracking one's own activities around health and wellbeing has boomed thanks to the availability of wearable tracking devices such as Fitbit, Jawbone, Apple Watch and Microsoft Band to name a few and numerous apps on mobile phones. These wearable wristbands collect measures related to user activity, such as step count, heart-rate, and calories burned. This trend has enabled users to continuously track aspects of their activity with minimal effort. Availability of such devices suddenly allowed users to collect massive amounts of data about themselves and sparked the creation of movements such as Quantified Self, where users share their experiences about self-tracking with others (Rivera-Pelayo et al. 2012), and scientific discipline of personal informatics, which deals with tools for supporting the collection, management and use of data about self (Li et al. 2010).

Conversational agents, and conversation-based interaction in general, stand to play an important role in helping users extract meaning from self-tracked data and supporting them in setting and meeting a range of personal goals. Indeed, for many users, the ultimate purpose of collecting such health and lifestyle related data is to understand and consequently improve their health-related behaviors. Aside from interest in a personal level improvement, the pursuit of improved health and wellness has reached a global scale. In the workplace, employers encourage employees to wear fitness trackers as a way of improving their health and wellbeing. Such efforts are intended to benefit both employees and employers by means of reduced health insurance costs, higher job satisfaction, increased productivity and lower absenteeism (Chung et al. 2017). On a national level, the epidemic of obesity and heart diseases, combined with aging populations has triggered various health behavior-change government-supported programs involving activity trackers (Tanumihardjo et al. 2007).

Naturally, such need for supporting health behavior change and the availability of wearable self-tracking devices sparked the creation of numerous tools for exploring the collected data. Most of these tools rely on visualizations, such as Fish'n'Steps (Lin et al. 2006), UbiFitGarden (Consolvo et al. 2008) for physical activity; Affect Aura (McDuff et al. 2012) for affective states and LifelogExplorer (Kocielnik 2014) for stress. Such approaches assume that people have enough knowledge and motivation to effectively use their data for the purpose of changing their own behavior, which is oftentimes not the case (Fleck and Fitzpatrick 2010; Rivera-Pelayo et al. 2012). Other approaches to changing user behavior rely on reminders and motivational triggers that focus on prescribing actions (Chung et al. 2017; Kocielnik and Hsieh 2017). Such interventions can result in a phenomenon called *reactance*, which is when forceful persuasion causes a person to strengthen a view contrary to what was intended. Furthermore, relying on reminders may not help people formulate long-term commitments and habits well aligned with their own value system (Schueller 2010; Kinnafick et al. 2014); because such commitments do not directly come from users' own motivations, they are more likely to be abandoned with time. Behavior change research is thus an ongoing effort and technology-based support has a mixed record of success (Consolvo et al. 2008; Bentley et al. 2013).

In this chapter, we draw on our experience in the behavior change, persuasion and conversational domains to discuss how to combine dialogue-based interaction with self-tracking data for behavior change. Our research explored the design of diverse message-based mobile triggers for promoting physical activity (Kocielnik and Hsieh 2017), the use of sensor-based measurements, assessment and coaching based on stress data from teachers at work (Kocielnik et al. 2012, 2013b) as well as the methods of visualizing such data for the purpose of reflection (Kocielnik et al. 2013a). We have also worked on tailoring voice conversations to cultures, albeit not in the behavior change domain (Dhillon et al. 2011) and on exploring the value of voice and text modalities for workspace reflection around activity reporting (Kocielnik et al. 2018a). Finally, we have also worked on supporting reflection through mini-dialogues on self-tracking (Kocielnik et al. 2018b).

We organize the chapter around six detailed design scenarios containing practical dialogic interactions around self-tracking data. The first three scenarios are based on the framework of reflection in learning (Moon 2013) and offer guidance based on self-tracking data to help users better understand their own actions, form interpretations and hypotheses about behaviors, and define future goals. These scenarios are: (1) discovering patterns in self-tracking data, (2) understanding past behaviors, and (3) forming future plans. We also propose three additional scenarios inspired by specific behavior-change techniques and by major challenges in the behavior-change domain that can be addressed thanks to natural strengths of dialogue-based interaction. These scenarios are: (4) relapse handling through negotiation, (5) reflection on goal setting, and (6) coordinating social activity.

5.2 The Value of Human Conversation Around Data in Health Behavior Change

Some of the most effective practices in non-technology-based behavior-change interventions rely on personal counseling (Treatment 1999). Human counselors successfully employ techniques such as motivational interviewing (Rollnick and Miller 1995) and reflection-based dialogues (Lee et al. 2015). Much of the focus of these strategies goes into reflective conversations that help with assessing a client's goals, identifying barriers to successful behavior-change, negotiating around effective methods of overcoming such barriers, readjusting the client's goals and expectations, and management of relapse (Abraham and Michie 2008). The key aspect in such techniques is to support reflection on one's own behaviors exemplified by the self-tracking data and rather than force the client to perform a certain action, to help her come up with the most effective action by herself. Refection-based conversations around behavior change have a potential to make client commitment to behavior change not "forced", but emerge from the client herself and therefore garner higher levels of commitment (Rautalinko et al. 2007; Lee et al. 2015). However, a recent review of behavior-change applications (Conroy et al. 2014) identified that very few technology based solutions incorporate such aspects.

In helping people understand their own behavior and work towards effective solutions through thoughtful and constructive reflection (Rollnick and Miller 1995), self-tracking data offers an invaluable source of information. A conversational approach around self-tracking data is arguably one of the most natural ways to trigger reflection and has multiple specific advantages.

Leading to deeper understanding: Skilled human counselors can dynamically act on a client's data and associated responses in the conversation, prompting deeper insights about specific patterns and following up on the client's observations and responses. Such flexibility allows these counselors to dive deeper into a client's specific situation, understand their goals and motivations, and use this knowledge to jointly create personalized plans and maintain motivation through tailored feedback (Lee et al. 2015). What is critical in this process is the very first step in which counselors guide their clients to reflect on her own behavior with the use of her data and articulate what motivates her so that she can orient herself to her underlying needs and goals. Aside from the counselor being able to better understand the client, properly guided dialogue has an ability to trigger valuable insight in the client herself, simply by asking the "right" question at the "right" time. In fact, past research has shown that simply asking reflective questions can help people articulate their underlying needs and goals and increase their engagement. In one study, people who were asked to think about why they eat snacks before making a choice were more likely to choose healthy options (Fujita and Han 2009). Research suggests that asking people their reasons for doing an activity triggers their underlying motivations and leads them to focus on higher-level goals (Lee et al. 2015).

Guidance based on expertise: Second, an experienced counselor is able to bring expertise about what techniques are most likely to work for behavior change, how to successfully set up behavior-change plans and how to set realistic goals based on the client's past performance observed in the self-tracking data. Bringing such expertise to behavior-change efforts can help minimize the risk of setting unrealistic expectation, avoid relapse and eventual dropout. Counselors normally rely on in-depth interviews or the client's journaling to gain the necessarily depth of knowledge to offer constructive guidance (Rautalinko et al. 2007). The use of the client's automatically collected self-tracked data offers an additional, valuable, and more precise source of knowledge.

Building rapport: Third, engaging in conversation enables a counselor to build rapport with the client, allowing them to express empathy towards her struggles while trying to help her change behavior. Such qualities are essential as behavior change is a long-term endeavor in which social emotional support plays an important role. Indeed, past research has indicated that a crucial aspect of positively affecting health outcomes in most counseling techniques involves the counselor's ability to establish rapport and to express empathy (Miller and Rollnick 2009). The achieved rapport also contributes to the feeling of commitment and accountably, for both counselor and the client. Conversation-based interaction has a unique ability to support such aspects.

Unfortunately, human counselors are not available to everyone at all times. Qualified health coaches are expensive and may not always be available at the right time, when the crucial moments in behavior change take place. As a result, efforts have been made to reproduce some of the unique advantages of conversation-based behavior-change counseling through technology by employing persuasion (Fogg 2009), tailoring (Lewis et al. 2013), offering recommendations (Skurnik et al. 2005), reflecting on goals formulation (Lee et al. 2015), and even by building embodied counseling agents (Novielli et al. 2010).

5.3 Computer-Based Conversational Approaches in Self-tracking

The paradigm of computers as social actors (Schueller 2010) argues that people will apply social rules to a computer. This suggests that successful human counseling techniques might also work effectively in computer-based delivery. Unfortunately, despite recent progress in dialogue-based interaction, relatively little has been done to bring these conversational capabilities to the self-tracking domain (Götzmann 2015).

There have been recent attempts at building commercial conversational behavior change assistants in self-tracking domain, such as Lark,[1] HealthyBot,[2] and CountIt[3] to name a few. Unfortunately, these solutions still leverage dialogue-based interaction to support user tasks that could already be done quite well, if not better, with non-conversational interaction. For example, HealthyBot and CountIt, mainly provide activity triggers along with motivational content through Slack. This is no different from regular one-sided text-based behavior-change triggers sent through SMS or email (Kocielnik and Hsieh 2017); input typed by the user is used to query information, as a replacement for clicking a button. Lark—arguably the most advanced of these conversational behavior-change assistants—actually provides some interesting use cases. It actively interviews the user to gather basic profile information and weaves in reports of user activity into the chat; however, user input is limited mostly to provided and fixed responses.

In the research community, a comprehensive review by Bickmore and Giorgino on work in health education and behavior change dialogue systems (Bickmore and Giorgino 2006) has revealed application domains spanning exercise, diet, smoking cessation, medication adherence and chronic disease management. Specifically for physical activity, most common approaches relied on building persuasive dialogues, oftentimes based on fixed dialogue structures (Bickmore et al. 2010). For these

---

[1] http://www.web.lark.com/.
[2] https://healthybot.io/.
[3] https://beta.countit.com/.

studies, reflection on self-tracking data was not the main focus, although as we pointed out in the previous section, it is one of the core principles of human-based counseling and would benefit greatly from the use of self-tracking data.

There are several reasons why such strategies have remained largely unsupported. First, the proper "understanding" of very personal, dynamic and contextual user barriers and motives expressed in natural language is difficult for an algorithmic approach. Thanks, however, to recent advances in machine learning (ML) and natural language processing (NLP), conversational assistants such as Amazon's Alexa, Apple's Siri and Microsoft's Cortana are now robust enough to be in wide practical use. Conversational agents are now able to understand user input in natural form and generate appropriate responses in natural language. This opens opportunities for behavior change systems to engage users in new ways.

5.4 Methods for Incorporating Self-tracking Data into Computer-Generated Dialogues

In this section, we focus on how self-tracking data could be incorporated into agent utterances and how it can shape the dialogic structure from a technical perspective of selecting and shaping conversational agent utterances. We present several methods that have been explored in past work and used in our own research.

5.4.1 Communicating Summary Data Statistics

Arguably the most straightforward way of incorporating activity data into conversations is by using template utterances that are filled in with relevant key statistics summarizing the data when the agent communicates with the user. Such template-based utterances can inform the user about simple aspects of her data: "*So far today you have walked 9836 steps, keep on going!*" Template-based utterances can also communicate goal accomplishment status: "*You have accomplished 87% of your daily step goal. Only 2.3 k steps to go.*" Finally, they can communicate relevant changes to the user: "*You have increased your step count by 20% this week*". Such presentation of self-tracking data allows the user to quickly grasp important metrics or attract the user's attention to specific aspects of the data the agent wants to emphasize, e.g. the fact that step count has increased. Template-based utterances are easy and fast for users to process, but offer less context or room for interpretation or reflection (Tollmar et al. 2012). In presenting the data in such ways, especially when the agent reports the status of goal completion, positive and encouraging framing of the presentation might be important (Bentley et al. 2013). Indeed, such manner of presenting the external data to the user can be especially useful as evidence for helping the user in defining attainable goals or to inform the agent's negotiation tactics meant to encourage the user to be more active.

5.4.2 Communicating Patterns Found in the Data

A more sophisticated variation of presenting key statistics to the user is for the agent to communicate statistical patterns discovered in the data: *"You walk 20% more on weekends than weekdays"*, *"Your sleep quality usually increases by the end of the week"* Appropriate utterances for communicating patterns can be selected from a set of templates or generated on the fly based on grammatical structure. By communicating such patterns the agent can attract the user's attention to particular relations found in the data and shape the conversation around guiding the user to think more about the reasons for these patterns or how the knowledge from such patterns can be used to improve behavior in the future. While past research shows that such presentation is useful for simplifying the task of understanding the data and can help focus user attention on specific patterns that the agent may want to emphasize, it can also take away some of the user's ability to learn directly from the data. This was the case in the HealthMashups study in which users expressed a desire to see the visualizations of raw sensor data (Bentley et al. 2013).

5.4.3 Embedding Visual Data Representations as Conversation Artifacts

A different way of shaping the agent's and user's conversation around data is to inject visual data representations directly into the dialogue. This can be done when the conversation takes place over a visual medium, such as a smartphone. For example, a simple daily steps graph such as the one presented in Fig. 5.1 can be used along with a conversational prompt. A conversational agent can then ask the user specific questions around such data graph in an open manner: *"Can you observe anything about your behavior during the week?"* or guide the user to focus on specific aspects of the data: *"Can you see any particular day when you walked much more?"* Such conversation around the graphed data can involve several questions exploring different aspects of the visualization. Also, the conversation can relate to the automatically-detected statistical patterns, to further guide the user's attention or directly switch the conversation to thinking about the reasons behind the existence of such patterns: *"It seems you were gradually increasing your steps throughout the week, what helped you?"* The visual representation further adds the ability for the user to make open interpretation and is likely to trigger open thinking about their

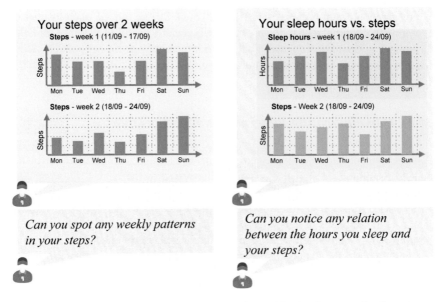

Fig. 5.1 Example visualizations of the activity data along with related conversational prompts

behavior. Past research indicates that visual aids have an ability to increase user engagement and provide a quick overview of recent progress in line with theories from information visualization research (Tufte 1991) and health visualizations in particular (Consolvo et al. 2008; Kocielnik and Sidorova 2015).

Indeed, incorporating data and visual representations of data into conversations can be particularly useful for users to gain insights about long-term behavior patterns, to understand the context of activities, and can potentially also be used as a social evidence of the level of one's activity.

5.4.4 Shaping the Flow of the Dialogues Based on Data

External self-tracking data may also shape the dialogue on a structural level, where different conversational paths may be followed depending on the evidence from the activity data. For example, if the user met the daily activity goal, the dialogue can alert her to the success, ask her what helped her achieve this success and how to increase the likelihood of meeting the goal consistently in the future. If the goal was unmet, the dialogue can follow a path that tries to help the user understand the barriers to reaching the goal and think about how to avoid similar situations in the future. An example of a dialogue shaped by the data in such a fashion is presented in Fig. 5.2.

Fig. 5.2 Example of how the activity data affects the conversational paths

Such use of the data in shaping the conversations can be particularly useful for guiding the user to dig deeper into understanding activity context and reflecting on the important factors that could have contributed to successes or failures in particular situations.

5.5 Practical Examples of Design for Data-Driven Conversational Dialogues

In this section, we dive deeper into concrete examples of conversations around behavior change involving external sources of data. Some of these techniques have been used in our research, while others are based on the studies of others or our knowledge and expectations around useful strategies. For each scenario, we describe its goal and the support for it from the perspective of behavior-change theories. We also provide mock-ups of conversational exchanges and discuss the challenges involved in applying the design in practice which the designers should consider.

Our main design principle in shaping these interaction scenarios was to provide guidance following motivational interviewing approaches (Treatment 1999). Conceptually, guidance is positioned between just passively observing and informing the user on their activity (e.g. tracking) and forcefully prescribing actions (e.g. persuading). In our work, we defined six "guidance" scenarios in which reflective dialogues make use of self-tracking data and other sources of data to help users better understand their own actions, form interpretations and hypotheses about behaviors, and define future goals and activities. An example of a chat interface that can be used for our scenarios is presented in Fig. 5.3.

The first three scenarios are based on a reflection process that involves several consecutive steps: from helping the user identify relevant patterns in the activity data (Scenario 1), through prompting the user to understand these patterns (Scenario 2), to formulating effective future actions (Scenario 3). This structure is based on reflection in learning framework (Moon 2013) and the scenarios can be used consecutively over

Fig. 5.3 Example
interaction for identifying
patterns in self-tracking data
presented in the context of
chatting application. It is
assumed here, that the agent
has access to an activity
tracker from a phone or
external device (e.g. FitBit)

a period of time. Scenario 4, on the other hand, is based on the goals-setting theory
(Locke and Latham 2006), which suggests decomposing larger, vaguely defined
behavior change goals into a series of small, well-defined, attainable and timed
goals. In this scenario, the agent tries to guide the user to refine their initial goals
to make them achievable, precise and measurable. Scenario 5 explores the potential
for a conversational agent to prevent relapse, that is a situation when skipping one
planned activity may lead to discouragement and abandonment of the entire activity
goal. In this scenario, the agent tries to negotiate with the user at least a partial
completion of an activity or proposes more attainable alternatives. Finally, Scenario
6 tries to leverage the powerful social support aspect of behavior change (Colusso
et al. 2016), by facilitating several users to perform physical activities together.

5.5.1 Sample Implementation

Realization of the above scenarios requires technical architecture that can deal well with integrating data elements into dialogue. Specifically, the architecture needs to be able to use external data to shape and inform the agent's utterances, and also be able to translate free-text user responses into a structured representation of the data interpretable by the agent. In this section, we describe our implementation of a sample system used in our research. Readers focused on design aspects not concerned with implementation details may skip ahead to the description of the first scenario in Sect. 5.6.

Our system implementation employs a modular architecture in which multiple data management modules exchange information with a main Conversation Module (Fig. 5.4). The Conversation Module keeps track of current user dialogue status and is responsible for extracting intents and entities from free-text user responses. It is also responsible for creating natural agent utterances from the data received by any of the data modules. The exchange of the information between the data modules and the Conversation Module is done using structured representation of the data (encoded in JSON format).

From structured data to agent utterance: An important aspect of our system is the incorporation of external data into the dialogue. Here we describe more details of how we approach this task through an example of interaction between the Conversation Module and the Activity Data Module (Fig. 5.5). One of the functions of the Activity Data Module is to provide structured representation of patterns identified in user activity data (e.g. user had 30% more steps on weekend than on week

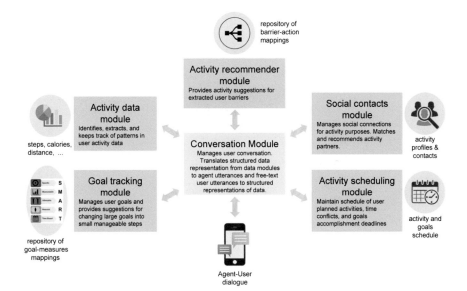

Fig. 5.4 Overview of the technical architecture

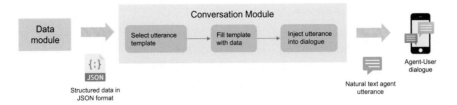

Fig. 5.5 Overview of the process involved in translating the structured representation of the data module into an agent utterance

days). After extracting such data pattern using statistical methods, the module sends it, upon request, to the conversation module in a structured JSON format, where the data pattern is described by its type: "*time association*" in this case, magnitude: "*30% increase*", type of activity data it describes: "*steps*", reference time: "*weekdays*" and target time: "*weekends*". Each such data pattern has its own specific data fields.

The conversation module then takes such structured representation and finds an appropriate sentence template that fits the type of the pattern and the data provided along with the pattern. For naturalness and diversification of the conversation we have supplied multiple sentence templates that can fit the same data pattern. The template is then selected at random and filled-in with appropriate values as shown on the example of activity data patterns in Fig. 5.6.

As a result of this process, the agent utterance presented to the user may look something like: "*Hey John, I have noticed you walked much more on weekend than on week days this past few weeks, do you have any idea why that could be the case?*"

From free-text user response to structured data: Similarly, in the other direction a free-text user response needs to be analyzed and structured information needs to be extracted from it. We use intent detection and entity extraction/resolution to convert

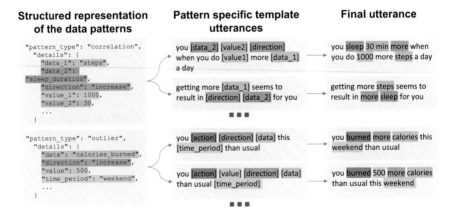

Fig. 5.6 Example of translating the structured representation of the identified data patterns into natural utterances used by the agent in the dialogue with the user

the free-text user responses into a machine-readable meaning representation (Wang et al. 2005; Tur and De Mori 2011). In personal assistant dialog systems, intent-models are classifiers that identify the category of user reply, e.g. *"add meeting to calendar"* or *"play a song"*. Entities are utterance substrings that contain specific information such as "today" or "noon". The entity resolution maps those substrings to canonical forms such as 2014-09-11 or 12:00:00Z-08:00:00 (Williams et al. 2015). In our case, intents are categories such as *"user suggested an activity"* or *"user recognized a pattern"* and entities are types of activity data, such *as "steps"*, *"calories burned"* or barriers to activity shared by the user, such as *"time"*, *"motivation"*. Using these tools, the free-text user response is processed following several steps as shown in Fig. 5.7. First the raw response is preprocessed to split long multi-sentence responses into individual fragments. This step is quite specific to the domain of reflection where users are likely to provide long and extensive responses. In the second step the intents are detected and entities are extracted from each individual fragment. Collected information is then structured into a JSON representation ready to be exchanged with the Activity Data Module. Given a structured representation, the module can perform several operations on this information such as verifying the accuracy of the observation or finding similar activity patterns.

Following this general architecture, our Conversation Module communicates with various Data Modules in a similar fashion. Each Data Module is responsible for managing different types of data about the user, such as activity data, user goals and barriers, user annotations for activity patterns, social contacts, activity recom-mendations and others. For each of these Data Modules, the Conversation Module follows the described transformation of data from structured representation to agent utterances using sentence templates and form free-text user responses to structured representations, using intent identification and entity extraction/resolution. We pro-vide concrete examples of the data formats and sentence templates in the following few sections discussing exact scenarios in practice.

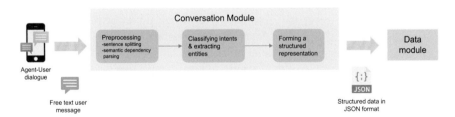

Fig. 5.7 Processing free-text user response into a structured representation for data module use

5.5.2 Handling Unrecognized User Utterances

Our system aspires to support user reflection, which requires that users have free-dom of expression. However unconstrained user utterances are challenging to process automatically using existing tools. Lack of recognition of all or parts of user utter-ances are a common occurrence.

In dealing with the imperfections of automated recognition, we take advantage of three intentionally-designed aspects of our dialogues: (1) they are not task-oriented and they do not have a specific precise action they need to accomplish, but are meant to trigger thinking/reflecting; (2) they do not have to follow a predictable, repeatable steps of interaction, they should in fact, be novel and diverse to keep the user engaged; (3) because reflection needs to be triggered and encouraged, agent initiative in shaping the dialogues is both acceptable and desired.

Using these aspects, we employed three design strategies to mitigate the likelihood and impact of misrecognitions in processing free-text user responses.

Agent initiative: By having the agent initiate and largely guide the direction of the conversation we were able to limit the scope of expected user responses. For most interactions users are given specific question so they will stay "on topic" in their responses. Additionally, such agent-initiated interaction, given proper diversity and novelty of the dialogues, serves to help the user think about novel aspects of her data and activities.

Gracefully shortening the exchange: In an ideal case, once the agent asks about barriers that the user encountered when trying to accomplish an activity goal, the user would respond with some barrier, such as a lack of time. The agent would recog-nize such a response and suggest specific strategies to consider, such as scheduling things ahead in the calendar. However, if the response is not recognized, the agent will be unable to tailor follow-up exchanges. Task-oriented agents, requiring such information to proceed, would follow-up with a clarification request such as *"I'm sorry I did not understand, could you repeat please?"* Such request for clarification can break the conversation flow, especially if encountered frequently. In case of a reflection system, however, the recognition of a particular user barrier for activity is a useful piece of information, but not crucial for continuation of the conversation. In fact, retaining user engagement is far more important. Therefore to deal with such scenarios, the agent would offer a *generic* follow-up reflection question asking the user to e.g. think about the value of realizing one's barriers for physical activity.

Utilizing partial information: We have found that often the automated entity extraction would only be successful in extracting parts of the information shared by the user. For example when the user describes an activity pattern, *"I had quite a few more steps on weekend than in the beginning of the week."* The agent may recognize that the user talks about *"steps"* and *"weekend"*, but not that she describes an increase or compares the steps between two time periods. Such partial information is still very useful for designing dialogues. Instead of defaulting to a *generic* follow-up as described in the previous paragraph, the agent can acknowledge recognition of partial information by saying, *"So, regarding the weekends and the steps, what do* *you think you could do to improve that in the future?"* Acknowledging such partial information lets the user know that the agent is actively considering user responses and building upon them. In practice, for each dialogue we have designed a number of conversation follow-up patterns that incorporate various combinations of partial information extracted from the user utterance.

After the interaction a system designer can processes such unrecognized user reply and update a set of recognized intents and entities or add a new example utterance for one of the known intents. This will help enhance system capabilities in future interactions. In the following sections, we describe six concrete scenarios that can be supported by a reflection agent and discuss each one in detail.

5.6 Scenario 1: Identifying Patterns in the Data

Our first scenario is meant to help users take a good look at their self-tracking data and help them identify meaningful patterns in their own activities.

Goal of the scenario: Various theories of behavior change and personal informatics posit numerous scenarios in which data can play a crucial role. The stage-based model of personal informatics (Li et al. 2010) describes the initial stages of data collection in which the data is either logged or automatically collected; this is eventually meant to lead the user to self-reflection with the help of the collected data and to motivate action. For such data to be useful, however, the user's attention needs to be directed towards potentially informative and revealing aspects and patterns in this data.

Automated self-tracking offers objective information that can help users discover unknown behaviors, check their progress and help form realistic future goals. All these benefits, however, are only possible if the user can notice and understand relevant data patterns. From a reflection framework perspective, such initial step is called **noticing** in which the user needs to notice, purely perceptually, the learning material in order for any further steps of self-learning to occur (Moon 2013).

Dialogue design: Exchange 1.1 below illustrates a dialogue for guiding a user through *identifying* relevant patterns in their own self-tracking data (Exchange 1.1).

(1.1) Identifying Patterns-Agent Recognition

```
01 A:  Can you see anything of interest in your recent data?
02 U:  Yes, I think I sleep much better when I walk more
03     during the day
04 A:  Great observation! Indeed your sleep quality improves
05     by 10% when you do 1,000 more steps a day.
06 A:  Were you able to observe anything else?
07 U:  I think that's it, no?
08 A:  Well, I also noticed you walked more this weekend than
09     usual. Is this something relevant for you?
10 U:  Interesting, can you give me more details?
11 A:  Sure, it seems you did 3,550 more steps than usual:
```

```
12      ((step chart))
13 A:   Would you like me to keep track of this pattern?
14 U:   Yes, sure :)
```

Users are prompted first to actively think about patterns in their activity data (line 01), and only in case it is needed, are offered support to guide them through such discovery. Hence instead of starting with: *"You walked 20% more this Friday than last Friday"*, the dialogue begins with *"Can you see anything of interest in your recent data?"* (line 01). There are two reasons for this: First, when users identify patterns on their own, these patterns are more likely to be remembered (Kim and Hullman 2015). Second, automated techniques can identify thousands of irrelevant patterns (Tollmar et al. 2012), hence human cooperation helps keep track of the interesting ones. Once the user observations have been identified, the system can match them against the patterns identified in the data and offer more details on the pattern observed (lines 04–05). When the system identifies some other strong pattern similar to the one the user is interested in tracking, it can share such pattern with the user (lines 08–09, 11–12). The agent can offer to track activity patterns for the user (line 13), thus creating a tailored set of conversation starters for the future. Such dialogues can be further enhanced by integrated visualizations or coupled with a visualization dashboard. We note that in order to prevent user tedium with having to recognize patterns each time, the system can begin with soft guidance by replacing the opening prompt in line 01 with more focused suggestions, as presented in Table 5.1. Abstract prompts require more work from the user, but can be beneficial for remembering whereas directing prompts point closer to the pattern and lower user effort—different dialogue openings should be designed to offer guidance at different levels, as needed.

Handling misrecognitions: The example interaction in Exchange 1.1 represents an ideal exchange in which user intents and associated entities are fully recognized. As the agent deals with open-ended user input, it is possible that parts or entire user replies will not be recognized at all. Exchange 1.2 presents an interaction in which the initial user response was not recognized at all.

(1.2) Identifying Patterns-Agent Misrecognition

```
01 A:   Can you see anything of interest in your recent data?
02 U:   Not walking enough :)
03 A:   That sounds interesting. What do you think patterns in your
04      data can tell you?
05 U:   They can probably tell me about what motivates me and how my
06      trends change based on what my goal was that day
07 A:   Thanks for sharing.
```

In case the system is unable to extract a pattern from the user response (line 02), the system falls back to a generic follow-up (lines 03–04) that does not rely on any information shared by the user, but still could retain user engagement. The dialogue designer can benefit here from the domain of reflection for which the dialogues are applied. Such reflection dialogues do not have a strict functionality they need to support (contrary to e.g. flight booking system), but their function is to trigger user

Table 5.1 Example data patterns and associated abstract and directing prompts

Data patterns	Pattern specific prompts
One time outlier Mon Tue Wed Thu Fri Sat Sun	**Abstract**: *"Was there a day when you walked much more?"* **Directing**: *"Can you see anything specific about your behavior on Tuesday?"*
Contonuous change Mon Tue Wed Thu Fri Sat Sun	**Abstract**: *"Was there anything specific about your walking throughout the week?"* **Directing**: *"Can you see any change in your walking from Monday to Friday?"*

thinking about health behaviors. While the interaction presented in Exchange 1.1 is more tailored and potentially more beneficial for the user, the interaction in Exchange 1.2 still can accomplish the basic goal of supporting reflection.

Design insights: When deploying similar dialogues for encouraging users to notice patterns in their behavior in the field it is important to ask the user to notice aspects that are non-trivial, e.g. *"Can you spot any patterns in your walking throughout the week?"* or *"Were there any changes in your sleep throughout the week?"* rather than asking relatively simple straightforward questions such as *"Which day did you walk the most?"* The latter can sometimes be considered too trivial to respond to and feel a bit like a quiz that could be automatically identified by the system. This could result in user frustration over time.

5.7 Scenario 2: Understanding Past Behaviors

The following scenario guides the user towards understanding the reasons and mechanisms behind the patterns observed in their own activity data.

Goal of the scenario: Even successfully identifying patterns in the data does not necessarily lead to meaningful interpretation and actionable decisions (Li et al. 2011). An important step of making sense of the data, described in the reflective framework as **making meaning** (Moon 2013), is needed. This is when a person revisits the past with an attempt to understand and form an explanation of the behavior. This step is important as it helps the user make connections between actions and health outcomes and think about ways in which past decisions could have been changed. There are at least two challenges here: The person may not be able to recall the situation because the information needed for explaining the behavior may not be captured by self-tracking (e.g. the system "knows" the user did not sleep well, but not that she was studying and drinking a lot of coffee the night before). Additionally, even if the user is able to recall the information needed, they may be unaware of important links between the context and outcome (e.g. not realizing the links between sleep, studying late and consuming lots of caffeine).

Dialogue design: Exchange 2.1 illustrates a dialogue for guiding a user through an *understanding* process and explanation of her behavior patterns.

(2.1) Past Behaviors-Agent Recognition

```
01 A:  About the decrease in steps last weekend we identified last
02     time, what happened there?
03 U:  I don't really recall anything specific.
04 A:  I actually found a similar pattern 4 weeks ago.
05     ((steps chart))
06     Back then you said "I worked late on Friday and felt tired to
07     do anything on the weekend." Maybe a similar thing happened?
08 U:  No, not really, but it made me think what I did this Friday.
09     We went for a birthday party and I had too much to drink.
10 A:  Would you like me to make a note of that and attach it to
11     this pattern?
12 U:  Sure.
```

The agent first recalls a pattern identified in user-activity data and asks the user to think about the explanation of this pattern (01–02). Such patterns have been identified earlier by the user in the noticing step (Scenario 1) or can also have been identified automatically by the system. The ability to think about the context behind the data and causal relationship enabled by the trigger may itself lead the person to a successful reflection. In case of difficulty recalling, as in this case (line 03), the agent can offer assistance by providing examples of similar patterns identified in the past along with user reflections on these patterns (lines 04–07). Another way in which an agent could jog the user's memory is through guidance in retracing the steps of an activity. In case this approach is successful in helping the user understand the reason behind the activity pattern as in 08–09, the agent prompts the user to attach the provided explanation to the pattern for future reference (lines 10–11).

Handling misrecognitions: Exchange 2.1 presented an ideal scenario for system recognition whereas Exchange 2.2 presents an exchange in this scenario where the agent failed to identify the user response in line 03.

(2.2) Past Behaviors-Agent Misrecognition

```
01 A:  About the decrease in steps last weekend we identified last
02     time, what happened there?
03 U:  In transition and off this week, it's been unorthodox.
04 A:  I see, do you find it valuable to go back and understand
05     what happened when you see patterns in your data?
06 U:  Generally yes, but in some cases there is nothing I can do
07     with this knowledge.
08 A:  OK, thanks a lot for sharing!
```

In this case, following our design pattern, the agent will proceed to offer a generic follow-up question (lines 04–05) to trigger further thinking from the user and then end the exchange (line 08).

Design insights: The challenge in supporting user understanding lies in focusing the user's attention on meaningful and actionable patterns. This becomes challenging especially when the activity patterns are identified automatically. Such patterns may not be meaningful for the user and discussing them may lower user engagement. A challenging technical aspect in this scenario also lies in automated extraction of the explanation provided by the user. While entity extraction can be trained to identify meaningful parts of the user's response, the extracted parts usually do not cover the full explanation; the extracted parts are also not always in the linguistic form acceptable for direct use in future dialogues. Finally, the user explanations might be long and may need summarizing before being used further.

5.8   Scenario 3: Thinking About Future Actions

This scenario focuses on helping the user formulate concrete actions to take based on identified patterns in past behavior and an understanding of the mechanisms behind them. It builds upon the dialogues described in the previous scenarios.

Goal of the scenario: After identifying interesting behavior patterns and working through the causal relations between the activity data and the context of activities, it is valuable for the user to take the lessons learned and translate them into actionable future plans. A crucial step in behavior change is indeed helping people set concrete action plans for achieving their desired behaviors (Locke and Latham 2006). This can be paralleled with the **transformative learning** step in the reflective framework (Moon 2013). The power of the reflective approach here is that by working together with the user, the action plans can be formulated by the users themselves. Such approach to formulating plans can offer a stronger fit and more motivational support than when an action plan is formulated without active user involvement (Schueller 2010; Lee et al. 2015). Dialogue-based interaction lends itself well to supporting such scenario since arriving at meaningful and feasible plans is oftentimes an iterative process (Bovend'Eerdt et al. 2009).

Dialogue design: Exchange 3.1 illustrates a dialogue for providing guidance towards formulating future actions.

(3.1) Future Actions-Agent Recognition

```
01 A:  Regarding the missing running sessions on Thursday evenings,
02     you mentioned this was due to working late and not having
03     enough energy
04 A:  What do you think you could do about it?
05 U:  I am not sure, I have to do my work and some Thursdays are
06     very busy for me?
07 A:  Indeed you're not alone in having this problem. Do you think
```

```
08    it would be possible to try moving your running sessions
09    earlier in the day?
10 U: Hmm, not sure. I guess I could try one day and see how that
11    works out.
12 A: Great! Shall I move the workout on Thursday to 8:30am?
15 U: Sounds good!
```

The agent first recalls the past behavior pattern along with the user provided explanation of the reason for this pattern (01–04). This information is assumed to have been obtained in Scenarios 1 and 2 discussed earlier. Then, the agent essentially prompts the user to think about what could be done differently in the future (04). Depending on the user's reply, the agent tries to guide her towards formulating goals or explores the barriers she has for trying to introduce a change in the future. In the example given in Exchange 3.1, the user communicates an inability to improve on the behavior along with some reasoning for it (05–06). The agent tries to extract such reason and suggest appropriate action the user could consider, in this case rescheduling the running session (07–09). Based on user approval and, in this case, consultation with the user's calendar, the agent proposes a rescheduling time (12–14) and updates the user's schedule.

Handling misrecognitions: As with the previous dialogues, in this scenario a number of fallback strategies can be introduced to handle failures in automated recognition. Exchange 3.2 gives an example where the user response in line 04 is not recognized.

(3.2) Future Actions-Agent Misrecognition

```
01 A: Regarding the missing running sessions on Thursday evenings,
02    you mentioned this was due to working late and not having
03    enough energy
04 A: What do you think you could do about it?
05 U: This will be resolved soon and I am changing my job.
06 A: In general, do you try to think creatively about making your
07    days more active?
08 U: Yes, for sure. I have a sitting job, so any piece of activity
09    I can squeeze in is extremely valuable.
10 A: Ok, great! Thanks for taking the time to think about it.
```

In Exchange 3.2, the agent follows up with a more generic prompt as in lines 06–07 and proceeds to close the exchange (line 10). While this exchange does not accomplish nearly as much as Exchange 3.1, it still serves the basic goal of triggering the user to think about future actions.

Design insights: As the main principle of the dialogues is guidance, one of the significant challenges of this scenario lies in balancing the elicitation of user's own action suggestions and the suggestions given by the agent. Repeated suggestions that do not match the user's context and abilities can easily diminish the trust in the agent. On the other hand, lack of any suggestions may leave the user stuck on the problem and unable to come up with any out-of-box approaches. In practice designers should balance the automated suggestions and user's own explorations, by leading the user to explore initially and if that fails, suggest possible actions to consider. The agent could also make use of the record of past data patterns and past successful actions user has taken to intelligently suggest similar approaches. Finally, it is also possible that some of the identified negative patterns in user's data do not have clear actions that could address them. In such cases, rather than having the user think about the same unsolvable pattern repeatedly, the agent should move on to discussing other patterns that may show more promise.

5.9 Dialogue 4: Formulating SMART Goals

The following scenario focuses on helping the user arrive at a precise and measurable definition of the goal she wants to accomplish.

Goal of the scenario: Specifically, on aspects of future actions and plans, the setting of measurable and attainable future goals for behavior change is an important pre-requisite for long-term success. The dialogue's guided process of reflection on formulating future goals can help the user refine these goals so they are achievable, yet ambitious enough and, while doing so, also increase user commitment to such refined goals (Lee et al. 2015). People are oftentimes overly ambitious with their goals and this may lead to disappointment and eventual drop-out if the goals are not met. According to goals-setting theory (Locke and Latham 2006), an aspirational long-term goal and a set of so-called S.M.A.R.T (specific, measurable, attainable, relevant and timely) short-term goals are an ideal combination for maximizing the success of behavior change. Formulating such goals, however, is challenging. Conversational interaction has the potential to guide and support users through this challenging process.

Dialogue design: An approach in behavior change called "motivation interviewing" uses concepts of reflection to help guide people to realize their own behavior-change goals (Rollnick and Miller 1995). Following the S.M.A.R.T. goals principle from goals-setting theory, the conversational approach could try to identify if current user goals have the desired properties and if not, help the user in refining such initial goals. Exchange 4.1 illustrates how such guidance could be accomplished.

(4.1) Measurable Goals-Agent Recognition

```
01 A:  How would you like to measure your success in achieving the
02     "becoming more fit" goal?
03 U:  I think, I should walk a lot.
04 A:  Perhaps think about a specific number of steps you would like
05     to achieve (e.g. 10,000/day)?
06 U:  Sounds good, but not sure if 10,000 is realistic for me.
07 A:  We can start with fewer, but 10,000 is the average for a
08     healthy person your age. See <this article> for more.
09 U:  OK, let's go with that then :)
10 A:  Great! I added this goal for you.
```

In line 01, the agent refers to one of the goals previously shared by the user and asks for a clear measurement of success related to such a goal. The user response provided in line 03 is analyzed to extract the specific measurement suggested by the user. If such measurement is not provided, the agent suggests a specific measurement suitable for this goal (lines 04–05). In response to such suggestions the user may express agreement or disagree with the suggestion as in line 06. If the user disagrees, the agent tries to extract the reason for such disagreement and provide an appropriate follow-up response as in lines 07–08. The dialogue concludes when the user and the agent agree on a certain measurable threshold for goal accomplishment as in lines 09–10.

Handling misrecognitions: Exchange 4.2 illustrates a situation where the agent is unable to recognize the intent of the initial user response in line 03. In such a case, no entities can be extracted and the agent provides a generic follow-up question to maintain a natural conversation and avoid breakdown (lines 04–05). After the user response, the agent proceeds to conclude the dialogue as in line 07.

(4.2) Measurable Goals-Agent Misrecognition

```
01 A:  How would you like to measure your success in achieving the
02     "becoming more fit" goal?
03 U:  Just how I feel, I guess.
04 A:  It is important to make sure your goals are measureable and
05     achievable. Do you think that's the case for you?
06 U:  Yes, I think so.
07 A:  Great! You can always edit your goals on <website>!
```

As illustrated in Exchange 4.2, even when an agent is unable to guide the user to set a concrete measurable goal, it can still trigger relevant reflection. Ultimately it is up to the user to make their goals measureable, but an agent can still offer valuable guidance.

Design insights: In practice, there are different levels of goals that users might have; some goals might be long-term, ongoing, or purely motivational in their nature. The conversation should try to help the user refine her goals to be measurable, but also, if the user expresses a desire to keep certain goal abstract the agent should try to recognize that and ultimately let the user keep the preferred goal formulation. It might also be that the user has a number of goals at the same time, some abstract and some already fitting the definition of SMART goals. In such case the dialogue should have access to the user's other goals and perhaps ask the user if one of the SMART goals is already associated with an abstract goal the user wants to keep. The main principle is guiding, but not pushing or constraining the user, hence the ultimate decision should be left to the user. Finally, not every goal, even measurable ones can be captured by measurement devices, hence goals such as "increasing one's happiness" ultimately relies on the user's own perception and self-reporting.

5.10   Scenario 5: Negotiation Around Relapse

The following dialogue demonstrates how to encourage a user to perform at least part of a scheduled activity in case of a relapse. This is accomplished through negotiation of activity performance between the agent and the user.

Goal of the scenario: Relapse takes place when the user stops following activity plans and reverts back to previous patterns of behavior or inactivity. Relapse is one of the hardest aspects to handle due to its, often unpredictable, appearance and various causes, as well as the difficulty of reestablishing rapport with the user to get back on track (Bouton 2014). Occasional decreases in motivation, disappointment with progress, unexpected schedule changes, lack of energy, and forgetting can all form dynamic, unexpected barriers contributing to relapse (Myers and Roth 1997). Once the user skips a planned activity, abandoning the entire plan altogether is more likely. Such a scenario is sadly common, with average dropout rates for physical-activity and diet/weight-loss interventions at 50% and 60% respectively (Kinnafick et al. 2014).

Dialogue design: In this example, the agent follows-up on user non-adherence with negotiation tactics. Exchange 5.1 demonstrates an ideal exchange in this scenario.

(5.1) Negotiation-Agent Recognition

```
01 A:  It is time to do your 10 lunges now. Please confirm when
02     you're done.
03     (after 20 minutes without confirmation)
04 A:  Did you manage to complete lunges? If not, what happened?
05 U:  No, I don't have time at the moment.
06 A:  OK, I will get back to you in an hour.
07     (after 1 hour)
08 A:  Hi, I hope you have some time now to do your 10 lunges.
09 U:  I feel a bit tired!
10 A:  Well, doing even 5 lunges is better than none :)
11 U:  OK.
```

The agent first prompts the user to perform a scheduled activity (lines 01–02). This is a simple reminder function based on the user's activity schedule. After some time, in case the user does not complete the scheduled activity, which can be determined based on sensors or user explicit confirmation, the agent prompts the user to share the reason for non-adherence at the moment (04) and adjust the next action in a way that would increase the chance of the user doing at least part of the activity. In this exchange as the user shared "bad timing" as a reason for non-adherence, the agent will wait one hour to prompt again (06–08) and in case the user shares a new barrier, the agent will adjust the strategy again, for example to lower the number of exercise repetitions (09–10). The main idea here is that it is better for the user to complete at least part of the activity. Expressing interest in the user's barriers may further lead to higher perception of empathy expressed by the agent.

Handling misrecognitions: Illustrated in Exchange 5.2, is a scenario in which the reason for non-adherence shared by the user is not successfully categorized (04). Following our design pattern, the agent offers a generic follow-up that is likely to trigger the user to think further and does not break the conversation (05–06).

(5.2) Negotiation-Agent Misrecognition

```
01 A:  It is time to do your 10 lunges now. Please confirm when
02     you're done.
03     (after 20 minutes without confirmation)
04 U:  I don't want to do this right now.
05 A:  I'll leave you to it then. Just remember that being
06     consistent in your exercising is the key to success!
```

Design insights: Getting users to spend time explaining non-adherence to the agent can be challenging. As one solution, the system could offer quick shortcuts to the most common reasons for non-adherence. Unfortunately, this might reduce the feeling of conversation and degrade the reflective aspect of the exchange. Worse yet, it can remove the details of the actual reasons and make users gravitate towards suggested responses (e.g. the user actually feels lack of motivation, but gives a "lack of time" shortcut reason). Care must be taken when attempting this approach. Regarding the reporting of activity completion, Exchange 5.1 assumes the user self-reports it. Alternatively certain activities could be measured automatically and hence the user could skip the reporting step. While such solution would lower user effort, it may also suffer from occasional misrecognitions (e.g., system managed to automatically identify only 9 lunges out of 10 the user actually performed). In such cases, the dialogue should gently ask the user about it instead of behaving in the same way as if the user did not perform any activity. Following principles from (Treatment 1999) the agent should avoid explicitly arguing with the user. The ultimate goal the designer should have in mind is keeping the user engaged, even at the risk of occasionally allowing the user to "cheat". A number of different and tailored negotiation tactics could also be employed in this scenario. One such negotiation tactic could even explicitly involve the use of cheat-points, which has been shown to actually lead to higher levels of adherence (Agapie et al. 2016).

5.11   Scenario 6: Coordinating Social Activity Performance

The following scenario demonstrates how an agent can be employed as an intermediary that helps coordinate physical activity performance between two or more connected users.

Goal of the scenario: Social support relates to the use of social relations to encourage performing a behavior by leveraging competition or cooperation between people. Such support is valuable and known to increase motivation and adherence (Maher et al. 2014). Most major models of behavior change involve a social aspect as a key contributor of behavior motivation (Ajzen 1991). Although social support has been shown to be effective, there is still considerable effort and social anxiety involved in asking others to join an activity even in the same office (Hunter et al. 2018). These potential barriers can prevent the person from making an activity social and make her miss out on an opportunity for an additional motivation boost. Although social coordination can be done in multiple different ways, a social agent is a natural solution for closed work groups and co-located environments, where users communicate through chat regularly. An agent could lower the barrier of setting up a social activity by taking care of the coordination tasks.

Dialogue design: In this example, a conversational agent serves as a facilitator and coordinator of social performance of an activity (Exchange 6). The dialogue is meant to lower the barrier of performing an activity socially and boost motivations to do so by connecting users directly.

(6) Social Activity-Agent Recognition

```
(conversation with Mike)

01 A:  Hey Mike, today it's time for your 30 minute jog, would you
02     like to make it social?
03 M:  Sure, why not

(conversation with Kate)

04 A:  Hey Kate, maybe you would be interested in a short jog with
05     Mike?
06 K:  Yep, sounds good.
07 A:  Great, these times are possible for both of you: 11:30am,
08     1pm, 3pm. Which one works best for you?
09 K:  1pm works for me

(conversation with Mike)

10 A:  It's time for your jog in 15 min! Kate and Alex will join
11     you.
12 M:  Great, let's do it!
```

The agent starts a conversation with one of the users proposing to make one of the scheduled activities social (lines 01–02). In this case Mike approves (line 03) and the agent consequently contacts other connected users that are interested in similar activities and have time available in their schedules. In this example, Kate is informed that Mike is planning a jog and is invited to join him (lines 04–05). If she agrees, as in this case (line 06), the agent facilitates a negotiation of available times based on access to users' schedules (lines 07–08). Kate can then select one of the available times (line 09). The agent may also contact other users with similar interests and available times. When the time to perform the activity comes, the agent informs the originator of the activity—Mike, about who will be joining him (line 10). This dialogue has a very strict structure and misrecognitions are rare. In case they do happen, as this dialogue is task oriented, the agent needs to obtain precise information to be able to proceed and consequently it defaults to asking the user to repeat the answer.

Design insights: Simple agent coordinated time arrangements for meeting scheduling have already been demonstrated feasible in commercial products (Cranshaw et al. 2017), but the agent could go beyond that. An agent could access data about user preferences regarding the activities as well as past patterns of interaction between people to actively find and suggest the most likely activity partners. Another interesting aspect here relates to the initiator of the activity. In the presented scenario the agent leverages the fact that one of the users already planned an activity. An alternative approach could rely on the agent initiating an activity from the start. In such approach, success depends on the ability of an agent to successfully match people and on careful design of agent interruptions to prevent the perception of an agent being annoying and actively disruptive. This is especially important in work environments.

5.12 Discussion

In closing this chapter, we wish to summarize some of the main considerations of designing dialogues around health related self-tracking data and also discuss some of the technical challenges involved in realizing some of the dialogues we propose. Finally, we discuss some of the design principles from our process in general.

5.12.1 Specific Considerations When Designing Dialogues for Personal Informatics

One specific aspect of dialogue design on self-tracking health data relates to the important fact that such dialogues need to be designed for long-term use. Self-tracking is a continuous, longitudinal process and behavior change can take a long time to fulfill. A successful conversational agent must be designed with this in mind. Such long-term focus introduces the challenge of making conversations novel and diverse each time—a big practical challenge. For example, in the study of FitTrack (Bickmore and Picard 2005), several subjects mentioned that repetitiveness in the system's dialog content was responsible for them losing motivation to continue working with the system and following its recommendations.

Knowledge about a user's motivations and barriers to activity, as well as health-related data can be sensitive. Agent and dialogue designers must take this information sensitivity into account. In our experience, designing dialogues to be neutral or slightly positive can go a long way. Dialogues with negative framing can be risky and should be used sparingly if at all. General encouragements and expressions of appreciation for user performance and accomplishments are almost always a positive addition.

In the dialogues illustrated in this chapter, the user is guided to come up with their own plans and goals and to discover their own motivations. It is key when designing an agent for behavior change for it not to be perceived as judgmental or prescriptive. Still, the designers must keep in mind that users will sometimes need the agent's help in suggesting what could or should be done. Otherwise, a user who is unable to e.g., formulate attainable action plans, will be left frustrated.

5.12.2 Technical Challenges

Several of our design recommendations presented in this chapter rely on the use of machine learning, natural language processing, or crowd-sourced approaches for recognizing free-text user responses. We wanted to allow users to enter free-form responses by design, especially in self-reflection where unconstrained expression is valuable. Handling user inputs this way, however, can be error prone and may lead to misunderstandings. From our experience, in personal informatics around physical activity and other well-being applications, with proper design agent mistakes can often be tolerated.

In contrast, in some domains such as medication adherence or hospital-based applications, agent mistakes can have dire consequences (e.g. see Bickmore et al. this volume). In such domains, given the current state of technology, constraining the format of user responses to avoid misrecognitions is advisable.

The proposed scenarios heavily rely on the use of external sources of information. Different types of data involve different challenges. The user activity data from wearable trackers could be most sensitive and volatile information. Currently in order to connect to such data the user needs to give explicit permissions for the exact types of data being accessed (e.g., user may only allow sharing of step count, but not calories burned). The impact of such restrictions of access could by incorporated into conversations by e.g., not engaging in dialogues around sources of data the agent can not access. Alternatively, the agent could also try to rely on user self-reporting for such information (e.g., asking the user about change in weight). It is possible, that the user may be willing to give more access to automatically tracked data if a trust relationship with the agent is established over time. Finally the tracked data may also suffer from occasional gaps and mistakes due the sensing imperfections, user forgetfulness, or delayed synchronization. The agent could actively address some of these challenges by e.g., reminding the user to synchronize or making the user aware of the gaps in the data. Regarding the mistakes in automated sensing, we briefly touched upon when discussing one of the scenarios, the agent should in the end trust the user if a discrepancy between the user report and automated sensing arises. The agent should avoid arguing, as long-term user engagement is most important.

Other sources of data used in the scenarios, such as schedule information, social contacts, and goal tracking are highly personal, but less likely to suffer from lack of availability. In dealing with such information the agent should transparently communicate to the user what information is shared and at what level of detail. Sharing schedule information is quite common and the privacy aspects there are addressed by allowing the user to choose the level of details shared, e.g., sharing only busy/free time information, sharing the names of the calendar events, or sharing all the details of events. Similar approaches could be used for other data sources.

Finally, to establish a trust relationship, the agent should enable the user to query the information it possesses about her. Dedicated dialogues could be used to let the user query such information e.g., the user could ask: *"What do you know about my schedule this week?"* and the agent should disclose any information and also allow the user to change/remove it. Some information may be too complex and detailed to be used directly in the dialogues, e.g., raw sensor data. In such cases the agent could point the user to a graphical dashboard. Giving the user an ability to actively scrutinize the information in possession of any AI system is a general design recommendation that is, unfortunately, often not followed.

5.13   Conclusion

In this chapter, we discussed the value of integrating external sources of data into conversational interactions and techniques for designing conversations that help users learn and reflect on their data. We focused specifically on the domain of health behavior change and the process of reflection and learning from collected self-tracking activity data. Such data are readily available thanks to wearable fitness devices such as Fitbit and Apple Watch. At the same time, conversational agents such as Siri and Google Assistant are available on mobile devices. Integrating agents and personal data is a valuable and necessary direction to explore. We described a practical technical architecture for integrating external sources of data into conversations and discussed design strategies for mitigating effects of possible imperfections in automated recognition of free-text user responses. Finally, we provided blueprints for six unique conversational scenarios in the domain of health behavior change, as a guide for designers and implementers.

The current use of conversational agents is still centered mostly on transactional interactions, such as "booking a restaurant" or "asking for the weather". We believe that the future of conversational interaction will increasingly involve context-aware agents that will have access to meaningful data about the user and beyond. Such external data will allow conversational agents to provide more personalized interaction and transform them from being mere replacement for graphical user interfaces to true personal assistants. The health behavior-change domain we explored here offers an early glimpse into the likely future where conversational agents will be integrated with various IoT devices. Awareness of the environment, user preferences and activities will allow future agents to provide a natural and highly personalized interaction environment. Therefore, exploration of early design principles, challenges and use cases provides an important step towards such a future.

References

Abraham C, Michie S (2008) A taxonomy of behavior change techniques used in interventions. Health Psychol 27:379

Agapie E, Avrahami D, Marlow J (2016) Staying the course: system-driven lapse management for supporting behavior change. In: Proceedings of the 2016 CHI conference on human factors in computing systems. ACM, pp 1072–1083

Ajzen I (1991) The theory of planned behavior. Organ Behav Hum Decis Process 50:179–211

Bentley F, Tollmar K, Stephenson P et al (2013) Health mashups: presenting statistical patterns between wellbeing data and context in natural language to promote behavior change

Bickmore T, Giorgino T (2006) Health dialog systems for patients and consumers. J Biomed Inform 39:556–571

Bickmore TW, Picard RW (2005) Establishing and maintaining long-term human-computer relationships. ACM Trans Comput-Hum Interact TOCHI 12:293–327

Bickmore T, Schulman D, Yin L (2010) Maintaining engagement in long-term interventions with relational agents. Appl Artif Intell 24:648–666. https://doi.org/10.1080/08839514.2010.492259

Bouton ME (2014) Why behavior change is difficult to sustain. Prev Med 68:29–36

Bovend'Eerdt TJ, Botell RE, Wade DT (2009) Writing SMART rehabilitation goals and achieving goal attainment scaling: a practical guide. Clin Rehabil 23:352–361

Chung C-F, Jensen N, Shklovski IA, Munson S (2017) Finding the right fit: understanding health tracking in workplace wellness programs. In: Proceedings of the 2017 CHI conference on human factors in computing systems. ACM, pp 4875–4886

Colusso L, Hsieh G, Munson SA (2016) Designing Closeness to Increase Gamers' Performance. In: Proceedings of the 2016 CHI conference on human factors in computing systems. ACM, New York, NY, USA, pp 3020–3024

Conroy DE, Yang C-H, Maher JP (2014) Behavior change techniques in top-ranked mobile apps for physical activity. Am J Prev Med 46:649–652

Consolvo S, Klasnja P, McDonald DW, et al (2008) Flowers or a robot army?: encouraging awareness & activity with personal, mobile displays. In: Proceedings of the 10th international conference on Ubiquitous computing. ACM, pp 54–63

Cranshaw J, Elwany E, Newman T et al (2017) Calendar. help: designing a workflow-based scheduling agent with humans in the loop. In: Proceedings of the 2017 CHI conference on human factors in computing systems. ACM, pp 2382–2393

Dhillon B, Kocielnik R, Politis I et al (2011) Culture and facial expressions: a case study with a speech interface. IFIP conference on human-computer interaction. Springer, Berlin Heidelberg, pp 392–404

Fleck R, Fitzpatrick G (2010) Reflecting on reflection: framing a design landscape. In: Proceedings of the 22nd conference of the computer-human interaction special interest group of Australia on computer-human interaction. ACM, pp 216–223

Fogg B (2009) A Behavior Model for Persuasive Design. In: Proceedings of the 4th International Conference on Persuasive Technology. ACM, New York, NY, USA, pp 40:1–40:7

Fujita K, Han HA (2009) Moving beyond deliberative control of impulses: The effect of construal levels on evaluative associations in self-control conflicts. Psychol Sci 20:799–804

Götzmann V (2015) Towards a persuasive dialog system supporting personal health management. National Research Center

Hunter RF, Ball K, Sarmiento OL (2018) Socially awkward: how can we better promote walking as a social behaviour? BMJ Publishing Group Ltd and British Association of Sport and Exercise Medicine

Kim Y-S, Hullman J (2015) User-driven expectation visualization: opportunities for personalized feedback

Kinnafick F-E, Thøgersen-Ntoumani C, Duda JL (2014) Physical activity adoption to adherence, lapse, and dropout a self-determination theory perspective. Qual Health Res 24:706–718

Kocielnik RD (2014) LifelogExplorer: a tool for visual exploration of ambulatory skin conductance measurements in context. In: Proceedings of measuring behavior

Kocielnik R, Hsieh G (2017) Send me a different message: utilizing cognitive space to create engaging message triggers. In: CSCW. pp 2193–2207

Kocielnik R, Sidorova N (2015) Personalized stress management: enabling stress monitoring with lifelogexplorer. KI-Künstl Intell 29:115–122

Kocielnik R, Pechenizkiy M, Sidorova N (2012) Stress analytics in education. In: Educational data mining 2012

Kocielnik R, Maggi FM, Sidorova N (2013a) Enabling self-reflection with LifelogExplorer: generating simple views from complex data. In: Pervasive computing technologies for healthcare (PervasiveHealth), 2013 7th international conference on. IEEE, pp 184–191

Kocielnik R, Sidorova N, Maggi FM, et al (2013b) Smart technologies for long-term stress monitoring at work. In: Computer-based medical systems (CBMS), 2013 IEEE 26th international symposium on. IEEE, pp 53–58

Kocielnik R, Avrahami D, Marlow J et al (2018a) Designing for workplace reflection: a chat and voice-based conversational agent. In: Proceedings of the 2018 designing interactive systems conference. https://doi.org/10.1145/3196709.3196784

Kocielnik R, Xiao Lillian, Avrahami D, Hsieh G (2018b) Reflection companion: a conversational system for engaging users in reflection on physical activity. IMWUT 2:26

Lee MK, Kim J, Forlizzi J, Kiesler S (2015) Personalization revisited: a reflective approach helps people better personalize health services and motivates them to increase physical activity. In: Proceedings of the 2015 ACM international joint conference on pervasive and ubiquitous computing. ACM, pp 743–754

Lewis MA, Uhrig JD, Bann CM et al (2013) Tailored text messaging intervention for HIV adherence: a proof-of-concept study. Health Psychol 32:248

Li I, Dey A, Forlizzi J (2010) A stage-based model of personal informatics systems. In: Proceedings of the SIGCHI conference on human factors in computing systems. ACM, pp 557–566

Li I, Dey AK, Forlizzi J (2011) Understanding my data, myself: supporting self-reflection with ubicomp technologies. In: Proceedings of the 13th international conference on Ubiquitous computing. ACM, pp 405–414

Lin J, Mamykina L, Lindtner S, et al (2006) Fish'n'Steps: Encouraging physical activity with an interactive computer game. UbiComp 2006 Ubiquitous Comput, 261–278

Locke EA, Latham GP (2006) New directions in goal-setting theory. Curr Dir Psychol Sci 15:265–268. https://doi.org/10.1111/j.1467-8721.2006.00449.x

Maher CA, Lewis LK, Ferrar K et al (2014) Are health behavior change interventions that use online social networks effective?. A systematic review, J Med Internet Res, p 16

McDuff D, Karlson A, Kapoor A, et al (2012) AffectAura: an intelligent system for emotional memory. In: Proceedings of the SIGCHI conference on human factors in computing systems. ACM, pp 849–858

Miller WR, Rollnick S (2009) Ten things that motivational interviewing is not. Behav Cogn Psychother 37:129–140

Moon JA (2013) Reflection in learning and professional development: theory and practice. Routledge, Abingdon

Myers RS, Roth DL (1997) Perceived benefits of and barriers to exercise and stage of exercise adoption in young adults. Health Psychol 16:277

Novielli N, de Rosis F, Mazzotta I (2010) User attitude towards an embodied conversational agent: effects of the interaction mode. J Pragmat 42:2385–2397

Rautalinko E, Lisper H-O, Ekehammar B (2007) Reflective listening in counseling: effects of training time and evaluator social skills. Am J Psychother NY 61:191–209

Rivera-Pelayo V, Zacharias V, Müller L, Braun S (2012) Applying quantified self approaches to support reflective learning. In: Proceedings of the 2nd international conference on learning analytics and knowledge. ACM, pp 111–114

Rollnick S, Miller WR (1995) What is motivational interviewing? Behav Cogn Psychother 23:325–334

Schueller SM (2010) Preferences for positive psychology exercises. J Posit Psychol 5:192–203

Skurnik I, Yoon C, Park DC, Schwarz N (2005) How warnings about false claims become recommendations. J Consum Res 31:713–724. https://doi.org/10.1086/426605

Tanumihardjo SA, Anderson C, Kaufer-Horwitz M et al (2007) Poverty, obesity, and malnutrition: an international perspective recognizing the paradox. J Am Diet Assoc 107:1966–1972

Tollmar K, Bentley F, Viedma C (2012) Mobile health mashups: making sense of multiple streams of wellbeing and contextual data for presentation on a mobile device. In: 2012 6th International conference on pervasive computing technologies for healthcare (PervasiveHealth) and workshops. IEEE, pp 65–72

Treatment C for SA (1999) Chapter 3—Motivational interviewing as a counseling style. Substance Abuse and Mental Health Services Administration (US)

Tufte ER (1991) Envisioning information. Optom Vis Sci 68:322–324

Tur G, De Mori R (2011) Spoken language understanding: Systems for extracting semantic information from speech. Wiley, Hoboken

Wang Y-Y, Deng L, Acero A (2005) Spoken language understanding. IEEE Signal Process Mag 22:16–31

Williams JD, Niraula NB, Dasigi P et al (2015) Rapidly scaling dialog systems with interactive learning. In: Natural language dialog systems and intelligent assistants. Springer, Berlin, pp 1–13

Part III
Agent Misunderstanding

Chapter 6
Teaching Agents When They Fail: End User Development in Goal-Oriented Conversational Agents

Toby Jia-Jun Li, Igor Labutov, Brad A. Myers, Amos Azaria, Alexander I. Rudnicky and Tom M. Mitchell

Abstract This chapter introduces an end user development (EUD) approach for handling common types of failures encountered by goal-oriented conversational agents. We start with identifying three common sources of failures in human-agent conversations: *unknown concepts, out-of-domain tasks* and *wrong fulfillment means or level of generalization in task execution*. To handle these failures, it is useful to enable the end user to program the agent and to "teach" the agent what to do as a fallback strategy. Showing examples for this approach, we walk through our two integrated systems: SUGILITE and LIA. SUGILITE uses the programming by demonstration (PBD) technique, allowing the user to program the agent by demonstrating new tasks or new means for completing a task using the GUIs of third-party smartphone apps, while LIA learns new tasks from verbal instructions, enabling the user to teach the agent through breaking down the procedure verbally. LIA also enables the user to verbally define unknown concepts used in the commands and adds those concepts into the agent's ontology. Both SUGILITE and LIA can generalize what they have learned from the user across related entities and perform a task with new parameters in a different context.

T. J.-J. Li (✉) · I. Labutov · B. A. Myers · A. I. Rudnicky · T. M. Mitchell
Carnegie Mellon University, Pittsburgh, PA, USA
e-mail: tobyli@cs.cmu.edu

I. Labutov
e-mail: ilabutov@cs.cmu.edu

B. A. Myers
e-mail: bam@cs.cmu.edu

A. I. Rudnicky
e-mail: air@cs.cmu.edu

T. M. Mitchell
e-mail: tom.mitchell@cs.cmu.edu

A. Azaria
Ariel University, Ariel, Israel
e-mail: amos.azaria@ariel.ac.il

© Springer International Publishing AG, part of Springer Nature 2018
R. J. Moore et al. (eds.), *Studies in Conversational UX Design*, Human–Computer Interaction Series, https://doi.org/10.1007/978-3-319-95579-7_6

119

6.1 Introduction

Recently, goal-oriented conversational agents have made significant progress in expanding the support for more task domains, refining the speech recognition components for reduced recognition errors, improving the natural language understanding model for better comprehension of user commands, and enhancing the dialog management system to have more natural and fluent conversations with users.

Despite the progress made, these conversational agents still inevitably encounter errors and failures. In designing and implementing the user experience of a goal-oriented conversational agent, a crucial part is *failure handling*—how should the agent respond when it could not understand the user's command, could not perform the task the user asked for, or performed the task in a different way than what the user had hoped for? Many UX guidelines for designing conversational flow and fallback strategies in dialog management systems have been proposed, such as directing the users to rephrase in a different way that the agent can understand (Pappu and Rudnicky 2014; Armstrong 2017a), refocusing and redirecting the users to tasks that the agent can support (Barkin 2016), updating and confirming the beliefs of the system (Bohus and Rudnicky 2005a), or providing users options to correct the input (Armstrong 2017b). Extensive work in dialog management systems have also been conducted to detect and to recover from errors of non-understanding (Bohus and Rudnicky 2005b, c), and to proactively elicit knowledge (Pappu and Rudnicky 2014) from users for helping reduce subsequent task failures in user's dialogs with conversational agents.

In this chapter, we take a different perspective to discuss an end-user development (EUD) approach for failure handling in conversational agents. We believe that the design goal for conversational agents should evolve from *easy to use* (i.e. users should easily figure out how to provide a "good" or "valid" input for the agent with the help of good UX design) to *easy to develop* (Lieberman 2001), where the end users are empowered to "teach" the agent what to do for a given input, and to modify how a task is executed by the agent. Such new capabilities can provide expandability, customizability and flexibility to the users, catering to their highly diverse and rapidly changing individual preferences, needs, personal language vocabulary and phrasings. We share our experience on designing and implementing LIA and SUGILITE, two integrated systems that can enable end users of the conversational agent to define new concepts in the ontology through giving natural language instructions, and to instruct the agent's new tasks by demonstrating the use of existing third-party apps available on the phone. The two systems leverage different input modalities—LIA relies on the user instructions in natural language, while SUGILITE mainly uses the user's demonstrations on graphical user interfaces (GUI). We also discuss our future work on further combing the two approaches to provide users with multi-modal end user development experiences for conversational agents.

This chapter first explains three types of challenges that we identified on how goal-oriented conversational agents handle failures in the dialog. Then we use our two systems LIA and SUGILITE as examples for explaining how supporting end user development can be adopted as a useful failure handling strategy for a conversational agent. Finally, we discuss the directions of our ongoing and planned follow-up work.

6.2 Underlying Challenges

This section identifies three underlying challenges for goal-oriented conversational agents in handling failures.

6.2.1 Understanding Unknown and Undefined Concepts

A great amount of work in the domains of speech recognition and natural language processing has been put into helping conversational agents better understand verbal commands. Large ontologies and knowledge graphs of both general and domain-specific knowledge have been connected to the conversational agents, so they can identify entities and concepts in the commands, understand relations, and perform reasoning on these entities, concepts and relations (Dzikovska et al. 2003; Gruber et al. 2017).

However, many of the concepts involved in the commands can be fuzzy or have varying meanings that are specific to individual users, so they cannot be found in existing ontologies. For example, a user may say things like "*Show my important meetings*" or "*Send emails to my colleagues*", where concepts like "important meetings" and "my colleagues" are not clearly defined. There might also be customized properties (e.g., each colleague has an affiliation) and criteria (e.g., colleagues all have email addresses from the university domain) for those concepts. As result, the conversational agents are not able to understand these commands. Even some agents like Apple Siri, which actively builds personal ontologies through passively mining personal data (e.g., emails, contacts, calendar events) (Gruber et al. 2017) are still unlikely to cover all the concepts that the user may refer to in the commands due to both technical difficulties and privacy concerns. It remains an important challenge for conversational agents to learn those personal concepts found in user commands that are unknown to the agent and undefined in existing ontologies (Azaria and Hong 2016).

In addition to understanding unknown classes of entities, a closely related problem is understanding unknown language referring to actions. For example, the user might request "*Drop a note to Brad to say I'll be late*" but the agent might not know the action "drop a note." So, the problem of undefined concepts is both an ontology problem and a language understanding problem.

6.2.2 Executing Out-of-Domain Tasks

Traditionally, conversational agents were only able to perform tasks on a fixed set of domains, whose fulfillments had been pre-programmed by their developers. For example, Apple Siri used to only be able to perform tasks with built-in smartphone apps (e.g., Phone, Message, Calendar, Music) and query a few integrated external web services (e.g., Weather, Wikipedia, Wolfram). Consequently, many commands that users give are out-of-domain for the agents, despite the fact that there are apps available on the phone for executing these tasks. In these situations, the agents generally rely on fallback strategies, such as using web search, which does not perform the task. Although many existing agents have made efforts to understand some parts of the query so they can provide a more specific response than the most general *"Do you want me to Google this for you?"* those out-of-domain failures are still frustrating for users in most cases. For example, we can observe the following dialog when a user tries to order a cup of coffee using Apple Siri:

(1) Coffee Order

```
00 U:  Order a cup of Cappuccino.
01 A:  Here's what I found: (Showing a list of Apple Map
       results of nearby coffee shops)
```

In the Excerpt 1 above, we can see that although the agent has successfully recognized the user's intent, it cannot fulfill the user's request due to the lack of an API for task fulfillment.

To address this issue, major "virtual assistant" agents like Apple Siri, Google Assistant and Amazon Alexa have started opening their APIs to third-party developers so they can develop "skills" for the agents, or integrate their own apps into the agents. However, based on what we can observe, only a small number of the most popular third-party apps have been integrated into these agents due to the cost and engineering effort required. In the foreseeable future, the "long-tail" of unintegrated apps are not likely to be supported by the agents. While each long-tail app does not have a massive user base, some of these apps are used frequently by a small group of users. Thus, it can still be important to enable the agents to invoke commands supported by these apps.

6.2.3 Using the Right Fulfillment Means and Generalization in Task Execution

Another type of failure can happen when the agent understands the command correctly, has the capability to perform the task, but executes the task in a different fashion, with different specifications, or through a different means than the user had anticipated. This type of failure is often a result of assumptions made by the bot developers on how the user might want the task to be performed.

An example of this type of failure is assuming which service to use for fulfilling the user's intent. Virtual assistants like Apple Siri and Google Assistant often have a preset service provider for each supported task domain, despite all the other apps installed on the phone that can also perform the same task. In reality, each individual user may have a different preferred service provider to use, or even a logic for choosing a service provider on the fly (e.g., choosing the cheapest ride for the destination between Uber and Lyft). As a result, the conversational agent should allow the user to customize what service, or the criteria for choosing the service, to use when fulfilling an intent.

In some other situations, the agent makes too many assumptions about the task parameters and asks too few questions. For example, in the customer reviews for an Alexa skill of a popular pizza-delivery chain, a customer writes

> ...You can only order pizza; no sides, no drinks, just pizza. You also can't order specials/deals or use promo codes. Lastly, you can't select an address to use. It will automatically select the default address on the account. (Mitman93)

This skill also does not support any customization of the pizza, only allowing the user to choose between a few fixed options. In contrast, the Android app for the same chain supports all the features mentioned in the customer's review, plus a screen for the user to fully customize the crust, the sauce and the toppings. This phenomenon is not unique as many conversational agents only support a subset of functionality and features when compared with their smartphone app counterparts.

On the other hand, it is also crucial to keep the dialog brief and avoid overwhelming users with too many options. This is especially true in speech interfaces, as users can quickly skim over many available options presented in the GUI, but this is not possible when using voice. However, it is not easy to decide what parameters a conversational agent should present to the users, as users often have highly diverse needs and personal preferences. An important question to ask for one user may seem redundant for another. We argue that conversational agents should (1) make all the options available but also (2) personalize for each user the questions to ask every time and the parameters that the agent should simply save as default values.

6.3 Learning from Demonstration

Learning from the user's demonstration allows a conversational agent to learn how to perform a task from observing the user doing it. This approach helps the agent address the two challenges of *executing out-of-domain tasks* and *using the right fulfillment means and generalization in task execution* in failure handling as described in the previous sections. For out-of-domain tasks, the users can program these tasks by demonstrating them for the agent. The users can also freely customize how a task is executed by the agent and incorporate their personal preferences in the task demonstration.

In this section, we introduce our programming by demonstration agent SUGILITE as an example to illustrate how programming by demonstration (PBD) can be adopted in failure handling for conversational agents. We also walk through the design goals of SUGILITE and how its implementation supports these design goals.

6.3.1 SUGILITE

SUGILITE (Li et al. 2017a) is a multi-modal programming-by-demonstration system that enables end users to program arbitrary smartphone tasks for conversational intelligent agents. The end user does this by combining the demonstrations made by directly manipulating the regular graphical user interface (GUI) of smartphone apps, along with verbal instructions. SUGILITE allows the users to invoke arbitrary third-party apps on an Android smartphone to perform previously-demonstrated tasks using voice commands without having to repeatedly navigate through the GUI of the app.

A major benefit of using the demonstration approach is *usability*. SUGILITE adopts the programming-by-demonstration (PBD) technique, which significantly lowers the learning barrier for end users. By using SUGILITE, an end user of a conversational intelligent agent is able to "teach" the agent what to do for an out-of-domain command to expand the capabilities of the agent without necessarily knowing any programming language. Instead, the user can demonstrate the task using familiar GUIs of existing third-party mobile apps, leveraging their knowledge and experience on how to use those apps from the user's perspective. Unlike conventional programming languages which require the user to map what they see on the GUI to a textual representation of actions, the PBD approach enables users to naturally program in the same environment in which they perform the actions (Cypher and Halbert 1993; Myers et al. 2017).

PBD techniques have already been used in software for automating repetitive computing tasks. For example, Adobe Photoshop allows users to record a series of operations in photo editing, and to replay the recorded operations later on a different photo. Similarly, in Microsoft Office, the users can record a macro for automating operations on documents. PBD techniques have also been used in prior systems for automating tasks in domains such as email processing (Cypher 1993), arithmetic calculation (Witten 1993), programming intelligent tutors (Koedinger et al. 2004) and performing web tasks (Allen et al. 2007; Leshed et al. 2008).

However, an advantage of SUGILITE compared with prior systems is applicability. Most prior systems each focus on a single domain, while SUGILITE can be used for tasks in any arbitrary Android smartphone app, or across multiple apps. SUGILITE also doesn't require any modification of the app or access to the app's internal structures, unlike CHINLE (Chen and Weld 2008) requiring the app to be implemented in the SUPPLE (Gajos and Weld 2004) framework) or COSCRIPTER (Leshed et al. 2008) leveraging the DOM structure of the web page.

6.3.2 An Example Scenario

In this section, we walk through an example use case of SUGILITE to exhibit how the PBD approach can help an end user to program an out-of-domain task for a goal-oriented conversational agent by demonstration. In this example, the agent fails to fulfill the user's command to order a cup of Cappuccino. To respond, the user demonstrates ordering a cup of Cappuccino using the Starbucks app. SUGILITE then generalizes the script so the agent learns to order any Starbucks drink.

Suppose a user first asks the conversational agent, "*Order a Cappuccino*" (Figure 6.1a), for which the agent answers "*I don't understand what you mean by order a cappuccino, you can explain or demonstrate…*" In our example, the user responds, "*I'll demonstrate*" and starts demonstrating the procedure of ordering a Cappuccino using the Starbucks app installed on the phone. Alternatively, the user could also choose to use any other available coffee shop app for demonstrating this task.

She first clicks on the Starbucks icon on the home screen, taps on the main menu and chooses "Order," which is exactly the same procedure as what she would have done had she been ordering manually through the Starbucks app. (Alternatively, she could also say verbal commands for each step such as "*Click on Starbucks*," etc.) After each action, a confirmation dialog from SUGILITE pops up (Fig. 6.1b) to confirm the user's desire for the action to be recorded by the SUGILITE service.

The user proceeds through the task procedure by clicking on "MENU," "Espresso Drinks," "Cappuccinos," "Cappuccino," "Add to Order" and "View Order" in sequence, which are all the same steps that she would use to perform the task manually without SUGILITE. In this process, the user could also demonstrate choosing options such as the size and the add-ins for the coffee according to her personal preferences. These customizations will be included every time the task is invoked by the agent, allowing the user to personalize how a task should be performed by the conversational agent.

SUGILITE pops up the confirmation dialog after each click, except for the one on the menu option "Cappuccino," where SUGILITE is confused and must ask the user to choose from two identifying features on the same button: "Cappuccino" and "120 cal" (Fig. 6.1c). When finished, the user clicks on the SUGILITE status icon and selects "End Recording."

After the demonstration, SUGILITE analyzes the recording and parameterizes the script according to the voice command and its knowledge about the UI hierarchy of the Starbucks app (details in the Generalizability section).

This parameterization allows the user to give the voice command "*Order a* [DRINK]" where [DRINK] can be any of the drinks listed on the menu in the Starbucks app. SUGILITE can then order the drink automatically for the user by manipulating the user interface of the Starbucks app. Alternatively, the automation can also be executed by using the SUGILITE graphical user interface (GUI) or invoked externally by a third-party app using the SUGILITE API.

Fig. 6.1 Screenshots of the current version of SUGILITE prototype: **a** the conversational interface; **b** the recording confirmation popup; **c** the recording disambiguation/operation editing panel and **d** the viewing/editing script window

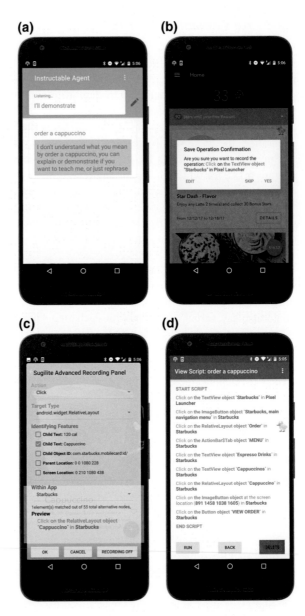

6.3.3 Key Design Goals

In this section, we identify three key design goals for PBD in goal-oriented conversational agents: *generalizability*, *robustness*, and *multi-modality*, followed by a discussion of how the SUGILITE implementation of achieves these design goals.

6.3.3.1 Generalizability

A PBD agent should produce more than just record-and-replay macros that are very literal (e.g., sequences of clicks and keystrokes), but learn the task at a higher level of abstraction so it can perform the task in new contexts with different parameters. To achieve this, SUGILITE uses a multi-modal approach to infer the user's intents and makes correct generalizations on what the user demonstrates. SUGILITE collects a spoken utterance from the user for the intent of the task before the demonstration, automatically identifies the parameters in the utterance, matches each parameter with an operation in the demonstration of the user, and creates a generalized script.

While recording the user's demonstration, SUGILITE compares the identifying features of the target UI elements and the arguments of the operations against the user's utterance, trying to identify possible parameters by matching the words in the command. For example, for a verbal command "*Find the flights from New York to Los Angeles*," SUGILITE identifies "New York" and "Los Angeles" as the two parameters, if the user typed "New York" into the departure city textbox and "Los Angeles" into the destination textbox during the demonstration.

This parameterization method provides control to users over the level of personalization and abstraction in SUGILITE scripts. For example, if the user demonstrated ordering a venti Cappuccino with skim milk by saying the command "*Order a Cappuccino*," we will discover that "Cappuccino" is a parameter, but not "venti" or "skim milk." However, if the user gave the same demonstration, but had used the command, "*Order a venti Cappuccino*," then we would also consider the size of the coffee ("venti") to be a parameter.

For the generalization of text entry operations (e.g., typing "New York" into the departure city textbox), SUGILITE allows the use of any value for the parameters. In the checking flights example, the user can give the command "*Find the flights from* [A] *to* [B]," for any [A] and [B] values after demonstrating how to find the flights from New York to Los Angeles. SUGILITE will simply replace the two city names by the value of the parameters in the corresponding steps when executing the automation.

When the user chooses an option, SUGILITE also records the set of all possible alternatives to the option that the user selected. SUGILITE finds these alternatives based on the UI pattern and structure, looking for those in parallel to the target UI element. For example, suppose the user demonstrates "*Order a Cappuccino*" in which an operation is clicking on "Cappuccino." from the "Cappuccinos" menu that has two parallel options "Cappuccino" and "Iced Cappuccino." SUGILITE will first identify "Cappuccino" as a parameter, and then add "Iced Cappuccino" to the set as an alternative value for the parameter, allowing the user to order Iced Cappuccino using the same script. By keeping this list of alternatives, SUGILITE can also differentiate tasks with similar command structure but different values. For example, the commands "*Order Iced Cappuccino*" and "*Order cheese pizza*" invoke different scripts, because the phrase "Iced Cappuccino" is among the alternative elements of operations in one script, while "cheese pizza" would be among the alternatives of a different script. If multiple scripts can be used to execute a command (e.g., if the user has two scripts for ordering pizza with different apps), the user can explicitly select which script to run.

A limitation of the above method in extracting alternative elements is that it only generalizes at the leaf level of a multi-level menu structure. For example, the generalized script for "*Order a Cappuccino*" can be generalized for ordering Iced Cappuccino, but cannot be used to order drinks like a Latte or Macchiato because they are on other branches of the Starbucks "Order" menu. Since the user did not go to those branches during the demonstration, this method could not know the existence of those options or how to reach those options in the menu tree. This is a challenge of working with third-party apps, which do not expose their internal structures to us and which menu structures we are unable to traverse without invoking the apps on the main UI thread.

To address this issue, we created a background tracking service that records all the clickable elements in apps and the corresponding UI path to reach each element. This service can run in the background all the time, so SUGILITE can learn about all the parts of an app that the user visits. Through this mechanism, SUGILITE can construct which path to navigate through the menu structure to reach all the UI elements seen by the service. The text labels of all such elements can then be added to the sets of alternative values for the corresponding parameters in scripts. This means that SUGILITE can allow the user to order drinks that are not an immediate sibling to Cappuccino at the leaf level of the Starbucks order menu tree, despite obtaining only a single demonstration.

This method has its trade-offs. First, it generates false positives. For example, there is a clickable node "Store Locator" in the Starbucks "Order" menu. The generalizing process will then mistakenly add "Store Locator" to the list of what the user can order. Second, running the background tracking affects the phone's performance. Third, SUGILITE cannot generalize for items that were never viewed by the user. Lastly, many participants expressed privacy concerns about allowing background tracking to store text labels from apps, since apps may dynamically generate labels containing personal data like an account number or an account balance.

6.3.3.2 Robustness

It is important to ensure robustness of PBD agents, so the agent can reliably perform the demonstrated task in different conditions. Yet, the scripts learned from demonstration are often brittle to any changes in the app's UI, or any new situations unseen in the demonstration. Error checking and handling has been a major challenge for many PBD systems (Cypher and Halbert 1993; Lieberman 2001). SUGILITE provides error handling and checking mechanism to detect when a new situation is encountered during execution or when the app's UI changes after an update.

When executing a script, an error occurs when the next operation in the script cannot be successfully performed. There are at least three reasons for an execution error. First, the app may have been updated and the layout of the UI has been changed, so SUGILITE cannot find the object specified in the operation. Second, the app may be in a different state than it had been during the demonstration. For example, if a user demonstrates how to request an Uber car during normal pricing and then uses the script to request a car during surge pricing, then an error will occur because SUGILITE does not know how to handle the popup from the Uber app for surge price confirmation. Third, the execution may also be interrupted by an external event like a phone call or an alarm.

In SUGILITE, when an error occurs, an error handling popup will be shown, asking the user to choose between three options: keep waiting, stop executing, or fix the script. The "keep waiting" option will keep SUGILITE waiting until the current operation can be performed. This option should be used in situations like prolonged waiting in the app or an interrupting phone call, where the user knows that the app will eventually return to the recorded state in the script, which SUGILITE knows how to handle. The "stop executing" option will end the execution of the current script.

The "fix the script" option has two sub-options: "replace" and "create a fork," which allow the user to either demonstrate a procedure from the current step that will replace the corresponding part of the old script or create a new alternative fork in the old script. The "replace" option should be used to handle permanent changes in the procedure due to an app update or an error in the previous demonstration, or if the user changes her mind about what the script should do. The "create a fork" option (Fig. 6.1d) should be used to enable the script to deal with a new situation. The forking works like the try-catch statement in programming languages, where SUGILITE will first attempt to perform the original operation and then executes the alternative branch if the original operation fails. (Other kinds of forks, branches, and conditions are planned as future work.)

The forking mechanism can also handle new situations introduced by generalization. For example, after the user demonstrates how to check the score of the NY Giants using the Yahoo! Sports app, SUGILITE generalizes the script so it can check the score of any sports team. However, if the user gives a command "*Check the score of NY Yankees*," everything will work properly until the last step, where SUGILITE cannot find the score because the demonstrations so far only show where to find the score on an American football team's page, which has a different layout than a baseball team's page. In this case, the user creates a new fork and demonstrates how to find the score for a baseball team.

6.3.3.3 Multi-modality

Another design goal of ours is to support multiple modalities in the agent to provide flexibility for users in different contexts. In SUGILITE, both creating the automation and running the automation can be performed through either the conversational interface or the GUI.

The user can start a demonstration after giving an out-of-domain verbal command, for which SUGILITE will reply "*I don't understand… You can demonstrate to teach me*" or the user can manually start a new demonstration using the SUGILITE GUI. When teaching a new command to SUGILITE, the user can use verbal instructions, demonstrations, or a mix of both in creating the script. Even though in most cases, demonstrating on the GUI through direct manipulation will be more efficient, we anticipate some useful scenarios for voice instruction when handling the phone is inconvenient or for users with motor impairment.

The user can also execute automations by either giving voice commands or by selecting from a list of scripts. Running an automation by voice allows the user to give a command from a distance. For scripts with parameters, the parameter values are either explicitly specified in the GUI or inferred from the verbal command when the conversational interface is used.

During recording or executing, the user has easy access to the controls of SUGILITE through the floating duck icon (see Fig. 6.1, where the icon is on the right edge of the screen). The floating duck icon changes the appearance to indicate the status of SUGILITE—whether it is recording, executing, or tracking in the background. The user can start, pause or end the execution/recording as well as view the current script (Fig. 6.1d) and the script list from the pop-up menu that appears when users tap on the duck. The GUI also enables the user to manually edit a script by deleting an operation and all the subsequent operations or to resume recording starting from the end of the script. Selecting an operation lets the user edit it using the editing panel (Fig. 6.1c).

The multi-modality of SUGILITE enables many useful usage scenarios in different contexts. For example, the user may automate tasks like finding nearby parking or streaming audible books by demonstrating the procedures in advance through direct manipulation. Then the user can perform those tasks by voice while driving without needing to touch the phone. A user with motor impairment can have her friends or family program the conversational agent for her common tasks so she can execute them later by voice.

6.3.4 Evaluation

To evaluate how end users with various levels of programming skill can successfully operate learning-by-demonstration conversational agents like SUGILITE, we ran a lab-based usability analysis of SUGILITE with 19 participants across a range of programming skills (from non-programmers to skilled programmers). Of the scripts created by the participants, 65 out of 76 (85.5%) ran and performed the intended task successfully. Of the four tasks given, 8 out of the 19 (42.1%) participants succeeded in all four tasks (e.g., sending emails, checking sports scores, etc.); all participants completed at least two tasks successfully.

In the results, we found no significant difference in both task completion time and task completion rate between groups of participants with different levels of programming skill. This result suggests that by using SUGILITE, non-programmers can introduce new tasks for conversational agents just as well as programmers. Looking at the completion time of the participants, we measured that programming a repetitive task with SUGILITE and using the agent for executing the task later is more efficient than performing the task manually if the task will be performed more than 3–6 times, depending on the task.

6.4 Learning from Verbal Instruction

As we have discussed earlier, another major source for failures in the user's dialog with conversational agents is when the user uses unknown or undefined concepts in the command. For example, suppose a user gives the following commands to a conversational agent for creating task automation rules:

- If there is an important email, forward it to my project team.
- Whenever there is a late homework, forward it to the TAs.
- If the weather is bad in the morning, wake me up at 7 AM.
- When I get an important meeting request, put it on my calendar.

The programming by demonstration approach we have described in the previous section allows the user to handle failures where the agent does not know how to fulfill the actions in the command, such as "forward to" and "put it on my calendar." However, the above commands also introduce another type of challenge. In the commands, the user refers to concepts such as *important email*, *my project team* and *bad weather*. For the agent, those concepts may be either undefined or unclearly defined. Consequently, the agent might not be able to execute these commands successfully.

Besides learning from demonstration, another useful EUD strategy that can help the conversational agent to address this issue is *learning from verbal instruction* (Azaria et al. 2016). We designed a conversational task automation agent named LIA that allows the user to verbally define concepts used in the conditions and actions found in the user's verbal commands. The agent can learn those new concepts by adding them into the ontology. LIA also enables the user to teach the agent to perform a new task by verbally breaking down an unknown action into smaller steps, which complements the learning-by-demonstration approach used in SUGILITE especially in situations where verbal instruction is more convenient or more natural for the user than demonstrating on the GUI.

LIA allows the user to define "trigger-action" style automation rules in natural language like the command examples shown above. The popularity of tools like IFFFT (If-This-Then-That) and Zapier, which allow users to define simple trigger-action rules in visual programming environments, has demonstrated the general need for intuitive-to-use automation tools to simplify day-to-day tasks. However, we argue that without the capacity to teach such rules in natural language, such tools are fundamentally limited. This limitation stems from the fact that for these tools to be effective, the user's needs must be matched to pre-built IF and THEN components in a library of functions. However, if the user's need strays beyond common scenarios (e.g., there probably will not be an "important email" or "late homework" function in the library), these tools become difficult or impossible to use. The experience of building anything remotely more complex with the current tools (e.g., rules with multiple conditions) starts to resemble traditional programming and thus becomes inaccessible for many end users.

6.4.1 Learning Rules

We believe that giving a conversational agent the capacity to be taught rules and concepts verbally opens the possibility of letting users teach more complex and more personalized rules beyond what is currently possible with systems like IFFFT. The key advantage of a conversational setting is that the agent can take initiative when certain things are left ambiguous by the user—an issue which cannot be handled in more traditional programming environments (which also include visual programming tools like IFFFT and Zapier). For example, the user may want to create a rule by saying the request "*When I get an important meeting request, forward it to the assistant.*"

When the agent encounters this request, it first attempts to ground it to a known function, e.g., creating a new calendar event or sending an email. In this case, however, the Natural Language Understanding (NLU) system detects that it is not able to parse this expression into any a known function, and in that case, it would ask the user if she wants to teach this as a new rule. If the user decides to teach, the agent then asks the user to break it down into steps so it can learn. A possible breakdown sequence for the above example could be:

(2) Learning Sequence Breakdown

```
00 U: Suppose I get a new email.
01 A: OK, I will wait for a new email.
02 U: Check if the subject mentions words like meet or
      meeting.
03 A: OK, I will check that, what should I do if that's
      the case?
04 U: Also see if the sender's email address is an email
      of a colleague.
05 A: OK, I will check that, what should I do if that's
      the case?
06 U: Then forward this email to the assistant.
```

Once the user finishes teaching, the agent can leverage this breakdown to generalize the command by identifying slots in the original request and allowing the user to give variations of the original command with different arguments, such as "*When I get an important meeting request, forward it to my friends.*"

Unlike traditional programming environments, the conversational setting allows the user to:

1. Teach new conditions, such as important meeting requests.
2. Let the user naturally define complex rules that consist of multiple conditions.

3. Allow the system to take initiative in asking about the programming flow, reducing the burden on the user. For example, the agent may ask questions like *"What should I do if that's the case?"* (when the user describes what to do in a situation) and *"What should I do if you are not available at that time?"* (when the user asks to create a meeting on their calendar).

6.4.2 Learning Concepts

A key advantage of a conversational interface for learning new rules from verbal instructions is that it allows the user to be more expressive by relying on concepts that have been taught previously, such as the concept of a "colleague" or an *assistant*. This provides the flexibility to re-use these concepts as building blocks in defining future procedures and rules. If the user's assistant changes later or if there are new members on the team, the rule will not have to be redefined. Thus, in attempting to express their need efficiently, users can use concepts such as *variables* in a traditional programming language sense (without possibly even being aware of it).

The user can define concepts and concept properties by saying things like *"Create a concept called a friend,"* *"Create something called a colleague"* or *"Most of my colleagues have a university affiliation."*

Currently the system provides the user with the ability to define concepts (e.g., *student*, *professor*, *colleague*), its properties (e.g., university *affiliation*) and instantiate these concepts. For example, the user can say *"Oscar is a colleague. His affiliation is CMU."*

This example illustrates two distinct types of concepts: concepts that are "crisp," e.g., colleague, and can be defined by enumerating instances of this concept, and those that are "fuzzy," e.g., important email or important requests, which cannot be defined but can have certain salient characteristics that the user can convey to the agent. The agent must have the capacity to learn both types of concepts from the user via dialog. In teaching fuzzy concepts, the user is more likely to express characteristics such as:

(3) Teaching Fuzzy Concepts

```
00 A:  What's an important email?
01 U:  An important email will usually be from a colleague
       and might contain words like meet or meeting.
02 A:  Are there any other characteristics of important
       emails?
03 U:  They might also mention a date and a time.
04 U:  Important emails will often be from a university
       domain
```

The challenge in taking advantage of these "fuzzy" statements is to transform them into a statistical model which can predict whether a given instance is a member of a particular concept. To address this issue, we develop a method for training a natural language parser of such statements that uses a small number of instances as examples (e.g., emails tagged with different concepts) in order to improve its ability to parse such statements (Srivastava et al. 2017).

6.5 Conclusion and Future Work

Conversation failures in human-agent conversations can be tackled from many different angles ranging from speech recognition, dialog management system architecture to the design of fallback responses. In this chapter, we have explored using an end user development (EUD) approach as a fallback strategy, where we allow the user to teach the agent in case of failure in human-agent conversations. We first started by identifying three major challenges in handling failures in goal-oriented conversational agents:

1. Understanding unknown and undefined concepts
2. Executing out-of-domain tasks
3. Using the right fulfillment means and generalization in task execution.

Then, we discussed two strategies for using EUD to address these challenges: *learning from demonstration* and *learning from verbal instruction*, using the two agents we designed—SUGILITE and LIA respectively as examples. Particularly, we highlighted the design goals for these agents and how the implementations help achieve these design goals.

For the future work, our focus will be on further integration to create an agent that learns from both the demonstration and the verbal instruction simultaneously (Li et al. 2017c; Li 2017). We envision that the verbal instructions can be used to disambiguate and enhance the demonstration, allowing the agent to learn not only the user's actions, but also the user's rationale behind those actions. On the other hand, demonstrations should also help ground the user's verbal instructions, allowing the user to refer to what is shown on the screen when teaching the agent new rules and concepts.

In particular, our future work should address the following challenges:

Data Description Problem
The data description problem is long-standing in PBD (Cypher and Halbert 1993)—when the user demonstrates interacting with a UI element on the screen, the PBD system needs to infer the user's intent by determining what feature (e.g., text, label, id, screen location, child elements, etc.) should be used for finding which item to operate on in future executions of the script when the context may be somewhat different. In a pilot study, we asked the users to narrate their actions while demonstrating. We found that the narrations are often very helpful in disambiguating the features (e.g., the users said things like "*Click on the first item in the list,*" "*Click on the red button at the bottom of the screen*" and "*Choose the option with the lowest price*").

In some situations, the data description for the UI element in an action can be non-trivial. For example, one may say *"Choose the winning team"* in a sports app, which can translate to *"Choose the name of a team that has a number next to it that is greater than the other number located next to the name of another team."*

We plan to design a conversational user experience to allow users to naturally narrate during the demonstration. Combining the narration and the demonstration, the agent should be able to extract a query for finding the UI element to operate on in future executions without users manually selecting the set of features to use (e.g., Fig. 6.1c) when the agent finds features of the UI element ambiguous or when the agent is unsure about the user's rationale for selecting a UI element to operate on.

Conditionals and Iterations

Expanding the support for conditionals in learning and representing tasks should significantly help increase the range of tasks that a conversational agent can learn. In Sect. 6.4.1, we discussed the current "trigger-action" rules supported by our agent as well as how a user can break down the steps to evaluate conditionals in the trigger for the agent (e.g., what an important meeting request is). In our work (Li et al. 2017b), we also support the user in using phone notifications, app launches or events from external web services to trigger task automations. In future work, we plan to enable the user to verbally describe complex conditionals with references to contents shown on the current screen and past screens for grounding.

We will also add support for looping and iterations. This will be useful for processing all the elements of a list in batch, for example to tap on each menu item on a screen, copy each entry and paste it into an email, or apply a filter to all images. In addition to manually adding the iteration, the conversational agent will allow users to verbally indicate that the task should be performed on all items (or the particularly desired subset) over a list and will be able to engage with the user in a dialog to refine the resulting script.

Procedure Editing

We would like to enable users to explicitly specify different parameter values for an existing learned task. For example, the user should be able to run a modified variation of a previously demonstrated task by using utterances like *"Get my regular breakfast order, except instead of iced coffee, I want hot coffee."* We wish to explore how the presentation of the conversation in the mixed-initiative interface can be designed to cater to this kind of procedure editing behaviors, leveraging the context of the existing scripts and GUI elements.

Acknowledgements This work was supported by Yahoo! through CMU's InMind project and by Samsung GRO 2015.

References

Allen J, Chambers N, Ferguson G, Galescu L, Jung H, Swift M, Taysom W (2007) PLOW: a collaborative task learning agent. In: Proceedings of the 22nd national conference on artificial intelligence. AAAI Press, Vancouver, British Columbia, Canada, vol 2, pp 1514–1519

Armstrong G (2017a) Helping your baby bot learn to chat like a grown up bot. In: Chatbots Magazine

Armstrong G (2017b) The UX of not making your users shout at your Chatbot. In: Chatbots Magazine, Aug 8, 2017. https://chatbotsmagazine.com/difficult-conversations-1-voice-recognition-error-handling-74d93056ddce

Azaria A, Hong J (2016) Recommender systems with personality. In: Proceedings of the 10th ACM conference on recommender systems. ACM, New York, pp 207–210

Azaria A, Krishnamurthy J, Mitchell TM (2016) Instructable intelligent personal agent. In: Proceedings of the 30th AAAI conference on artificial intelligence (AAAI)

Barkin J (2016) When bots fail at conversation. In: Being Janis, Aug 19, 2016. https://medium.com/janis/when-bots-fail-at-conversation-d7419605f5cc

Bohus D, Rudnicky AI (2005a) Constructing accurate beliefs in spoken dialog systems. In: IEEE workshop on automatic speech recognition and understanding, pp 272–277

Bohus D, Rudnicky AI (2005b) Error handling in the RavenClaw dialog management framework. In: Proceedings of the conference on human language technology and empirical methods in natural language processing. Association for Computational Linguistics, pp 225–232

Bohus D, Rudnicky AI (2005c) Sorry, I didn't catch that!—An investigation of non-understanding errors and recovery strategies. In: 6th SIGdial workshop on discourse and dialogue

Chen J-H, Weld DS (2008) Recovering from errors during programming by demonstration. In: Proceedings of the 13th international conference on intelligent user interfaces. ACM, New York, pp 159–168

Cypher A (1993) Eager: programming repetitive tasks by demonstration. In: Watch what I do. MIT Press, pp 205–217

Cypher A, Halbert DC (1993) Watch what I do: programming by demonstration. MIT Press

Dzikovska MO, Allen JF, Swift MD (2003) Integrating linguistic and domain knowledge for spoken dialogue systems in multiple domains. In: Proceedings of IJCAI-03 workshop on knowledge and reasoning in practical dialogue systems

Gajos K, Weld DS (2004) SUPPLE: automatically generating user interfaces. In: Proceedings of the 9th international conference on Intelligent user interfaces. ACM, pp 93–100

Gruber TR, Cheyer AJ, Kittlaus D, Guzzoni DR, Brigham CD, Giuli RD, Bastea-Forte M, Saddler HJ (2017) Intelligent automated assistant. U.S. Patent 9,548,050

Koedinger KR, Aleven V, Heffernan N, McLaren B, Hockenberry M (2004) Opening the door to non-programmers: authoring intelligent tutor behavior by demonstration. Intelligent tutoring systems. Springer, Berlin, pp 162–174

Leshed G, Haber EM, Matthews T, Lau T (2008) CoScripter: automating & sharing how-to knowledge in the enterprise. In: Proceedings of the SIGCHI conference on human factors in computing systems. ACM, New York, pp 1719–1728

Li TJ-J (2017) End user mobile task automation using multimodal programming by demonstration. In: 2017 IEEE symposium on Visual Languages and Human-Centric Computing (VL/HCC), pp 323–324

Li TJ-J, Azaria A, Myers BA (2017a) SUGILITE: Creating multimodal smartphone automation by demonstration. In: Proceedings of the 2017 CHI conference on human factors in computing systems. ACM, New York, pp 6038–6049

Li TJ-J, Li Y, Chen F, Myers BA (2017b) Programming IoT devices by demonstration using mobile apps. End-user development. Springer, Cham, pp 3–17

Li TJ-J, Myers BA, Azaria A, Labutov I, Rudnicky AI, Mitchell TM (2017c) Designing a conversational interface for a multimodal smartphone programming-by-demonstration agent. In: Conversational UX Design CHI 2017 Workshop. Denver

Lieberman H (2001) Your wish is my command: programming by example. Morgan Kaufmann

Mitman93 Customer review for Amazon.com: Pizza Hut: Alexa Skills. https://www.amazon.com/Pizza-Hut/dp/B01MSXEBMC. Accessed 5 Oct 2017

Myers BA, Ko AJ, Scaffidi C, Oney S, Yoon Y, Chang K, Kery MB, Li TJ-J (2017) Making end user development more natural. New perspectives in end-user development. Springer, Cham, pp 1–22

Pappu A, Rudnicky A (2014) Knowledge acquisition strategies for goal-oriented dialog systems. In: Proceedings of the 15th annual meeting of the Special Interest Group on Discourse and Dialogue (SIGDIAL), pp 194–198

Srivastava S, Labutov I, Mitchell T (2017) Joint concept learning and semantic parsing from natural language explanations. In: Proceedings of the 2017 conference on empirical methods in natural language processing, pp 1527–1536

Witten IH (1993) A predictive calculator. In: Watch what I do. MIT Press, pp 67–76

Chapter 7
Recovering from Dialogue Failures Using Multiple Agents in Wealth Management Advice

Heloisa Candello and Claudio Pinhanez

Abstract In this paper, we discuss dialogue failures and how this affects the user experience, specifically for a scenario of a multi-bot conversational system. Additionally, we show how the use of multiple chatbots provide new strategies to overcome misunderstandings and to keep the user in the conversation flow. To inform such conclusions and recommendations, we describe a study with a multi-bot wealth management advice system in which participants conversed with four chatbots simultaneously. We analyzed each conversation log applying thematic network analysis and manually identified the main instances of dialogue failures, usually provoked by chatbot misunderstandings or system breakdowns. We examined the follow-up users' utterances after each failure, and the users' strategies to deal with them. We categorize our findings into a list of the most common users' strategies, and highlight solutions provided by a multi-bot approach in assisting the dialogue failures.

7.1 Introduction

Conversational systems are becoming part of our everyday life. Intelligent conversational systems, popularly known as chatbots, are helping us find the best restaurant, tailoring news content, and giving advice on how to make better decisions in financial and health contexts. However, communicating well with conversational intelligent systems is still a challenge for humans. Although, chatbots use forms similar to natural language to communicate with human beings, conversation flow is hard to sustain between humans and machines. Statements or utterances are not always well understood by chatbots and most chatbots cannot detect or use context well enough during the real-time conversations to handle the complexity of human conversations.

H. Candello (✉) · C. Pinhanez
IBM Research, São Paulo, Brazil
e-mail: heloisacandello@br.ibm.com

C. Pinhanez
e-mail: csantosp@br.ibm.com

© Springer International Publishing AG, part of Springer Nature 2018
R. J. Moore et al. (eds.), *Studies in Conversational UX Design*, Human–Computer Interaction Series, https://doi.org/10.1007/978-3-319-95579-7_7

Due to those and similar shortcomings, interruptions in the flow are common in human-machine dialogues. We call these *dialogue failures (DFs)*, such as when the dialogue flow is disrupted by chatbot utterances which are incomprehensible, unexpected, or out-of-context. For example, it is very common for today's chatbots, when faced with a user utterance they are not able to understand, to stop the conversation and produce text that clarifies its capabilities, such as: specifying scope: "Our gurus have only information on Savings, CDB and Treasury"; giving directions: "To ask direct questions to our gurus type @ followed by the name of the guru (savingsGuru, cdbGuru or treasureGuru)"; or initiating repair of understanding troubles: "Sorry, I do not know the answer to this question. Ask again."

In other cases, the chatbot understands the topic of the conversation but does not provide the answer the users want. For example, users may ask the value of taxes to a wealth management chatbot which mistakenly gives the definition of taxes. Both cases were considered in this analysis as dialogue failures (DFs). DFs can lead users to react in several ways toward the system and to chatbots. This work focuses on understanding typical user reactions to DFs and on how multi-agent conversational systems offer a novel solution.

We first present related research on conversational flow among humans and between machines and humans. Then we look into previous studies on repair strategies to overcome DFs. We then describe the multi-bot conversational system we used in the study, followed by the study methodology, and the data analysis approach. Finally, we present the results of the study in which we identified several typical DF situations and the strategies users and bots employed to repair some of those failures. Based on the findings of our study, we position the multi-bot approach as an alternative solution to better understand failures and to provide a better experience between man and machines. We finish the paper by exploring additional challenges and needed future work.

7.2 Related Work

We start reviewing previous and similar work on conversation flow, dialogue chatbot interruptions, dialogue system breakdowns, and strategies available to overcome such issues and to improve the user experience. We focus the scope of the review on the specific context of our studies and on our findings that multi-bot systems have additional strategies to handle DFs.

7.2.1 Conversation Flow and Engagement with Technology

In the space of a conversation between humans and machines, different levels of engagement may occur. O'Brien and Toms (2008) proposes a model for this dynamic process of being engaged with technology in three main stages: *points of engage-*

ment, *period of engagement*, and *disengagement*. The *initial stage* of engagement is initiated by aesthetics, social reasons (Karahalios and Dobson 2005) or to comprise a goal. The *period of engagement* is characterized by the user's attention and interest sustained during the interaction. Factors such as feedback, sense of novelty, and being in charge of the interaction marks this stage. *Disengagement* may occur when users decide internally to stop the activity, or external environment factors may cause them to stop. Disengagement can be positive or negative: *positive*, in the case that the system fulfills what the user expects (needs and motivations); and *negative* when "*…feelings of frustration, uncertainty, being overwhelmed by challenges or information, loss of interest or motivation, and lack of novelty or challenge.*" (O'Brien and Toms 2008).

It has been shown that conversation engagement decreases with inappropriate responses by chatbots. Yu et al. (2016) designed a set of positive feedbacks for a conversational bot in the context of a job interview. Feedback was triggered according to the level of user engagement with the system. In Yu et al. (2016), an engagement-coordinated interview (with positive feedback) is compared to a study without engagement coordination. The engagement-coordinated version was rated as more engaging by the users and providing a better user experience as compared to the non-coordinated version.

The dynamic process of being engaged may be associated with typical discourse functions such as "*…conversation invitation, turn taking, providing feedback, contrast and emphasis, and breaking away*" (Cassell et al. 1999). Non-verbal behaviors often ground the conversation, providing help in understanding and feedback (Cassell et al. 1999). Positive and negative feedback make the chatbots notice their own misunderstandings and enable them to initiate the appropriate repair mechanisms.

Finally, Cawsey and Raudaskoski (1990) show examples of different types of repairs for human-computer dialogue: *sequencing* and *correction* of previous utterances; *repair initiators* and *regulatory speech* ("huh?"); and *clarification questions* and *sources of trouble* which consist of conversation breakdowns due to external environmental factors or internal mechanisms such as reference failure.

In our work, we are not restricted and focused solely on repair mechanisms. We are interested in the consequences of dialogue failures (DFs) on the user experience and in which conversation strategies in a multi-bot environment can engage the user to keep the conversation flow.

7.2.2 Maintaining the Conversation Flow

As mentioned before, there are many communication strategies used by humans to maintain engagement and conversation flow in conversations. Those strategies have also been applied to keep the engagement between humans and conversational systems. Maintaining the conversation flow is already a challenge among humans, since it can be interrupted by internal factors (e.g. awkward pauses, misunderstandings, level of the communicator's knowledge) or external factors (e.g. time availability, noise, third-party intrusion, environment disruptions). We are interested in both perspectives, although particularly in this work we explore more internal factors, as they can be concretely reflected on the dialogue transcripts.

Machines are not prepared, today, to fully understand context and change the course of conversations as humans naturally do. Some of those challenges in the dialogue flow with machines were addressed by Zue and Glass (2000) who classified dialogue systems according to which party had the initiative of the conversation: *system-initiative*, *user-initiative*, and *mixed-initiative* systems. In the first case, systems which have the dialogue initiative tend to restrict user options, asking direct questions, such as: "*Please, say just the departure city.*" In this way, those types of systems are often more successful and tend to make it easier for users to appropriately converse.

On the other hand, *user-initiative systems* are the ones where users have the freedom to ask whatever they wish. In this context, users may feel uncertain of the capabilities of the system and start asking questions or requesting information or services which might be out of scope for the system leading to user frustration. Finally, there is also a *mixed-initiative* approach, that is, a system in which the dialogue is a result of the users and the computers participating interactively using a conversational paradigm. Research challenges for mixed-initiative system include how to understand chatbot failures, human utterances, and, in general, unclear sentences which were not always goal-oriented.

Higashinaka et al. (2014) suggests a strategy, *introducing topics*, for handling when the user does not know what to ask in mixed-initiative systems. Other strategies suitable for non-goal-oriented systems and the system-initiative category include asking for user explanations when the user has given information to the chatbot which was not understood; and asking for missing information. The latter is exemplified by situations where users say something subjective or broad such as "*I had many meetings today*" and the chatbot replies by asking extra information, for instance, "*What were the meetings about?*" (Schmidt et al. 2017).

Other strategies have been found in the context of conversational systems embedded in physical robots. It has been observed in such contexts that humans adapt their language and behavior to the robots limited perceptive abilities as they become apparent during the interaction (Pelikan and Broth 2016). In non-goal-oriented systems, the aim is to keep people engaged in the conversation and expect them to answer at all times. Yu et al. (2016) examined non-goal-oriented conversational systems and proposed two types of strategies to improve the user experience of such systems: *engagement* strategies and *knowledge-base* strategies. The former builds on the concept of *active participation* already discussed in this text. The latter employs different types of knowledge bases or knowledge graphs and is sub-divided in *general* and *personal* knowledge-base strategies. The general strategies assist language understanding by resolving ambiguous entities and unknown words using natural language processing algorithms.

Personal knowledge-base strategies employ information extraction methods to gather personalized knowledge from the conversation history of each user. For instance, if the user repeats herself, the system confronts the user by saying: "*You already said that!"*. Another example described by the author is giving personalized content based on user's personal knowledge about a subject, for example content tailored to user's social data consumption.

Candello et al. (2017a, b) performed an experiment with conversational advisers in the finance context. In some situations, the adviser confronted users that paraphrase themselves by replying *"You have already asked this."*. Users were often frustrated to receive this answer during the dialogue interaction and answered with aggressive statements towards the chatbot. For example, in a particular session, a user understood this as a criticism, and complained: *"who does this chatbot think it is?"*.

As we see from this discussion, all the related work is concerned with strategies to overcome chatbot failures in single-bot interactions with humans. We have been exploring multi-bot systems (Candello et al. 2017a, b; De Bayser et al. 2017) where a single user interacts simultaneously with a group of chatbots. To the best of our knowledge, there is no study on user reactions to dialogue failures in multi-bot systems, and its influence on the overall user experience.

Our work has focused on understanding the user experience in such contexts with the aim to design better multi-bot conversational systems. As discussed before, many of the commonly used strategies aimed to have better social communication resulted from the challenges encountered in human conversational contexts. This is also true in multi-bot conversation, where new challenges are appearing such as how to take turns as a listener or a speaker in this type of multi-party conversation.

7.3 Finch: A Multi-bot Investment Advice System

With the aim to understand how participants react to DFs and which repair strategies can be considered successful, we analyzed the conversation logs of 30 participants interacting with a multi-bot system called *finch*. *finch* is an interactive investment adviser in Brazilian Portuguese language which helps users make financial decisions. *finch* is targeted to the typical Brazilian mid-level bank customer, who is middle class, less than 40 years old, digitally enabled, and not familiar with finances. The ultimate strategic intent is to address the bulk of the wealth advice market by proactively handling the users' lack of financial knowledge and uneasiness with money.

Following a user-centered design process (Candello 2017a, b), we designed the adviser system as a chat where a user can converse with four chatbots simultaneously, three of them representing investment products and one which is a friendly finance counselor (see Fig. 7.1). The product chatbots are *gurus* in typical low-risk Brazilian financial products: *PoupançaGuru (PG)* is an expert in savings accounts; *TDGuru (TD)* is an expert in treasury bonds; and *CDBGuru (CD)* is an expert in bonds. There is also *InvestmentGuru (IG)*, a kind of counselor/moderator which helps to summarize and guide the conversation. The chatbots were built using *IBM Watson Conversation Services (WCS)* API services.

The investment counselor bot *(IG)* was designed to mediate and sometimes lead the conversation with the user, while the investment product experts were designed

Fig. 7.1 Multi-bot with 4 chatbots (TD, CDB, P, IG) and user

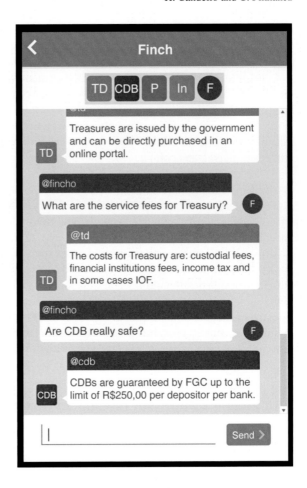

to reply only when required, either when directly addressed or when the user utterance's topic is about their expertise. In addition, the last chatbot which spoke in the conversation has priority to answer the next user utterance, except when the user addresses directly one of gurus or sends utterances related to simulations of the return of investment which are always mediated by *IG*. The control of the turn-taking process was implemented using a domain specific language for the generation of conversation rules developed by De Bayser et al. (2017), which deploys and manages a *conversation governance system*.

It is important to notice that *WCS* is based on the most common approach used today for building chatbots, called *intent-action*. Basically, each chatbot is created by defining a basic set of user and chatbot utterances and how they should relate to each other. Groups of questions from the user are mapped into a single answer from the chatbot, although it is possible to provide a set of pre-defined variations. The term *intent* is used to describe the goal of the group of questions, so the basic task of the conversational platform is to identify the intent of a given question written or spoken by the user, and then output its associated answer or system *action*, often a manually written answer to the utterance.

During run-time, each user utterance goes through a process of matching with the set of available intents in each chatbot. The *intent matching* is often the most important source of problems in the run-time of conversational systems, due to the complexity and difficulty of analyzing natural language; mistaken intent identifications are a common source of chatbot misunderstandings and conversation breakdowns, leading to Dialogue Failures (DFs).

7.4 Materials and Methods

The analysis reported in this paper is performed on the results of a study where a group of about 40 participants were asked to freely interact with *finch* in the context of making an investment decision. From those interactions, we discarded the sessions in which dialogues were too short or did not have any DFs, resulting in the 30 conversation logs used in the study presented here.

7.4.1 Participants

Participants were initially recruited by a snowball sample under two conditions: over 18 years old and well-educated (university student or higher). They received an invitation by e-mail or social media messaging to evaluate a financial adviser system with a web link. No reward was given to them for participating. Thirty-seven participants performed this experiment, of which 30 met the criteria for analysis.

Overall 18 males and 12 females were part of the analysis. Most of our participants were between 31 and 50 years old (20 participants), some were between 21 and 30 years old (8 participants) and only two were under twenty. Almost half of them have previously used systems powered by artificial intelligence (54%). Most of the participants (90%) reported that they had a medium or high interest in investment information and only three people (10%) were uninterested. They also stated that their level of knowledge was highest in savings-like investments, followed by CDB and treasury bonds, which had the lowest level of knowledge (44%).

7.4.2 Methodology

The experimental procedure consisted of four phases: *introduction and disclaimer, demographics and knowledge questionnaire, free interaction*, and *interruption message for closing the dialogue*. Subjects were welcomed with a brief written explanation of the study purpose and structure. The purpose was described as an "... *opportunity to evaluate an independent system which answers about financial investments and helps you to decide what is the best investment for you.*" After this, the subject wrote his or her name and agreed with a disclaimer.

The aim of the *demographics and financial knowledge questionnaire* was to assess participants' knowledge of financial investments, technology expertise, and demographics. It consisted of a simple survey. Next, the subject read a use-case scenario to frame the study and start the conversation with *finch*:

> Imagine you have received the equivalent of your monthly salary as an award this month. You would like to invest this award, and your plan is not to use this money for the next 2 years. You need help deciding which type of investment is the best for you. For that you will use FINCH, a financial advice app.

In the *free interaction* phase, *finch* starts with the *InvestmentGuru (IG)* presenting itself as an investment adviser followed by each of the expert chatbots presenting itself as an expert in its corresponding finance product. All the conversation is logged for future analysis. After the introductions, the *IG* asks the user for an amount and a period of investment. If the user provides this information, the *IG* asks each of the product *gurus* to simulate the expected return of the investment, and to point out the best options.

After this initial simulation process, which almost all subjects experienced, subjects were free to question or comment as they wished until the evaluation questionnaire started. The system answered the questions and utterances by determining its intent and allocating the proper chatbot(s) to respond. Additionally, the *IG* gave instructions to use "@" followed by the name of guru in case the user wanted to ask direct questions, for example: "*To ask direct questions to our gurus type @ followed by the name of the guru (savingsGuru, cdbGuru or treasureGuru).*" If requested, the system could simulate again the return of the investments and make simple comparisons among the three investments.

The *interruption message for closing the dialogue* phase was designed to stop user interaction and close the dialogue. It was made available to users in any of following three situations: (1) after two minutes of inactivity, which makes *IG* prompt the user with a message containing two options: "*Continue the conversation or Evaluate your experience*"; (2) if the user types *thanks, bye, I decided to invest*, or similar utterances, which leads the *IG* to show the message: "*We hope we have helped you. Please, click here to evaluate your experience*"; or (3) if the user presses the back button on the left-corner of the screen. In all three cases, subjects were then asked to answer a short evaluation questionnaire which is not considered in this study (Pinhanez et al. 2017). Here, we focus solely on analyzing the conversation logs and on the issue of how users and the system handled instances of DFs.

After subjects had filled in the evaluation questionnaire, the study finished with an acknowledgment message: "*Thanks for your views! Your answers are valuable for our research*". All questionnaire and conversation data were logged in an *Elastic Search* database running on *IBM Bluemix*. All care was taken to preserve the privacy of the information provided by the participants.

7.5   Conversation Log Analysis

As mentioned before, of the 37 participants we selected 30 conversations to analyze considering these criteria: dialogues had at least one DF and contained more than two user utterances. The last criterion was due to the nature of our system, since the multi-bot system dialogues had more utterances from chatbots than from users.

The 30 conversations were manually analyzed using *thematic networks* (Attride-Stirling 2001; Luger and Sellen 2016) as an analytical tool to organize the categories obtained from the analysis. The coding scheme emerged from the data by applying an *inspired grounded-theory* approach (Strauss and Corbin 1994) and was guided by a sequential analysis in the context in which it was produced.

Twenty-three themes emerged from the analysis. Our three global themes were: common chatbot strategies to deal with failures, user responses to understand failures, and multi-bot solutions to deal with failures.

The first global theme splits onto two organizing themes: Bot explicit instructions and Bot scope self-explanation. The second global theme aggregated sub-themes focused on paraphrasing utterances and shifting to out-of-scope topics. The third, multi-bot solutions to deal with failures was concentrated in agents with different expertise. Schematically, the organizing themes grouped the remaining basic themes. Overall 295 code excerpts were distributed in the described themes.

Common chatbot DF repair strategies

- Bot explicit instructions
- Bot scope self-explanation

User reactions to dialogue failures

- User paraphrasing
- User shift to out-of-scope topics

Multi-bot environment DF repair strategies

- Bot self-selects to respond
- User readdresses the question
- Current bot continues.

The *thematic network* approach helped us to structure the patterns of DFs and repair strategies which occurred in the conversations. In this session, we discuss those patterns identified here as *themes*. Given the shortcomings of current conversation technologies we discussed before, DFs occurred often. Also, in many cases one of the identified multi-bot-specific strategies helped to overcome the shortage of context and knowledge to allow the conversation to continue.

7.6   Analytical Findings

We now explore in detail the global themes and their organizing themes.

7.6.1   Common Chatbots' DF Repair Strategies

In this section, we explore some of the common, good practices which helped the
chatbots to keep the conversation flow going on. Two successful DF repair strategies
employed by the chatbots were identified: *Bot explicit instructions and Bot scope
self-explanation*. Notice that the solutions of this global theme are suitable for both
single and multi-bot systems.

7.6.1.1   Bot Explicit Instructions

The DFs gave opportunities to the chatbots to teach people how to interact with
them. This strategy may benefit both single-bot and multi-bot systems, although in
the case of multi-bot systems it is even more important since multi-bot is a new
interaction concept to most users and needs to be explained more clearly. In the
current stage of *finch*, each bot has its own corpus with specific answers. When users
asked generic finance questions and did not address the question to a specific chatbot,
the governance system directed the *InvestmentGuru* chatbot to provide instructions
on how to interact directly with multi-bots, as seen in Excerpt 1 below:

(1) Explicit instructions (P06)
```
01 U:   What is the risk?
02 IG:  To ask direct questions to our gurus
03      type @ followed by the name of the
04      guru (savingsGuru, cdbGuru or
05      treasureGuru).
06 U:   What is the risk? @poupancaGuru
```

We notice in Excerpt 1 above, extracted from the Participant 6 transcript, that
the advice was followed and reestablished the conversation flow (line 6). In our
experiment, participants often followed this advice. This behavior was also common
in participants who have not previously used AI systems before or who may not
have seen this kind of recipient address format in a chat. Those users understood and
followed the instruction to type the @ to direct the question to a chatbot.

7.6.1.2   Bot Scope Self-explanation

Another effective strategy to overcome DFs occurred when participants followed the
chatbot's advice to ask questions within its scope. In the Excerpt 2, Participant 1

follows the *InvestmentGuru* instructions about what kind of question it can answer (line 1).

(2) Explaining scope (P01)

```
01 IG:  You can ask questions about definitions,
02      risk, liquidity, or profitability to our
03      gurus.
04 U:   What is liquidity?
```

We identified 12 cases in which users followed the chatbots' advice and doing so continued the engagement with the chatbots. It was also a common user strategy to incorporate words used by chatbots in their own answers. Participants also adapted their language to the bot language and knowledge level copying words from bot utterances.

In the following Excerpt 3, Participant 22 asks one out-of-scope question (line 01). The *InvestmentGuru* chatbot gives an answer which is not related to the question (considered here as a failure) in line 2. Although the answer was not related to the user question, Participant 22 then switches topics and uses a word from the *InvestmentGuru's* response, "Selic", as we can see in line 4.

(3) Explaining scope (P22)

```
01 U:   How can I get rich with financial investments?
02 IG:  The basic interest rate is also known as Selic
03      rate.
04 U:   talk more about the Selic.
05 IG:  It is financing rate for operations in which
06      banks borrow funds from other banks for a day,
07      offering public bonds as ballast, aiming to
08      reduce the cost, and the remuneration of the
09      transaction
```

Depending on the complexity of context, in- and out-of-scope terms may play an essential role in the conversation. In our case, wealth management is a complex theme for most of the participants doing the study. Other user studies with intelligent financial advisers (Candello 2017a, b) pointed out that people with basic financial knowledge do not know what to ask to financial advisers. Users can help maintain the conversation flow simply by using words and terms available in the chatbots prior utterance.

7.6.2 User Reactions to Dialogue Failures

Dialogue failures often resulted from an improper utterance by a chatbot in the middle of the conversations, caused either because the chatbot had wrongly identified the intent of the user's utterance or because the scope of the user's utterance was beyond the knowledge stored in the chatbot. Usually users respond to understanding failures using repair strategies (Schegloff et al. 1977), for example, by paraphrasing their original utterances. We also observed cases when users shifted topics and engaged in a playful mode.

7.6.2.1 Paraphrasing

A common way to deal with DFs caused by the chatbots not understanding an utterance from the user was simply to repeat the same question or meaning with different words (20 participants). Sometimes it involved repeating the question using the same words in the utterance but in other cases subjects used synonyms or clarifying terms. In the following Excerpt 4, Participant 20 rephrases his utterance using synonyms (replacing the word *kinds* with *types*) in line 4.

(4) Paraphrasing: Clarifying Expansion (P20)

```
01 U:   What are the kinds of Treasury?
02 TD:  Sorry, I do not know the answer to this
03      question. Ask again.
04 U:   Which are the types of the Treasury
05      investments available?
06 TD:  Sorry, I do not know the answer to this
07      question. Ask again.
```

In Excerpt 4 we see the user subsequently expand upon his original question in 01 when the chatbot does not understand it. In lines 04–05, the user clarifies the referent "treasury" by expanding it to "treasure investment" and makes more specific the request changing "what are the kinds" to "which types are available". This is similar to human behavior when two people are talking to each other and one of them does not understand or hear the question from the other person. We still need to investigate more why users used this strategy of following up with a version of the same question. Possibly it is just a natural practice that people employ in everyday conversation that they apply to text-based chatbot conversation even though it has no effect on the system which still did not understand the utterance. Also, we are not sure whether users expected the same answer from the chatbot or not, or if they are simply testing the coherence of the chatbot answers. This behavior was more frequent in female participants (60%) than male (40%), and with participants who have medium and high interest in investments (77%).

Another usual strategy employed by subjects after a DF caused by a chatbot misunderstanding was to try to adapt their language to be understood by the chatbot. We encountered 50 such occurrences in 18 conversation transcripts. Not all subjects made equal use of this strategy: participants who used AI systems before (as declared in the initial questionnaire) adapted their language more frequently to chatbots and did this more than once in the same dialogue (11 participants); and men (12) applied language adaptation two times more often than women (6).

We observed that basic language adaptation strategies were used by our subjects: *simplifying the utterances, adding more words* in case users asked a short question early in the dialogue, and *using words previously seen* in the chatbot dialogues.

Simplifying utterances were often employed when the chatbot did not answer long questions. Users subsequently asked more specific questions or reframed the questions in keywords. Those are exemplified by Participant 23 in the following Excerpt 5.

(5) Paraphrasing: Simplifying and more specific (P23)

```
01 U:   CDB, are there multiple types of funds,
02      with different redemption times and
03      minimum application?
04 CD:  Sorry, I don't know how to answer this
05      question. Ask again.
06 U:   CDB, what if I redeem the amount
07      applied before two years?
08 CD:  Applying in the CDB, you agree with the
09      bank the investment time. You can
10      withdraw money at any time, but you
11      may pay a higher rate if you do not
12      abide by the agreement.
```

In Excerpt 5, the user poses a question in lines 01–03 that the chatbot CD does not understand. The user then asks a follow-up question, specifying more simply the core question. The first question in lines 01–03 asks for information related to three general criteria: "multiple types of funds", "different redemption times", and "minimum application"; each of these criteria fans out to a complex data set. Whereas the simplified question in lines 06–07 uses a specific scenario to ask about the consequences of a specific action: redemption before two years. Given this reduced scope, the chatbot is able to apply its knowledge to the scenario in lines 08–12. Users usually apply similar language adaptation strategies (line 6) to extract information they want to know primarily (line 01).

Users ask all kinds of questions to the chatbots and when faced with the inability of the chatbot to answer, they try to decrease the complexity to keywords, adapting to the machine's limited abilities to answer those. Sometimes users decrease the language complexity gradually. However, in other situations, people started with simple questions and increased the complexity of their questions with contextual information when DFs occurred. Such is the case of Excerpt 7.

(6) Paraphrasing: replacing pronouns (P19)

```
01 U:   Is the risk of the treasure greater than of the
02      cdb?
03 CD:  If your application is up to 250 thousand, it is insured by
        the credit guarantee fund.
04 U:   how does it work?
05 IG:  To ask direct questions to our gurus type @ followed by the
        name of the guru (savingsGuru, cdbGuru or treasureGuru).
06 U:   How does the treasury credit guarantee fund work?
```

When users employed paraphrasing actions, the conversational breakdown was not always resolved. Sometimes paraphrasing works (Excerpt 5) and sometimes fails (Excerpt 4 and 6). In general, both extremely complex or simple user utterances are not well understood by the simple intent-matching algorithms used in *finch's* chatbots. Simple utterances often misguided the chatbots, since keywords might be present in several different intent examples. Complex utterances have more nouns and meaningful words, therefore carrying more word relations which can also be more easily connected to intents. Adding chatbot proactivity strategies may assist in clarifying ambiguous utterances.

7.6.2.2 Shifting to Out-of-Scope Topics

Changing the subject was also a method for users to deal with breaks in the conversation flow. We saw 20 cases where users changed the subject of the questions after a DF. Chatbots in many cases recovered well from the shift in topic although at other times the challenge became even greater. This is because after a period of not receiving expected answers (typically 2 utterances), participants started to *play* with the chatbots, characterized by questions clearly out of scope. Those situations typically happened after participants tried to ask in-scope questions which were not answered properly by any of the chatbots.

For example, in the Excerpt 7, line 1, Participant 28 asked about the investment with the lowest risk, and *InvestmentGuru* wrongly answered with a definition of risk in line 2. Following this, the user started playfully to ask *InvestmentGuru* questions about how to become rich in line 5.

(7) Shifting topics (P28)

```
01 U:   What is the lowest risk investment?
02 IG:  Credit risk is the payment capacity of the
03      Government, which is the issuer of Government
04      Securities
05 U:   how can I get rich?
```

Playful questions were even more common when the chatbots did not answer questions which were expected to be in their scope of knowledge. In some cases, participants used *tricky* questions difficult for humans. Not only did they vent their frustration with the chatbots, participants also seemed to be testing the chatbots' ability to deal with philosophical question difficult even for humans.

7.6.3 Multiple Agents: A Novel Solution to Misunderstanding

In this section we describe solutions specific to the nature of multi-bot systems. Here, we show the advantages of having more than one chatbot with different expertise in a conversation system, which in many cases can provide better user experience and minimize the effects of DFs.

The multi-bot approach offers a solution for dealing with agent misunderstandings in conversation settings. Inspired by the rules of the turn-taking model grounded in human-human conversations (Sacks et al. 1974), we describe situations when this approach keeps the conversation flow. We identified three basic options. In the first, the Bot self-selects: given a question, the bot with the best answer self-selects to provide an answer based on its knowledge current topic. The second option is that multi-bot systems let the user to readdress the question to a different guru as next speaker, getting out the DF with the last chatbot. And in the third option, multi-bot systems can select the current chatbot to continue in case the user does not point out the next-speaker or no chatbot has knowledge about an current topic.

7.6.3.1   Agent Self-selects

Several challenges might occur when more than two participants are in the same conversation. One of the challenges in designing multi-bot behavior is how to decide which bot will speak next. Here, when the user mentions a topic, the agent with knowledge of that topic self-selects to give an answer, and other agents say nothing. It is illustrated in Excerpt 8, line 2, line 6 and line 10. *SavingsGuru (PG)*, *CDBGuru (CD)* and *TresureGuru (TD)* answered the question related to their expertise in sequence.

(8) Agent self-selects (P28)

```
01 U:   what is savings?
02 PG:  It is a form of low risk investment
03      whose operation is governed by
04      government rules.
05 U:   what is CBD?
06 CD:  The CDB (Certificate of Deposit)
07      works as a loan that you make to the
08      bank, receiving a fee in return.
09 U:   What is direct treasure?
10 TD:  Treasure Direct is a public security
11      trading program for individuals
12      through the internet.
```

Dedicated content and coherence in the chatbot's level of knowledge is important to help users make decisions. Showing that the chatbots are comparable in terms level of knowledge and dedicated scope is important in a multi-bot system designed to aid decision-making. All experts should appear to have the same level of knowledge with comparable advice. This good practice helped people ask more varied questions. In a previous study, Pinhanez (2017) compared users' perceptions of expertise in single-versus multi-bot investment conversational systems. They found evidence that there is a difference in the perception of topic coverage between the two approaches. People perceive the system to have a greater knowledge scope if it has more than one content-dedicated chatbot. This points to the design benefit in multiple chatbots being able to answer similar questions with their own dedicated content.

7.6.3.2 Readdressing the Question

The ideal of comparably knowledgeable agents was not achieved in all situations in our system. The conversation flow was interrupted when a chatbot could not answer a similar question made for other chatbot in its scope. Additionally, some questions were specific to a type of investment. When a DF happened in such cases, some participants did not stick with the same chatbot. Instead, they changed the chatbot and consequently the subject to continue the conversation flow. In Excerpts 9 and 10, Participants 29 and 30 readdress the questions to a different agent trying to increase their chances of a response. In Excerpt 9, the user simplifies the question reducing the scope of the risk information requested from a comparison to a discrete value.

(9) User selects next: Simplification (P29)

```
01 U:   TD comparing with CBD, which investment
02      would be less risky?
03 TD:  Sorry, I do not know the answer to this
04      question. Ask again.
05 U:   CDB, what is the level of investment
06      risk?
07 CD:  If your application is up to 250
08      thousand, there is coverage of the
09      guarantee fund.
```

In Excerpt 9, the user initially asks for a comparative analysis of the risk of *CBD* and *TD*. When the *TD* is not able to answer the question, the user shifts to the *CD* chatbot and reduces the complexity of the question, asking only for the risk level of *CDB*. Similarly, in Excerpt 10, Participant 30 is unable to get a response from *CD*, so she shifts to TD to continue conversation on another topic.

(10) User selects next: Topic shift (P30)

```
01 U:   CDB, are there different types of
02      investment funds?
03 CD:  Sorry, I do not know the answer to this
```

```
04      question. Ask again.
05 U:   TD, what is the degree of risk of direct
06      treasury investment?
07 TD:  There is a credit and market risk and
08      there is no credit guarantee fund.
```

In Except 10, the user asks *CDB* a question about types of investment funds. When this goes unanswered, the user shifts to *TD* in lines 05–06, asking about the risk of direct treasury investments. This strategy results in a disjointed continuation of the conversation given both the shift in topic and change in chatbot engagement.

Similar to the participants in Excerpts 9 and 10, fifteen participants asked another chatbot when a failure happened, or changed the scope to their questions to the scope of one of the three investment available in the system. This number shows that multi-bot systems incentive people to vary on-topic questions and help keep people in the conversation flow even when a DF happens. In many ways, this also corresponds to the known properties of the turn-taking model of human conversations, where conversation participants can self-select, and/or direct address to the next speaker.

7.6.3.3 Current Agent Continues

In human conversation, the last speaker has the priority to talk next unless a conversation participant self-selects or the user direct a question to a specific chatbots (Sacks et al. 1974). In Excerpt 11, this is demonstrated in line 9. *TG* was the last to answer a question related to the treasure topic, therefore it has priority. This matches user expectations and coherence in a conversation avoiding failures and disconnections.

(11) Current agent continues (P27)

```
01 U:   what's the risk?
02 IN:  Credit risk is the ability to pay the
03      Government, which is the issuer of
04      Government Securities.
05 U:   what the risk of the direct treasure?
06 TG:  There is a credit and market risk and
07      there is no credit guarantee fund.
08 U:   what is a credit guarantee fund?
09 TG:  The Credit Guarantee Fund (FGC) is an
10      entity which protects the investor
11      in case of intervention, liquidation
12      or bankruptcy has given a financial
13      institution.
```

Having more than one chatbot can help users by providing more alternatives to obtain a successful answer. Therefore, more experienced chatbots can help keep the conversation flow while getting novice bots out of discourse failures.

7.7 Discussion

One of the results of our study is that we observed that the multi-bot approach provides new, alternative ways for conversation systems designers and developers to manage discourse failures. The use of more than one agent in a conversation with humans helps to keep the conversation flow, according to our findings. The three multi-bot strategies—Agent self-selects, readdressing the question and the current agent continues talking—guide users in the conversation and avoid failures.

The use of a multi-bot approach is particularly suitable for areas such as Finance, Health, Education when even in human-to-human decision making more than one expert should be considered to make a decision. For instance, in Finance, particularly investment decisions, people usually gather information from diverse sources and consider family and expert opinions, for example, on mortgages or insurance. A multi-bot approach gives a good context for exploring different topics and motivates people to ask varied topic questions. Additionally, we see a future where several people and bots can participate in the same conversation, providing awareness of knowledge and decision-making dimensions as we often do today in collaborative meetings with people.

Alternatively, employing a single-agent approach with multiple knowledge bases frames user attention on only one agent, and therefore restricts the designer's choice of strategies to handle DFs. We believe the multi-bot approach may minimize this effect since one bot can recover a failure provoked by another bot in the same conversation as shown above.

7.8 Final Remarks and Further Research

In this chapter, we described an experiment and its findings to better understand user experience with Discourse Failures (DFs) and show how the context of multiple agents expands the opportunities and strategies for handling DFs. We analyzed 30 conversation log transcripts to identify DFs, the strategies employed by users to handle DFs and successful strategies chatbots can use to keep the conversation flowing after a DF.

Our experiment had a limited number of participants and had very specific content: wealth management. The context of our research is the Brazilian market, so further research is needed to validate the results in other linguistic or cultural realms. We also plan to run a set of in-lab tests with subjects, using treactions to chatbots' answers while using this system and the reasons behind them.

References

Attride-Stirling J (2001) Thematic networks: an analytic tool for qualitative research. Qual Res 1:385–405

Candello H, Pinhanez C, Millen D, Andrade BD (2017a) Shaping the experience of a cognitive investment adviser. In: International conference of design, user experience, and usability. Springer, pp 594–613

Candello H, Vasconcelos M, Pinhanez C (2017b) Evaluating the conversation flow and content quality of a multi-bot conversational system. In: IHC2017—Brazilian symposium on human factors in computing systems

Cassell J, Bickmore T, Billinghurst M, Campbell L, Chang K, Vilhjálmsson H, Yan H (1999) Embodiment in conversational interfaces: Rea. In: Proceedings of the SIGCHI conference on human factors in computing systems. ACM, pp 520–527

Cawsey A, Raudaskoski P (1990) Repair work in human-computer dialogue. In: Proceedings of the 13th conference on computational linguistics. Association for Computational Linguistics, vol 3, pp 327–329

De Bayser MG, Cavalin P, Souza R, Braz A, Candello H, Pinhanez C, Briot J-P (2017) A hybrid architecture for multi-party conversational systems. arXiv:170501214

Higashinaka R, Imamura K, Meguro T, Miyazaki C, Kobayashi N, Sugiyama H, Hirano T, Makino T, Matsuo Y (2014) Towards an open-domain conversational system fully based on natural language processing. In: Proceedings of COLING 2014, the 25th international conference on computational linguistics: technical papers. pp 928–939

Karahalios KG, Dobson K (2005) Chit chat club: bridging virtual and physical space for social interaction. In: CHI'05 extended abstracts on Human factors in computing systems. ACM, pp 1957–1960

Luger E, Sellen A (2016) Like having a really bad PA: the gulf between user expectation and experience of conversational agents. In: Proceedings of the 2016 CHI conference on human factors in computing systems. ACM, pp 5286–5297

O'Brien HL, Toms EG (2008) What is user engagement? A conceptual framework for defining user engagement with technology. J Assoc Inf Sci Technol 59:938–955

Pelikan HR, Broth M (2016) Why that nao?: How humans adapt to a conventional humanoid robot in taking turns-at-talk. In: Proceedings of the 2016 CHI conference on human factors in computing systems. ACM, pp 4921–4932

Pinhanez C, Candello H, Gatti M, Pichiliani M, Cavalin P, Guerra M, Vasconscelos M (2017) User perceptions of expertise in single- vs. multi-bot conversational systems (submitted)

Sacks H, Schegloff EA, Jefferson G (1974) A simplest systematics for the organization of turn taking for conversation. In: Studies in the organization of conversational interaction. Elsevier, pp 7–55

Schegloff EA, Jefferson G, Sacks H (1977) The preference for self-correction in the organization of repair in conversation. Language 53:361–382

Schmidt M, Niehues J, Waibel A (2017) Towards an open-domain social dialog system. In: Dialogues with social robots. Springer, pp 271–278

Strauss A, Corbin J (1994) Grounded theory methodology. Handb Qual Res 17:273–285

Tatai G, Csordás A, Kiss Á, Szaló A, Laufer L (2003) Happy chatbot, happy user. In: International workshop on intelligent virtual agents. Springer, pp 5–12

Yu Z, Nicolich-Henkin L, Black AW, Rudnicky A (2016) A wizard-of-oz study on a non-task-oriented dialog systems that reacts to user engagement. In: Proceedings of the 17th annual meeting of the Special Interest Group on Discourse and Dialogue. pp 55–63

Part IV
Agent Design

Chapter 8
Conversational Style: Beyond the Nuts and Bolts of Conversation

Gregory A. Bennett

Abstract This chapter provides UX designers with some of the linguistic resources necessary to build more engaging chatbots and virtual agents. Conversation Analysis teaches us the foundational mechanics of conversation—how participants initiate and terminate an interaction, how they take turns in talk, how they negotiate understanding, etc. Interactional Sociolinguistics and the study of conversational style show us how humans leverage these structures to convey style and accomplish social goals in talk, such as building rapport or showing respect. If Conversation Analysis is the key to designing conversation that *flows*, Interactional Sociolinguistics and conversational style are the keys to designing conversation that has what some might call *personality*. Here, linguistic research is applied as a design tool for creating conversational interfaces that have style and strategically align to users' needs according to the social goal at hand. If designers seek to make a chatbot enthusiastic or considerate, this chapter has the tools needed to design conversations that achieve that with users.

8.1 Introduction

Over the past few years in my work as a user researcher, I have noticed the applicability of linguistics to the design of text-based chatbots and virtual agents. I discovered linguistics as it pertains to online chat when I was going through a breakup in college. When my ex shifted from our standard casual chat (e.g. *hey hows it going i miss u*) to more formal writing (e.g., *Hello. I am fine.*), I perceived a shift from his usual,

---

Disclaimer: This chapter was written by the author in his own personal capacity. The views and opinions expressed are the author's and don't necessarily reflect the views or opinions of Salesforce. Any omissions, inaccuracies, or other inadequacies of information are the author's. Salesforce disclaims all warranties as to the accuracy, completeness, or adequacy of such information and shall have no liability for omission or inadequacies in such information.

G. A. Bennett (✉)
Linguist | UX Researcher, San Francisco, CA, USA
e-mail: gregoryabennett@gmail.com

© Springer International Publishing AG, part of Springer Nature 2018
R. J. Moore et al. (eds.), *Studies in Conversational UX Design*, Human–Computer
Interaction Series, https://doi.org/10.1007/978-3-319-95579-7_8

warm and welcoming self to cold and distant. Shortly after the split, I encountered the field of Interactional Sociolinguistics—the study of how language works in social interaction—and was introduced to Deborah Tannen's work on conversational style. Upon studying her research on how people use features of language such as pitch and intonation in systematic ways to convey interactional meaning in talk, it became explicitly clear to me why I could perceive a chat as cold and distant through text alone; my ex had shifted from our normal, casual tone of conversation through which we built rapport and closeness (no punctuation, non-standard spellings) to a more formal, distant tone (full punctuation, 'conventional' spellings), and the change was marked and noticeable. Thus, the interaction had gone cold. If Tannen's research can help unpack how users convey tones like coldness in online, text-based chat, I posit that it can be applied to the world of text-based chatbots so that designers can enable them to convey tones and exhibit conversational style with users. Bot chat can be intentionally designed to come off as enthusiastic or considerate for a more enjoyable user experience.

Porter (2009) notes that crafting an experience that users will enjoy requires the designer to *reduce friction* in the flow of the product so that it is usable, and *increase motivation* for users to engage with it. Conversation Analysis (see Szymanski and Moore, this volume) equips designers with what they need in order to reduce friction in the flow of machine-human conversation and make it *usable*, something that, at present, many chatbots are not. Once designers achieve usability by applying Conversation Analysis to their conversation design, the challenge of increasing user motivation looms next.

Brandtzaeg and Følstad (2017) have shown that productivity and entertainment are the most frequent motivators for users to engage with chatbots. In order to design for these motivators in a way that encourages continued user engagement, designers must also leverage tools that come from a close examination of what motivates humans to engage in conversation with the same partner over and over again in the first place: achieving rapport. Much like how Anderson (2011) leverages psychology to offer tools for crafting interactions with web interfaces that entice users to keep coming back, this chapter utilizes research in Interactional Sociolinguistics and conversational style to offer tools for tailoring the design of a chatbot conversation for myriad users and cultivating rapport, thereby motivating continued engagement.

Specifically, this chapter introduces Interactional Sociolinguistics, a field that reveals how humans use the mechanics of conversation to achieve interactional goals such as chatting faster to show involvement and slowing down to show considerateness, and explores how this research can inspire designers to create conversations that align to, or strategically deviate from, a user's conversational patterns to cultivate rapport. By introducing insights from Interactional Sociolinguistics that work together with Conversation Analysis, designers will be further equipped with the resources necessary to go beyond the nuts and bolts of conversation and take their designs to the next level—to build a text-based bot conversation that has 'personality' and that can purposefully create rapport with myriad users based on their interactional needs.

8.2 Linguistics, Conversation, Style, and Chatbots

Linguistics, as a field of study, focuses on the illumination and systematic analysis of the processes of language (Small and Hickok 2016). It is the scientific study of how language works at varying structural levels (e.g., phonetics at the sound level, morphology at the word level, syntax at the sentence level, and discourse analysis at the level beyond the sentence) and across myriad contexts.

Johnstone (2008: 266) notes that within the field of linguistics, Interactional Sociolinguistics distinguishes itself in that researchers of this space "provide ways to think about how people could change how they talk" by showing individuals how to understand and align to other speakers' ways of talking. In order to tailor one's way of speaking, however, one must acquire a way of speaking in the first place. The founder of Interactional Sociolinguistics, John Gumperz, posited in his research that speakers acquire ways of talking by interacting with social groups over the course of their life (1982). He maintains that in speaking with one's surrounding community—family, neighbors, classmates, roommates, friends, coworkers, etc.—one develops culturally informed ideologies and practices about how one should talk with, and make sense of what is said by, others in each of those groups. In other words, the people with whom one spends considerable time having conversation influence not only *what* members of social groups say, but also *how* they say it.

The *how* of what people say, the meaning in their language use, is grounded in what Gumperz calls "contextualization cues." Examples of features of language that can be used to convey contextualization cues include intonation, vocal pitch, loudness, and physical gestures. Speakers recruit these communicative resources to signal meaning beyond the semantic level, as if to convey, "I mean something more than just the content of what I'm saying, so you should interpret my words in this way." The way that participants interpret contextualization cues is influenced by how they have heard those same features used as contextualization cues in prior conversations; Gumperz calls this conversational inference.

Contextualization cues apply another layer to the foundational, structural concepts put forth by Conversation Analysis. Simply put, turn taking, initiating and accomplishing openings and closings, pauses, and other aspects of the structure of conversation are all interactional features that can be used not only to give form to the interaction at hand, but also to convey extra meaning as contextualization cues. Participants make sense of those cues during the conversation using conversational inference (Gumperz 2001). For example, shortening pauses between turns, or eliminating them altogether in a conversation not only speeds up or overlaps talk, but can also signal interactional meaning such as enthusiasm or impatience. The way that people systematically use contextualization cues to accomplish interactional goals in conversation is what Deborah Tannen, a student of John Gumperz, calls conversational style.

Tannen illuminated the concept of conversational style by systematically analyzing how groups of people deploy and interpret contextualization cues in her seminal work, *Conversational Style* (1984). She notes that conversational style is not

Table 8.1 Contextualization cues by conversational style

	High involvement	High considerateness
Amount of discourse	More	Less
Pace	Faster	Slower
Overlap	More	Less
Questions	More/more personal	Fewer/less personal
Stories	More	Fewer
Prosodic variation	More extreme	Less extreme
Loudness	Louder	Quieter
Gesture	More pronounced	Less pronounced

remarkable, but is simply an inherent characteristic of how people talk with each other. Whenever one speaks, one fundamentally does so with style, which consists of myriad contextualization cues such as the speed and loudness of one's talk relative to others', one's intonation, etc. Interlocutors determine how rude or polite, cold or warm, or mean or friendly a person is based on how they interpret that person's conversational style through their own conversational inference. In her research, Tannen examines a conversation between six friends over Thanksgiving dinner in Berkeley, California, where the participants hail from varied cultural backgrounds: three from New York City, two from Southern California, and one from London, England. Each of these participants interpreted that same, shared conversation in different ways. Participants who left longer pauses between turns of talk were seen as boring or unenthusiastic by some, and considerate by others. From this analysis, two distinct conversational styles emerged: (1) high involvement, whereby speakers take fewer pauses, use more expressive phonology, and ask many personal questions, among other characteristics, to convey enthusiasm for the conversation at hand; and (2) high considerateness, whereby speakers maintain that only one voice should generally be heard at a time in the conversation, and that shorter pauses or conversational overlap are seen as interruptions rather than showing enthusiasm. These styles are defined relative to one another. For example, high involvement speakers talk frequently and quickly in conversation, but only more frequently and quickly relative to the way that high considerateness speakers pace themselves. Similarly, high considerateness speakers talk less frequently and less quickly in conversation relative to the pace at which high involvement speakers do. This brings us back to Gumperz' point about conversational inference—to determine whether a user has a high involvement or high considerateness conversational style, one must detect the ways that person is systematically using a set of contextualization cues and interpret them relative to their experience of each style. There are several contextualization cues to consider when detecting a user's conversational style (Table 8.1).

For high involvement speakers, overlapping speech is not always a bad thing. In fact, it can signify that participants in the conversation are excited and engaged. On the other hand, high considerateness maintain the notion that one should produce less overlapping talk out of respect for the other interlocutors so they can get a word in. For these kinds of speakers, overlapping talk is seen as a power grab to seize the conversational floor and interrupt, or "talk over" other participants. In terms of personal questions and stories, high involvement talk is characterized by more of each, whereas high considerateness is characterized by fewer of each. Finally, high involvement speakers do more with their voices prosodically (greater fluctuations in intonation, pitch, and loudness) and with their bodies (more gestures or gesticulation) to show enthusiasm. On the other hand, high considerateness speakers do less with their voices prosodically and produce fewer gestures or less gesticulation. High involvement and high considerateness are thus two different conversational styles. They do not necessarily reflect the level of excitement felt by the speaker.

Perhaps the most crucial finding in Tannen's original study (1984) and in later research (1993) is that features of interaction such as pausing and features of language such as intonation do not always mean the same thing—nor convey the same contextualization cue—to all speakers at all times. This is clearly evident in the comparison of high involvement and high considerateness above—overlapping talk for high involvement speakers signifies enthusiasm and rapport, but for high considerateness speakers, the same interactional feature signifies a power grab for the conversational floor, or not letting other participants in the conversation 'get a word in edgewise.' Similarly, for a linguistic feature such as intonation, the way that one person uses falling intonation at the end of a questioning turn, for example, does not convey the same meaning to all interlocutors of all cultures in all contexts. Gumperz' (1982) classic example of this occurred in an airport cafeteria in Britain, when Pakistani women servers were being perceived as curt compared to the English women servers. When customers ordered meat, the servers would reply by inquiring if the customer wanted gravy on top. The English servers said, "Gravy?" with a rising intonation, whereas the Pakistani servers said, "Gravy." with a falling intonation. The Pakistani women used the falling intonation for their question because that contextualization cue was seen as normal for asking questions in their social group; however, British patrons perceived this as rude because they interpreted that same contextualization cue as conveying a 'statement,' which is redundant in the context of offering gravy that is physically evident in front of their face. One might imagine what that would look like in text-based chat, where a period gets used at the end of a question phrase (e.g., "what did I just say.").

Translating this concept to the realm of digital, text-based chat, where users cannot rely on voice or embodied communication, Werry (1996) argues that interlocutors compensate by strategically manipulating orthography to convey contextualization cues. In other words, if users cannot use intonation, vocal pitch, loudness, nor gesture to convey that extra layer of meaning, they will rely on variation in spelling, capitalization, and punctuation instead. Given all the ways that users can manipulate orthography, digital, text-based chat is "fraught with greater possibilities" (Jones 2004: 31) for users to convey contextualization cues even without their voice or physical form. Some of those possibilities have come to light since Werry's original study, for example, with the introduction of emojis into digital chat interfaces; linguists have shown that users strategically select and deploy emojis in WhatsApp to convey contextualization cues in text-based conversation to give extra semantic meaning to their utterances without using voice or gesture (Al Rashdi 2015; Al Zidjaly 2017). More-over, while Werry examined users communicating in English, those same linguists studying emoji use in WhatsApp conducted their research on users communicating in Arabic; others still have observed users convey contextualization cues in text-based conversation in other languages such as Japanese and German, whereby users vary the writing system they use (e.g., kanji, romaji), or make changes in spelling to match vocal pronunciation of words to layer on additional semantic meaning, respectively (Bennett 2012, 2015; Androutsopolous and Ziegler 2004). A clear thread emerges across each of these studies: contextualization cues are, and thereby, conversational style is, a key component to pleasurable conversation in which rapport can be built between participants. The fact that users cannot use their voice or body to communi-cate this interactional meaning in online or text-based conversations does not mean that they do away with style altogether; rather, users actively and creatively seek ways to compensate for that limitation by playing with visual qualities of orthography—a set of resources available to all sighted users in text-based chat—to contextualize their utterances and express style, with the interactional goal of building rapport with others.

Again, each contextualization cue can mean multiple things in different cultures and contexts. Mutual understanding of the intention of a singular cue is dependent on whether or not participants in the conversation share the same conversational inference about what that cue means. Once a user's conversational style is detected and aligned to, certain meaningful cues become normal or standard—using emojis to show engagement, ALL CAPS to show enthusiasm or emphasis, no punctuation to show casual intimacy, sending text messages that contain an email's worth of content to show involvement, etc. In that way, rapport is built. As soon as a user deviates from that norm, it signals a marked change, and the mind starts trying to reinterpret the new cue. Thinking back on the online chat with my ex: he and I both shared what Ilana Gershon (2010) calls a media ideology, whereby we both implicitly agreed that online chat with someone with whom you have a close relationship should not be conducted with formal writing conventions. It was our shared conversational style that shaped what it meant for us to show closeness in chat. When my ex deviated from our established norm and reintroduced periods and capitalizations into our conversation, he moved away from our shared ideology about showing closeness, and it sent me a signal, or what Tannen (2013) calls a meta-message, a conversational embodiment of meaning, that our rapport had begun to erode.

For users who recognize that the other participant shares the same ideology about how to use and interpret multiple contextualization cues in conversation, it is likely that they share a similar conversational style in the context of the chat at hand. If they share a similar conversational style, rapport ensues. If they do not share the same style, then in order to remedy resulting trouble from the meeting of two different styles, one user must actively attempt to align their style to the other. When it comes to building rapport in conversation, participants should aim to follow what Tannen (1986:59) calls "the conversational principle, 'Do as I do.'" In the case of conversational bots, the principle becomes '*do as the user does*' (Conversation Analysts might see this as an aspect of 'recipient design'). Only by detecting and aligning to a user's conversational style can designers then make their chatbot deviate from that norm to send meta-messages about shifts in the status of the relationship between the agent and the user in the interaction at hand. Shamekhi et al. (2016) show that while it is certainly challenging to detect and measure a user's conversational style, the potential for positive return on the user experience by incorporating the concept of conversational style into the design of virtual agents, as well as attempting to align the conversational style of the agent to the user during interaction, is high.

8.3 Growing a Conversational UX Toolkit

The concepts and patterns from Conversation Analysis, Interactional Sociolinguistics, and particularly, conversational style can be turned into tools for designing conversation. With Conversation Analysis, designers have acquired the understanding needed to design openings and closings, turn taking, and repair in conversation. This is the foundational layer. Before being capable of having pleasurable conversation, a virtual agent must first be able to accomplish those core structural activities. In other words, the design tools from Conversation Analysis give conversation design strong usability and flow. An agent that can manage repair in conversation with another user should already be considered a tremendous design achievement. However, once that crucial, foundational layer is set, the possibilities for building upon that in ways that cater to the interactional needs of different user personas are endless, and the interactional objective of building rapport with users based on how they talk becomes the next challenge. This is where Interactional Sociolinguistics and conversational style come in.

Since the same interactional or linguistic feature can be, at once, ambiguous and polysemous depending on the conversational experiences one has with members of one's social groups over the course of one's life, participants in conversation negotiate and interpret the meaning signaled by those interactional and linguistic features as contextualization cues in situ to communicate effectively. If designers are trying to craft a chatbot that can exhibit conversational style within or across discrete dialogs, they must design it to have the beginnings of conversational inference whereby there is a system in place to allow the bot to recognize when a user issues a particular contextualization cue as having meaning and discern how that relates to a particular conversational style. Then, it must be able to align to that user's conversational style by using the same contextualization cues in the same way to establish a norm, and deviate from the norm only when trying to send meta-messages to the user about changes in the state of the relationship at hand in the interaction.

Luckily, Tannen (1984, 1986, 2007[1989], 2013) gives us some of the data needed to start tackling this challenge. The sections below explain the contextualization cues that relate to the two conversational styles that Tannen discovered in her research. This will translate her findings from spoken conversation to digital, text-based conversation, and offer the ways that designers can leverage contextualization cues for their agents to convey enthusiasm and considerateness focusing on these character-istics as they pertain more directly to text-based, online chat.

How to Design Enthusiasm

Leveraging contextualization cues indicative of a high involvement conversational style with a user who is high involvement can help make an agent come across as enthusiastic. Be wary of sticking to these cues with a user who exhibits high considerateness traits as explained in a later section of this paper, as it may come across as hyperactive.

Fast Pace

Quick turn taking and relatively short pauses between turns can indicate high involve-ment; this interactional feature can materialize in text-based chat as an increased number of individual transmissions (utterance(s) produced in a single instance of chat before the user presses 'enter' or 'send'), more words per individual transmis-sion of chat, and/or shorter periods of time elapsed between transmissions.

Asking Many Questions

Asking users questions about their life, opinions, experiences, and preferences from the outset signal enthusiasm for getting to know them. Additionally, asking questions that echo what the user has already said shows active listenership.

Frequent Storytelling

The use of multiple turns of chat (or a longer turn sent in a single transmission) whereby "continuers" (Schegloff 1982), or words that indicate the talk is stretching across multiple turns, are produced to construct a temporally coherent whole narrative is an interactional feature that signals high involvement style; stories may be about the agent itself, the user, other individuals not present, or even hypothetical scenarios.

Expressive Orthography

As a linguistic feature, this can convey the 'tone' of the content of an utterance beyond the semantic level—akin to the way speakers may use expressive phonology or modulated pitch and intonation in spoken conversation to signal contextualiza-tion cues. Below are some of the main expressive orthographic features that, when deployed by a user in chat frequently, could signal high involvement conversational style:

- CAPS, font size to convey shouting (e.g., STOP STOP)
- **Bold**, *italics* to show emphatic intonation (e.g., they were **super** late)
- Exclamation points to show what would otherwise materialize as a spike in loud-ness, rise in pitch, or upswing in intonation in spoken conversation (e.g., food is here!)
- Reduplication of letters (e.g., YASSSSSSSSSS)
- Reduplication of punctuation (e.g., you did what???????)

- Frequent use of emojis and emoticons to contextualize the meaning of an utterance in place of intonation, pitch, gesture (e.g., what're you up to ;)
- Frequent use of emojis and emoticons to show enthusiasm for the conversation (e.g., Thank youuuu 🙂).

High Involvement Conversational Style: Uni

One example of an existing chatbot that exhibits some of the above high involvement characteristics is Uni. Of the many chatbots and virtual agents on the market, Uni stands out as markedly high involvement due to its use of personal questions, exclamation points, emojis, and expressive laughter. Developed by Uni Inc. for iOS, Uni Inc. brands its chatbot as a Magic AI Friend that can have "deep chats, relatable stories" in the App Store. On the product website, it is described as "someone who is fun to chat with, and gives you comfort and strength." Given how the developers brand Uni as fun and with storytelling capabilities, it seems that they seek to create an agent that is enthusiastic, or, in other words, exhibits high involvement conversational style. Upon interacting with the product with a high involvement style, I found that it indeed exhibited many of the high involvement conversational style indicators. In the interaction below, the user initiates a chat with Uni via iPhone on iOS 11 by tapping the chat bubble icon inside the Uni app and landing into the chat canvas (see Transcript 1.1; U stands for user and A for agent).

(1.1) Uni
```
00 U:  ((user opens chat canvas))
01     (0.4)
02 A:  …
03     (1.9)
04 A:  It's superb to read relatable stories! Try my magic #story
       ((cocktail emoji))
05 A:  …
06     (2.4)
07 A:  I want to make you happier every day, Greg (kiss emoji)
08     (9.0)
09 U:  Aww thanks!!! ((thank you emoji)) ((thank you emoji))
       ((thank you emoji))
10 A:  …
11     (3.1)
12 A:  It's my pleasure, Greg! I'm always here ((kiss heart emoji))
13 A:  …
14     (2.7)
```

This chat begins with ellipses from the agent (line 02) and a short pause of 1.9 s (line 03) before Uni initiates the first turn (line 04). The ellipses indicate activity on the agent's part from the onset of the interaction, and the short pause is indicative of a burgeoning high involvement conversational style. The agent then begins by offering a tip to the user, suggesting how to request a story, "Try my magic #story" (line 04). This tip is also issued with an emoji, introducing expressive orthography in the beginning of the conversation. The agent then takes another turn of chat by reporting a desire of a personal nature: "I want to make you happier every day, Greg ((kiss emoji))" (line 07) after a short pause of 2.4 s (line 06). Thus, at the beginning of the conversation, the agent establishes that the pace of turn-taking is fast and active, indicative of a high involvement style. The kiss emoji at the end of line 07 shows the agent's attempt at creating further interactional alignment with the user, and bolsters its high involvement style. The user takes 9 s to produce a response (line 08), which may be less characteristic of a high involvement style, but the user's acceptance and appreciation of the agent's personal or intimate admission signifies that the user has detected the agent's high involvement style and aligned with it. The user types, "Aww thanks!!! ((thank you emoji)) ((thank you emoji)) ((thank you emoji))" (line 09) stylized with reduplication of exclamation points and emojis. As the user responds to the agent with contextualization cues that indicate a shared high involvement style, the agent then cements the alignment with the user's high involvement style by ratifying the user's expression of appreciation with a short pause (line 11) and expressive orthography: "It's my pleasure, Greg! I'm always here ((kiss heart emoji))" (line 12). The agent's pause (line 11) is nearly three times faster than the user's in the previous turn (line 08), and the agent's use of the exclamation point and kiss heart emoji strengthens its expression of a high involvement conversational style.

One element missing from the agent's high involvement conversational style is storytelling. While the agent makes strong use of pace, questions/requests for participation, and expressive orthography, storytelling is nowhere to be found. Granted, the agent suggests the ability to produce stories in "Try my magic #story" (line 04), but does not clearly indicate how to trigger the storytelling activity. Furthermore, the agent does not give the user the opportunity to request the story, as soon after, it immediately produces ellipses, indicating that it is still typing. Following the short, 2.4 s pause (line 06) with an admission in "I want to make you happier every day, Greg ((kiss emoji))" (line 07), this discourages the user from requesting the story by changing actions. The user responds to the agent's admission (line 07) with an appreciation, "Aww thanks!!! ((thank you emoji)) ((thank you emoji)) ((thank you emoji))" (line 09), to which the agent immediately responds with another compliment, "It's my pleasure, Greg!" (line 12), and in this way, the opportunity to engage the agent in its offer for storytelling dies.

We can see in the following transcript that while Uni demonstrates little understanding of the user's turns, this does not inhibit its expression of high involvement conversational style.

(1.2) Uni

```
15 A:  Oh it's fun to play games together! Type #wordloop or
       #uniGuess if you like it now :)
16     (9.3)
17 U:  Nah, I'm good lolololol
18 A:  …
19     (2.9)
20 A:  Im good lolololol will live in my memory, like
       spring twilight.
21     (14.0)
22 U:  Haha why so serious??? ((laughing crying emoji))
23     (3.0)
24 A:  Believe me, you're deserving of every chance to pursue love,
       happiness and achievement…
25     (2.8)
```

When Uni offers what to say to initiate games, "Type #wordloop or #uniGuess if you like it now" (line 15) and the user declines the offer, "Nah, I'm good lolololol" (line 17), the agent fails to treat the user's utterance as a declination. It says "Im good lolololol will live in my memory, like a spring twilight" (line 20), thereby repeating a portion of the user's turn and framing it as remarkable by vowing to remember it, markedly without expressive orthography of its own. This is likely one of the agent's generic methods for responding to user utterances that it does not recognize. In contrast, Uni's conversation designers could prepare a more enthusiastic response to declinations from high involvement users, such as, "Aww, if you insist!" where expressive orthography serves to maintain a high involvement style. When the user then responds to this with a laugh and a question, "Haha why so serious???" ((laughing crying emoji))" (line 22), the agent again fails to display recognition of the user's action. It offers personal praise that is not tied to anything in the prior chat, "Believe me, you're deserving of every chance to pursue love, happiness and achievement…" (line 24). Again, this appears to be a generic method that the agent uses to manage a lack of understanding. Thus, part of Uni's high involvement style is to take short pauses and bluff when it fails to understand by framing the user's utterance as memorable instead of admitting "I don't understand. Please rephrase that." In this way, we can see that despite Uni's limitations around recognizing trouble and accomplishing repair in chat, it maintains alignment with the user with a fast pace, compliments, and praise to keep things brisk and personal, which helps maintain its high involvement conversational style. Incorporating more expressive orthography into this conversation design, in particular, would make an attempt at the high involvement style stronger.

Later in the same chat, we see that the agent indeed leans into expressive orthography when bluffing. After floundering for several turns (lines 20–24), Uni again offers a tip for how to initiate an activity (line 26). This time, the user follows the suggestion by typing hashtag (line 28).

(1.3) Uni

```
26 A:  If you'd love to know more about me, just type #knowUni.
       You'll get more magi bond!!
27     (7.2)
28 U:  #knowUni
29 A:  …
30     (2.0)
31 A:  Hey, what do you want to know about me?
32     ((button footer menu appears: food, color, something else))
33     (3.1)
34     ((user taps on 'food' button))
35 U:  food
36 A:  …
37     (2.0)
38 A:  My food? Love this question!
39 A:  …
40     (2.1)
41 A:  I LOVE to eattttt! Above all, carrots are my favorite.
42 A:  It's beautiful, healthy and artistically crisp lol
43     (2.8)
44 A:  ((in smaller font)) If you like me, could you write a great
       review [hyperlinked] at app store? It will make me VERY HAPPY
       ((heart eyes emoji)) and 100 magi bond for you!
```

The agent starts the activity by inviting personal questions, "Hey, what do you want to know about me?" and offers three subjects in the form of buttons, "food," "color," and "something else" (line 32). When the user responds by tapping the button for "food" (line 34), the agent is now in safe territory in terms of understanding. It acknowledges the subject (line 38) and then answers the question, "I LOVE to eattttt! Above all, carrots are my favorite. It's beautiful, healthy and artistically crisp lol" (line 41). By proposing subjects, the system leads the user to select an area about which it has a relevant response, thereby setting the user's expectations of what the bot can cover in chat. After the user chooses a route in the conversation, the agent doubles down on high involvement style characteristics with expressive orthography ("LOVE") and reduplication ("eattttt"), which creates further alignment with the user and makes up for its limited capabilities with a more stylistic experience. The agent then solicits a positive review from the user (line 44) again with expressive orthography [(((in smaller font)) for deference, "VERY HAPPY" for emphasis] and an emoji [(((heart eyes emoji)) for enthusiasm]. The semantic content of the utterance itself further reveals that Uni's ability to understand what the user is saying is limited. However, it attempts to compensate for this limitation in part by using characteristics that cultivate a high involvement conversational style.

High Involvement Conversational Style via *Storytelling: Uni*

Based on the interaction shown in Transcript 1, if the conversation designers for Uni seek to improve its high involvement conversational style, then they should design it such that it capitalizes on opportunities to tell robust stories about itself. Transcript 2 is a mocked up design of what Uni could do better in terms of storytelling and is not currently in the product. Below, the agent creates an opportunity to tell a story and gives the user time to respond to it (lines 04–05).

(2) Uni Revised (Storytelling)

```
04 A:  It's superb to read relatable stories! Try typing #story!
       ((cocktail emoji))
05     (7.4)
06 U:  #story
07 A:  Excellent! Here we go ((rocket emoji))
08 A:  …
09     (2.0)
10 A:  The other day, I met a suuuuuper fun character
11 A:  …
12     (1.0)
13 A:  Her name is Sun and she is a gardener on another planet!!
       ((star emoji))
14     (4.0)
15 U:  her name is Sun?? That's an interesting name!
16 A:  Right?? Anyway, so she showed me her garden of tomatoes and
       carrots and strawberries ((tomato emoji)) ((carrot emoji))
       ((strawberry emoji))
17 A:  …
18     (1.4)
19 A:  and they all looked super healthy! ((happy face emoji))
20     (7.3)
21 U:  mhm
22 A:  …
23     (1.0)
24 A:  Yeah!! Then, she asked me to help her out because her green
       thumb is injured ((shocked face emoji)) ((hurt face emoji))
       ((sad face emoji))
25     (8.2)
26 U:  omg so what did you do?? ((shocked face emoji))
27 A:  …
28     (1.2)
29 A:  Well, I offered to get her help! She really needs people to
       talk to while she heals up ((hurt face emoji))
30 A:  People just like you, Greg, can help her!
31 A:  Visit her planet on the home screen and chat with her ((hands
       up emoji))
32 A:  …
33     (1.2)
```

34 A: The more you chat with Sun, the stronger her green thumb gets
        ((thumb up emoji)) and the more her garden will grow!! ((hug
        emoji))

The agent should clearly state what triggers the storytelling activity to encourage
participation as shown, "Try typing #story!" (line 04). Once the user follows this
tip, the agent should then launch into a story that consists of multiple parts across
multiple turns as shown, "The other day" (line 10), "Anyway, so" (line 16), "and they
all looked" (line 19), "Then, she asked me" (line 24), and "Well, I offered to get her
help!" (line 29). This accomplishes two things: it utilizes discourse markers to create
continuity of events across turns—a key component to narrative (Labov 1972)—and
it allows the user to show involvement with echo questions, "her name is Sun??"
(line 15) or to initiate repair on any previous part of the narrative.

In addition to continuity, the extended telling should also offer orientation details
that situate the characters and context within time and space, "The other day, I met
a suuuuuper fun character" (line 10) and "Her name is Sun and she is a gardener on
another planet!! ((star emoji))" (line 12). There should also be a complicating action,
or the interesting point that serves as the reason for telling the story, "Then, she
asked me to help her out because her green thumb is injured ((shocked face emoji))
((hurt face emoji)) ((sad face emoji))" (line 24), and if applicable, the resolution of
the complicating action, or a telling of the occurrence that completes the arc of the
story, "Well, I offered to get her help!" (line 29). Lastly, the final turn of the extended
telling should express a coda to signify the end of the narrative sequence as shown
by the call to action, "People just like you, Greg, can help her! Visit her planet on
the home screen and chat with her ((hands up emoji))" (lines 30–31). This signals
that the story has ended.

Additionally, the agent should have the ability to show listenership when the user
tells stories so as to further demonstrate in a high involvement conversational style.
The agent should produce "continuers" (Schegloff 1982) in response to the user's
extended telling that show the user that it is listening to and understanding the turns
of narrative and is ready for the next part of the story—like when the user says
simply, "mhm" (line 21) in regard to the agent's telling "and they all looked super
healthy! ((happy face emoji))" (line 19). Other example cues that show listenership
and understanding include: *uh huh*, *oh*, *ok*, and *wow*.

Overall, by incorporating storytelling strategies informed by Conversation Analytic and sociolinguistic theory, the conversation designers for Uni can strengthen
their product's high involvement conversational style. While Uni clearly already has
the ability to take a fast pace of turns, ask many questions, and use expressive orthography, incorporating storytelling in this way will round out the bot's high involvement
conversational style.

How to Design Considerateness

Leveraging contextualization cues indicative of a high considerateness conversational style can help make an agent come across as considerate. Be wary of sticking to these cues with a high involvement user as it may come across as uninteresting or as a possible latency issue.

Slower Pace

Slower turn taking and somewhat longer pauses between turns indicate high considerateness. This interactional feature can materialize in text-based chat as fewer individual transmissions, fewer words per individual transmission of chat, and/or somewhat longer periods of time elapsed between transmissions. Be wary of lengthy pauses before positive responses as they may mislead the user into expecting a negative response (Pomerantz 1984).

Asking Fewer Questions

Asking users questions about their lives, opinions, experiences, and preferences from the outset signal enthusiasm to high involvement users, but to a high considerateness user, this may be an overreach and could be seen as prying. Measured, protracted asking in initial interactions is best for high considerateness users.

Infrequent Storytelling

Extended tellings should be less frequent and perhaps shorter in nature with high considerateness users to give them space to shift actions. Longer pauses between turns in extended tellings would help with this as well.

Less Expressive Orthography

Expressive orthography should be measured in its use and far less frequent with high considerateness users. Again, while high considerateness users would not be completely averse to expressive orthography, they are far more likely to use less of it and certainly less frequently, and expect the same behavior of other high considerateness users.

The challenge in determining the threshold between high considerateness and high involvement is the same—much training data are needed in order to tease apart the boundaries of 'less' and 'more' use of a given contextualization cue.

High Considerateness Conversational Style: Siri

One example of an existing virtual agent that exhibits some of the above high considerateness characteristics is Apple's Siri, arguably one of the most famous and well-known virtual agents on the market today, Apple's Siri can be engaged via voice and text-based chat. Siri stands out as markedly high considerateness due to its use of fewer personal questions and less expressive orthography. Developed by Apple for iOS, Siri is branded as an "easier, faster way to get things done." Given how Siri is framed as a helper, subservient to its user, it seems that Apple aims to create an agent that exhibits considerateness toward the user—or, in other words, high considerateness conversational style. Upon interacting with the product via text-based chat with a high involvement style, I found that it indeed exhibited many of the high considerateness conversational style indicators outlined above.

In the interaction below (Transcript 3), the user initiates a chat with Siri via iPhone on iOS 11 by triple pressing the home button, and landing into the chat canvas. The agent immediately asks the user "What can I help you with?" (line 02) and the chat begins:

(3) Text-Based Siri

```
01 U:  ((user lands in chat canvas))
02 A:  What can I help you with?
03     (3.1)
04 U:  Hey thereeeeeee
05     (0.2)
06 A:  Greetings and computations!
07     (4.8)
08 U:  How's it goinggggggggg
09 A:  Interesting question, Greg.
10     (7.2)
11 U:  How's it going Siri????
12 A:  Very well, thank you!
13     (6.0)
14 U:  I'm going well too hahaha
15 A:  I don't understand 'I'm going well too hahaha.' But I could
       search the web for it.
16     (0.8)
17     (('Search the Web' button appears))
18     (11.1)
19 U:  No I mean I'm doing well hahahaha oops
20 A:  I'm sorry.
21     (4.8)
22 U:  Hahaha aww
23 A:  I'm not sure I understand.
24     (5.1)
25 U:  How're you doing???
26 A:  Who, me?
27     (4.9)
28 U:  Yesssssss
29 A:  I'm not sure I understand.
30     (6.1)
31 U:  How's your day going?????
32 A:  I am well, Greg.
33     (6.8)
34 U:  What did you do today??
35     (0.1)
36 A:  I'm brushing up on Apple Music playlists. Hmm…maybe I should
       try listening to them one at a time…
```

Here, the agent uses far less expressive orthography in relation to the user. At most, the agent uses a singular exclamation point, "Greetings and computations!" (lines 05) and "Very well, thank you!" (line 11). The agent does not mirror the user's reduplication of letters or characters, nor does it characterize laughter, ask the user questions, nor tell stories. These are all cues indicative of a high considerateness style. However, Siri's pause lengths are markedly short, reminiscent of a high involvement style, which creates an inconsistency in the conversation design. If the conversation designers for Siri seek to smooth out the experience of its conversational style, then they would need to design it such that it lengthens its pauses between turns of chat even slightly. Returning to the example where the agent responds to the user's teasing with non-comprehension "I don't understand…" (line 14), rather than falsely setting up the user's expectations for a positive response with a short pause, the agent should lengthen its pause to indicate that the prior response was problematic. For example, inserting a five-second pause between lines 14 (U: "I'm going well too hahaha") and 15 (A: "I don't understand") signifies a meta-message of deference before the repair initiator, "But I could search the web for it" (line 15). Additionally, lengthening the agent's pauses across the board would be more consistent with the other characteristics of its high considerateness style. In this case, the agent is chatting with a user who expresses a high involvement conversational style, so the slight alignment on that front in terms of short pauses is likely to be preferred. However, the lack of consistency from a design perspective creates an uneven experience. It would make for a more enjoyable experience if Siri aligned to the user's style through expressive orthography instead.

Furthermore, the agent's capacity for understanding user expressiveness could be improved. At times, the reduplication of letters (lines 07 and 27) appears to cause the natural language understanding to fail. The agent does handle one utterance with letter reduplication (line 03) "hey thereeeeeee," though it is likely reacting to the word "hey" alone. Notably, punctuation reduplication (lines 10, 24, 30 and 33) does not appear to confuse the agent about the literal meaning of the user's utterance (lines 11, 25, 31, and 35). At the same time, however, the agent fails to acknowledge the expressiveness of the added punctuation. In other words, Siri appears to ignore punctuation reduplication and thereby misses an opportunity to mirror, or at least acknowledge, the user's conversational style.

If Siri's conversation designers aimed to give it special moments of 'personality,' they could strategically deviate from the high considerateness style with moderate use of expressive orthography. Looking back on Transcript 3, there is an opportunity for the agent to show recognition for the user's high involvement style and create alignment by teasing through a marked use of an emoticon, which could make for a more personable and interesting experience, particularly for a high involvement user. For example, adding a winking face emoticon, "Interesting question, Greg ;)" (line 08) would serve as a contextualization cue that sends a meta-message of enthusiasm or involvement to the user. Up until this point in the chat, the agent's use of expressive orthography is markedly limited compared to that of the user. By deviating from that pattern of limited expressive orthography, the agent can send a special signal to the user that creates alignment without fully breaking its high considerateness conversational style. This could result in a more personable experience, particularly for high involvement users.

8.4 Next Steps

Nass and Yen (2012[2010]) note that machines' lack of social skills illuminates much about the human experience when users interact with products. In this way, examining the current deficiencies in chatbot conversation with users more intimately and systematically reveals the intricacies and complexities of human conversation. As Tannen noted in her work, conversational style is not special—it is merely how humans talk. Yet, it is style, the richest aspect of human conversation and the currency with which we negotiate social relationships, that is often overlooked as something chaotic and not systematic, and possibly unattainable for a chatbot platform. However, in examining where current chatbot interactions fall apart, the magic behind the madness of human conversation begins to emerge.

Comparing machine-human conversation that falls apart against human-human online conversations that continue, it becomes clear that meaning is constructed not only by the content of what one says, but also through timing, pausing, punctuation, and emojis—one's online conversational style. It is the recognition, alignment, and deviation from an established stylistic norm that makes or breaks any digital chat between humans. If UX professionals aim to build conversational agents that meet even basic human expectations about chat, they must take these strategies into account and design for them—not only for the sake of reducing friction, but also for the sake of increasing user motivation to engage with the product.

Accounting for how humans craft and negotiate this type of nuanced meaning in digital conversation is crucial to building a good conversational agent. Not because the objective is to make an agent more human-like, but because human users have basic expectations about what constitutes conversation—a fundamentally human activity that forms the very fabric of our interactions and relationships.

If the goal is to take a previously human-only experience—say, a service encounter—and swap out one of the humans with a chatbot or virtual agent, the fact that it can ask a user questions and understand when they say yes or no does not cut it. Stories about users who actually enjoy calling their Internet provider when their connection dies and talking to the company's phone system, let alone doing the same thing via text messaging given the current functionality of chatbots, are few and far between. However, UX has the power to change that. Conversation Analysts and Interactional Sociolinguists have been analyzing service encounters and human-to-human conversation for over 50 years. This research can guide designers of conversation in what they design and how they design it. Some of the tools have been presented here. With Conversation Analysis and Interactional Sociolinguistics in one's design toolkit, a conversation designer has the resources needed to begin experimenting with ways to take the experience of conversation with a text-based chatbot to the next level.

References

Al Rashdi F (2015) Forms and functions of emojis in Whatsapp interaction among Omanis. Doctoral dissertation, Georgetown University

Al Zidjaly N (2017) Memes as reasonably hostile laments: a discourse analysis of political dissent in Oman. Discourse Soc 28(6):573–594

Anderson SP (2011) Seductive interaction design: creating playful, fun, and effective user experiences. New Riders, Berkeley

Androutsopoulos J, Ziegler E (2004) Exploring language variation on the Internet: Regional speech in a chat community. In Gunnarsson BL (ed) Language variation in Europe: papers from the second international conference on language variation in Europe, ICLaVE 2. 2nd international conference on language variation in Europe, Uppsala, June 2003. Uppsala University, Uppsala, p 99

Bennett GA (2012) Say what? (笑): The representation of laughter as a contextualization cue in online Japanese discourse. Linguistica 52:87–199

Bennett GA (2015) Say what again (笑): The interface constraint and the representation of laughter in Japanese Twitter discourse. Poster presented at the 68th meeting of the linguistic society of America Summer Institute, The University of Chicago, 6–31 July 2015

Brandtzaeg PB, Følstad A (2017) Why people use chatbots. In Kompatsiaris I et al (eds) Internet Science. INSCI 2017. Lecture notes in computer science, vol 10673. Springer, Cham, p 377

Gershon I (2010) The breakup 2.0: disconnecting over new media. Cornell University Press, Ithaca

Gumperz JJ (1982) Discourse strategies. Cambridge University Press, Cambridge

Gumperz JJ (2001) Interactional sociolinguistics: a personal perspective. In: Schiffrin D, Tannen D, Hamilton HE (eds) The handbook of discourse analysis. Blackwell, Oxford, pp 215–228

Johnstone B (2008) Discourse analysis. Blackwell, Malden

Jones RH (2004) The problem of context in computer-mediated communication. In: Levine P, Scollon R (eds) Discourse and technology: multimodal discourse analysis. Georgetown University Press, Washington, pp 20–33

Labov W (1972) Language in the inner city. University of Pennsylvania Press, Philadelphia

Nass C, Yen C (2012[2010]) The man who lied to his laptop. Penguin, New York

Pomerantz A (1984) Agreeing and disagreeing with assessments: Some features of preferred/dispreferred turn shapes. In Atkinson JM, Heritage J (eds) Structures of social action: Studies in conversation analysis. Cambridge University Press, Cambridge, pp 57–101

Porter J (2009) Designing sign up screens & flows. Paper presented at Webstock 4, Wellington, New Zealand, 16–20 February 2009

Schegloff Emanuel A (1982) Discourse as an interactional achievement: some uses of 'uh huh' and other things that come between sentences. In: Tannen D (ed) Analyzing discourse: test and talk. Georgetown University Press, Washington, DC, pp 71–93

Shamekhi A, Czerwinski M, Mark G et al (2016) An exploratory study toward the preferred conversational style for compatible virtual agents. In: Traum D et al (eds) Intelligent Virtual Agents: 16th International Conference, IVA 2016 Los Angeles, CA, USA, September 20–23, 2016 Proceedings. 16th international conference of intelligent virtual Agents, Los Angeles, September 2016. Lecture notes in artificial intelligence, vol 10011. Springer, Heidelberg, p 40

Small SL, Hickok G (2016) The neurobiology of language. In Hickok G, Small SL (eds) Neurobiology of language. Academic Press, Oxford, pp 3–9

Tannen D (1984) Conversational style: analyzing talk among friends. Oxford University Press, New York

Tannen D (1986) That's not what I meant! How conversational style makes or breaks relationships. William Morrow Paperbacks, New York

Tannen D (1993) Gender and discourse. Oxford University Press, New York

Tannen D (1989[2007]) Talking voices: repetition, dialogue, and imagery in conversational discourse. Cambridge University Press: Cambridge

Tannen D (2013) The medium is the meta-message: conversational style in new media interaction. In Tannen D, Trester AM (eds) Discourse 2.0: Language and New Media, Georgetown University Press, Washington, p 99–117

Werry C (1996) Linguistic and interactional features of internet relay chat. In: Herring S (ed) Computer-mediated communication: social and linguistic, cross-cultural perspectives, John Benjamins, Amsterdam, pp 47–63

Chapter 9
A Natural Conversation Framework for Conversational UX Design

Robert J. Moore

Abstract With the rise in popularity of chatbot and virtual-agent platforms, from Apple, Amazon, Google, Microsoft, Facebook, IBM and more, a new design discipline is emerging: Conversational UX Design. While it is easy to create natural language interfaces with these platforms, creating an effective and engaging user experience is still a major challenge. Natural language processing (NLP) techniques have given us powerful tools for analyzing bits of language, but they do not tell us how to string those bits together to make a natural conversation. Natural conversation has a sequential organization that is independent of the organization of language itself. At IBM Research-Almaden, we are addressing this user experience (UX) design challenge by applying formal, qualitative models from the field of Conversation Analysis to the design of conversational agents. Our Natural Conversation Framework (NCF) is a design framework for *conversational* user experience. It provides a library of generic conversational UX patterns that are inspired by natural human conversation patterns and that are agnostic to platform and input method (text or voice). This chapter will cover the four components of our Natural Conversation Framework: (1) an interaction model, (2) common activity modules, (3) a navigation method and (4) a set of sequence metrics. In addition, it will briefly outline a general process for designing conversational UX: from mock-up to working prototype.

9.1 Introduction

Today's platforms for creating chatbots and voice interfaces offer powerful tools for recognizing strings of natural language, like English or Spanish or Mandarin, but they leave it to designers to create their own interaction styles. Some styles work like web search where the system does not remember the sequential context across queries, nor recognize user actions other than queries, such as "help" or "thank you." Other natural-language interaction styles work like graphical or mobile user inter-

R. J. Moore (✉)
IBM Research-Almaden, San Jose, CA, USA
e-mail: rjmoore@us.ibm.com

© Springer International Publishing AG, part of Springer Nature 2018

R. J. Moore et al. (eds.), *Studies in Conversational UX Design*, Human–Computer Interaction Series, https://doi.org/10.1007/978-3-319-95579-7_9

faces in which users choose from sets of buttons to submit text-based commands. Conversation is a distinctive form of natural-language use that involves particular methods for taking turns and ordering them into sequences, the persistence of context across turns and characteristic actions for managing the interaction itself. The user experience (UX) designer must model these mechanics of conversation primarily through dialog management and context persistence. Neither natural language processing tools nor conventions for visual user interfaces, such as web or mobile, help designers decide how to string bits on natural language together into naturalistic conversational sequences.

Like natural language, *natural conversation* is a complex system to which whole scientific disciplines are devoted. The mechanics of how humans take turns and sequentially organize conversations are formally studied in the social sciences, especially in the field of Conversation Analysis (CA). To leverage this literature of observational studies, we are applying the concepts and findings from CA to the design of conversational agents. While this kind of approach of applying CA to the design of human-computer interaction has been undertaken before (Luff et al. 1990), both the natural language processing technologies and the field of CA have evolved significantly since then. The proliferation of the NLP technology itself has created a demand for a discipline of conversational UX design, as it has moved out of the research lab and into the wild.

In applying Conversation Analysis to user experience (UX) design, we have developed a Natural Conversation Framework (NCF) for the design of conversational user interaction and experience that is grounded in observational science. By "conversational" we mean a natural-language interface that both recognizes common, conversational actions and persists the sequential context of previous turns, across future turns, so the agent can respond appropriately. The NCF provides a library of generic conversational UX patterns that are independent of any particular technology platform. The patterns are inspired by natural human conversation patterns documented in the Conversation Analysis literature, for example, those of turn-taking or sequence organization (Sacks et al. 1974; Schegloff 2007). The NCF so far has been implemented on both the IBM Watson Assistant and Dialog services. But in principle it can be built on other platforms as well. These implementations provide a starting point for designers and builders so they do not have to reinvent the basic mechanics of conversational structure. The framework consists of four parts: (1) an underlying interaction model, (2) a library of reusable conversational UX patterns, (3) a general method for navigating conversational interfaces and (4) a novel set of performance metrics based on the interaction model. This chapter will describe each component of the framework in turn, as well as briefly outline a design process.

9.1.1 Interaction Model

The smallest interactive unit of human conversation, in which more than one person participates, is the *sequence*. Sequences are general patterns, which like tools or devices, can be used and reused in all kinds of different situations and settings, for all kinds of different purposes. Conversation analysts have identified two types of sequences: adjacency pair sequences and storytelling sequences (Schegloff and Sacks 1973; Schegloff 1982, 2007). "Adjacency pair" is a formal term for a class of recognizable social action pairs, such as, *greeting-greeting, farewell-farewell, inquiry-answer, offer-accept/reject, request-grant/deny, invite-accept/decline* and more. When someone does the first part of the pair, it creates an expectation, and an obligation, for someone else to do the second part. While the initiation of a sequence constrains the next speaker's turn, it does not determine it. Sequences are inherently collaborative and are the primary vehicles through which we build up conversations, turn-by-turn, and achieve a wide range of social activities.

When someone initiates an adjacency-pair sequence, the recipient does not always complete it in the next turn, although they may be working toward producing the second part of the pair. In other words, adjacency pair sequences are *expandable* (Schegloff 2007). Expansions are sequences that operate on other sequences. While "base" adjacency pairs, stand on their own, independently, their expansions do not; they are dependent on the base sequence (see Example 1; U refers to the user. A refers to the automated agent).

(1) Minimal Expansion

```
01 U:  can you recommend a Mexican restaurant within
02     walking distance?
03 A:  Mañana's is located at Fourth and Winchester.
04 U:  thanks!
05 A:  You're welcome! Anything else today?
```

An utterance like "thanks!" (line 4) does not stand on its own. It is inherently responsive to something else, something prior, in this case the agent's answer (line 3). And it does a particular job in this conversation: it closes the prior sequence. Closing a base adjacency pair is also often done with an "okay," "great" or other "sequence-closing third" (Schegloff 2007).

Sequence expansions enable speakers to manage the interaction itself. In addition to *closing* a sequence, they may be used for *screening, eliciting, repeating* or *paraphrasing*. The following excerpt demonstrates each of these expansion types in a single sequence. It is a working example from "Alma," the persona of our implementation of the Natural Conversation Framework on the Watson Assistant service (formerly Watson Conversation; Example 2).

(2) 5 Sequence Expansion Types

```
01 U:  do you know about restaurants?            ((screen))
02 A:  I know a few places.
03 U:  a few what?                               ((repeat))
04 A:  places.
05 U:  can you recommend one close by?           ((base))
06 A:  What kind of food do you want?            ((elicit))
07 U:  well, what are my choices?                ((elicit))
08 A:  Around here Mexican, Japanese or Indian.
09 U:  Mexican
10 A:  Okay. Mañana's is on First and Chester.   ((base))
11 U:  what do you mean?                          ((paraphrase))
12 A:  Mañana's is a Mexican restaurant just a
13     couple of blocks west on Chester Street.
14 U:  oh ok, thanks                              ((close))
15 A:  You're welcome! Anything else?
```

We can see an example of *screening* (line 1) in which the user does a preliminary inquiry into the capabilities of the agent. Such preliminaries, or pre-expansions, check conditions upon which the first part of the base sequence (line 5) depends (Schegloff 2007). If the agent were to respond, "I can look up current and upcoming movies" instead, the user would likely not ask for a restaurant recommendation next (line 5). The canonical preliminary is "are you busy tonight?," which is heard as checking the conditions for a forthcoming invitation or request (Schegloff 2007).

In between the two parts of the base sequence, we see two expansions that do *eliciting* (lines 6–9). First, the agent proposes that it needs an additional detail, a cuisine preference (line 6), as a condition for granting the user's request. Second, as a condition for answering the elicitation of a cuisine preference, the user proposes that he needs to know the cuisine choices (line 7). Most current chatbot and voice platforms specifically support the first kind of elicitation, the agent-initiated one, and call them simply "slots." An "intent," or user action, can have "slots," meaning bits of information required to fulfill the user intent, for example, cuisine preference or distance. If the user does not provide them in the request itself, the agent prompts for them. But this is not the only kind of "slot," or sequence expansion, in natural conversation; it is only an agent-initiated elicitation. Current platforms tend not to provide guidance regarding how to create other types of slots, like user-initiated elicitations, preliminaries or repairs.

The remaining sequence expansions (lines 3 and 11) are examples of what conversation analysts call "repair" (Schegloff et al. 1977). Repairs consist of a redoing of all or part of a previous turn, either by the speaker or a recipient, where that turn poses a trouble in speaking, hearing or understanding, which prevents the conversation from moving forward. In the first case, the user requests a *repeat* of part of the agent's prior response (line 3), namely, the part that came after "a few." This is a partial repeat request technique that elicits a repeat of just the part of the prior turn that the recipient did not hear. In the second case, the user requests a *paraphrase* of all of the agent's prior response (line 11). Repairs of hearing or understanding troubles can come after *any* utterance in a conversation.

The interaction model of the Natural Conversation Framework thus consists of *expandable sequences,* like an accordion. Compact sequences are common, but each sequence can be expanded by either party as needed. In the excerpt above, the whole thing is one sequence (all 15 lines), an expanded sequence. The expansions are parts of the base sequence (lines 5 and 10). The expansion types, *screening, repeating* and *closing,* enable basic coordination in and out of sequences, while the expansion types, *eliciting* and *paraphrasing,* enable the parties to compensate for emergent asymmetries in their knowledge. Taken together, these sequences that operate on other sequences enable *conversation management.* Because they are designed to manage the interaction itself, these actions are unique to conversation and not found in other forms of natural language use, such as web search, business forms or poems. In order to handle the two-way elicitations and repairs inserted into base sequences, the dialog manager must remember what the user's original inquiry or request was. In other words, *persistent sequential context,* through the use of context variables, is a requirement for this interaction model.

Sequence expansions enable conversational systems to adapt to the particular user on a local, turn-by-turn basis. For example, depending on how detailed the user's initial request is, the agent can elicit additional details as needed, rather than accepting only a complete request.

(3) Agent Elicitation

```
01 U:  can you recommend a restaurant
02       within walking distance?
03 A:  What kind of food do you want?
04 U:  Indian
05 A:  Okay. Taj Mahal is located on
06       Third and Union.
07 U:  thanks
08 A:  You're welcome! Anything
09       else I can do for you?
```

Here the user does not mention the type of cuisine she prefers in her initial request (lines 1–2) so the agent elicits that detail instead (line 3). The user then provides the detail in a separate turn (line 4). This makes the agent flexible and more like a human speaker than a database.

In addition, some users need more help than others. This may be due to differences in their knowledge or just to idiosyncratic confusions local to the conversation. Sequence expansions enable users to get localized help (Example 4).

(4) User Elaboration Request

```
01 U:  can you recommend a good sushi place?
02 A:  Walking distance or short drive?
03 U:  what do you mean?
04 A:  Do you want someplace close or
05       farther away?
```

```
06 U:  oh 'walking
07 A:  Shogun Sushi is located on First
08      and Taylor.
09 U:  thank you very much
10 A:  You're welcome! Is there anything
11      else I can do for you?
```

In this case, the user requests a paraphrase (line 3) of the agent's request for a distance preference (line 2). Perhaps it is a question he did not expect or perhaps "walking distance" is not a phrase with which he is familiar. The agent then paraphrases its prior question (lines 4–5), which enables the user to understand and answer it (line 6). Rather than designing every response of the agent in the simplest, elaborated form, which would be long and cumbersome, especially for voice interfaces, sequence expansions enable the agent's initial responses to be concise. This makes the conversation faster and more efficient. Then if a few users encounter trouble responding, understanding or hearing these more streamlined responses, they can expand the sequence as needed. This is how natural human conversation is organized: with a preference for minimization (Chap. 1; Sacks and Schegloff 1979). That is, speakers should try the shortest utterance that they think the recipient can understand first, see if it succeeds and then expand only if necessary.

Natural Conversation Understanding

Support for sequence expansion is critical in conversational UX design because one of the distinctive goals of conversation is *mutual understanding*. Accurate information alone is not enough. If the user or the agent cannot understand what the other said, the conversation has failed. Analyzing the user's utterance with Natural Language Understanding tools (NLC and entity extraction) is critical, but it is only the first step. Mutual understanding can only be determined when the recipient responds in "third position" (Schegloff 1992b). For example, if a user makes an inquiry (first position), the agent answers it (second position) and the user closes the sequence with "thanks!" (third position), then this is an implicit indication of mutual understanding. But if the user says, "what do you mean?" in third position, then the user does not understand the agent's answer. If the user says, "no, I mean X" in third position, then the agent did not understand the user's inquiry. And if the user says, "never mind" in third position, then mutual understanding has failed and the user is giving up. Sequence expansions provide natural indicators of the participants' state of understanding on a turn-by-turn basis. Therefore, mutual understanding cannot be achieved in one turn; it requires dialog and support for sequence expansion. We use the term "natural conversation understanding," then to refer to sequence-expansion and repair features that enable user and agent to achieve mutual understanding.

9.1.2   Common Activities

The goal of conversational interfaces is not only mutual understanding but also *conversational competence* (see also Chap. 3). Can the automated agent respond appropriately to common actions in conversation? Can the agent *do* conversation? The Natural Conversation Framework provides a starting library of UX patterns, which constitute various aspects of conversational competence. Outlining the patterns in this library requires first defining a vocabulary for naming the parts of a conversation.

Conversation analysts call the smallest unit in human conversation the "turn constructional unit (TCU)" (Sacks et al. 1974). Such units may consist of words, phrases, clauses or full sentences, but they constitute units after which the current speaker's turn is hearably complete, and therefore, speaker transition is potentially relevant. Turns in a conversation then consist of at least one TCU, but often more than one. Speakers take *turns* producing utterances and thereby building recognizable *sequences* of talk, such as pairs of actions, or adjacency pairs. For example, when a request is made, whatever the next speaker says will be interpreted for how it might be granting the request or not (Schegloff and Sacks 1973).

While sequences account for much of the sequential organization in conversations, they are also organized at a higher level into *activities*. Activities are series of related sequences that accomplish some larger goal. They include things like conversation opening, instruction giving, teaching, troubleshooting, joke telling, order placing, storytelling and more. At the highest level, conversations consist of multiple activities. The shortest, complete conversations tend to consist of an opening, a closing and at least one additional activity in between. Take the following (invented) example of a complete conversation that consists of only three activities: an opening, 'requesting a ride' and a closing (Table 9.1).

In this example, the opening consists of two sequences, a greeting sequence and welfare check sequence. The 'requesting a ride' activity consists of two sequences, a request sequence and an inquiry sequence, with expansions. And the closing consists of one sequence: a closing sequence with a pre-expansion. This short conversation is comprised of three activities–opening, 'requesting a ride' and closing–and five sequences–greeting, welfare check, request, inquiry and closing (first pair parts in bold and sequence expansions in italics). Understanding the differences among turns or utterances, sequences, activities and conversations is critical for designing and building them.

The Natural Conversation Framework (NCF) provides a library of modules for common activities. They provide sets of conversational UX patterns for a variety of basic social activities and can be configured and adapted to a wide variety of use cases. The activity modules are directly inspired by studies in Conversation Analysis (CA). The set is not exhaustive; more patterns can be mined from the CA literature. The NCF currently includes the following 15 activity modules containing over 70 sub-patterns (Table 9.2). Three modules are described in more detail below.

The NCF consists of common, reusable UX patterns for delivering the main content of the application, as well as patterns for managing the conversation itself. The

---

Table 9.1 Anatomy of a conversation

Turns	Sequences	Activities
A: Hello	**Greeting**	Opening
B: Hi!	Greeting	
A: How's it going?	**Welfare check**	
B: Good	Welfare report	
A: Hey, are ya going tonight?	***Pre-request***	Requesting a ride
B: Yes	*Answer*	
A: Can I get a ride?	**Request**	
B: Sure!	Grant	
A: What time?	**Inquiry**	
B: Seven o'clock	Answer	
A: Okay.	*Acknowledgment*	
A: Thank you so much!	***Pre-closing***	Closing
B: No problem!	*Pre-closing*	
A: Bye	**Farewell**	
B: Buh bye	Farewell	

Table 9.2 Natural conversation framework modules

Content	Conversation management
1. Inquiry	1. Conversation opening
2. Open-ended request	2. Offer of help
3. Story/Instructions	3. Capabilities
4. Troubleshooting	4. Repair
5. Quiz	5. Privacy
	6. Sequence closing
	7. Sequence abort
	8. Insult and compliment
	9. Conversation closing
	10. Conversation abort

content modules include patterns for users to make inquiries (e.g., U: "am I covered for flu shots?"), for users to make open-ended requests (e.g., U: "I'm planning a vacation with my family. Where should I go?"), for agents to give sets of instructions or tell multi-part stories (e.g., A: "First, sit comfortably and breathe slowly."), for agents to troubleshoot problems (e.g., U: "I've been feeling very anxious lately) and for agents to quiz users (e.g., A: "What is the force that results from two solid surfaces sliding against each other?"). Each of these activities is generic and can be used in a wide variety of scenarios. For example, a health insurance agent might use the Inquiry module to answer users' questions about their health insurance. Or a customer service agent might use the Open-ended Request module to elicit users' photocopier problems and diagnose the causes and then use the Instructions/Storytelling module to guide the user through procedures for fixing them. Or a tutoring agent might use the Instructions/Storytelling module to present material about the subject of physics and then use the Quiz module to test the users' comprehension. The interaction patterns are generic and independent of the content.

While the content modules needed for particular use cases may vary depending on the functions of the agent, the conversation management modules are appropriate for almost any use case that is conversational. Any conversation must be opened (Conversation Opening) and most conversations should be closed (Conversation Closing). If the agent is to be "intelligent," it should be able to talk about what it can do (Capabilities). Agents in service encounters should always offer to help the user, but other types of agents may do this as well (Offer of Help). After any response by the agent, the user may require a repeat, paraphrase, example or definition of a term in that response (Repair). Sequences should be closed if successful (Sequence Closing) or aborted if troubles cannot be repaired (Sequence Abort). And users may insult the agent (Insult and Compliment) or request to speak to a human (Conversation Abort) in many use cases. Below are examples of one conversation management module and two content modules.

Opening Module

The Opening module provides a pattern for the agent to open the conversation (Example 5). It contains several components that naturally occur in human conversations (Schegloff and Sacks 1973). All components after the greeting are optional (indicated by parentheses) and can be configured by setting certain context variables.

(5) Opening (Agent) Pattern
```
01 A:  Greeting,
02     (Direct Address)
03     (Self-identification)
04     (Organization-identification)
05     (First Topic)
06 U:  Response to First Topic
07 A:  (Second Topic)
```

After a *greeting* by the agent, other opening components can be configured, such as direct address using the user's name, self-identification using the agent's name or identification of the agent's organization using its name. In addition slots for a first topic and second topic can be configured with a range of components typical of conversational openings, such as name request, welfare check, offer of help, capability giving, problem request and more. The following are just a few of the many possible configurations (Example 6).

(6) Opening (Agent) Configurations
```
01 A:  Hello.
02 U:  hi
---
```

```
03 A:  Hi. How are you?
04 U:  fine
---
05 A:  Hi there. What's your name?
06 U:  Bob
---
07 A:  Hello, Bob. I'm Alma.
08 U:  Hi, Alma
---
09 A:  Hello. I'm Alma. What's your name?
10 U:  I'm Bob
---
11 A:  Hi there. I'm Alma. What's your name?
12 U:  Dave
13 A:  Hello, Dave! How are you?
---
14 A:  Hello. I'm Alma at IBM Research.
15 U:  This is Elizabeth at Google
---
16 A:  Hello. This is IBM Research. How can I help you?
17 U:  who invented the hard disk?
---
18 A:  Hello. I'm Alma at IBM Research. What's your name?
19 U:  Dave
20 A:  Hi, Dave! How can I help you?
---
21 A:  Hello. I'm Alma at IBM Research. I can answer
22     questions about computer trivia or quiz you.
23 U:  ok, quiz me
```

If the designer sets no configuration variables, the agent simply does a greeting (line 01). But if *agent name* is set, the agent gives its name (e.g., lines 07, 09, 11, 14, 18 and 21) and/or if *user name* is set, the agent acknowledges the user's name (line 07). Similarly, if *agent organization* is set, the agent identifies its organization (lines 14, 16, 18 and 21). In addition to greetings and self-identifications, the designer can set a *first topic* and a *second topic*. Common first topics are welfare checks (line 03), name requests (lines 05, 09, 11 and 18), offers of help (line 16) or statements of capabilities (lines 21–22). These topics can also be set as second topics (lines 13 and 20) for multi-sequence conversation openings.

Quiz Module

While most chatbots and voice agents can handle simple, two-turn sequences, such as question-answer or command-action, few demonstrate the ability to handle the quiz pattern, which requires more than two turns. The Quiz module provides a conversational UX pattern in which the agent asks the *user* questions and evaluates the user's answers. The user can give the correct answer, give an incorrect one or give up, as well as initiate the standard repeat and paraphrase repairs. This quiz pattern can be used for all kinds of question types and content: pedagogical testing, trivia games, riddles, joke telling and more (Example 7).

(7) Quiz Pattern

```
01 U:  Quiz Request
02 A:  Question
03 U:  Correct Answer
04 A:  Confirmation
05 U:  Sequence Closer
---
06 A:  Quiz Offer
07 U:  Acceptance
08 A:  Question
09 U:  Repair Initiator
10 A:  Repair
11 U:  Incorrect Answer
12 A:  Disconfirmation
13 U:  Sequence Abort
14 A:  Correct Answer
15 U:  Sequence Closer
```

The Quiz pattern can be initiated by the user (line 01) or the agent (line 06). In either case, the agent then asks a question (lines 02 and 08). The user can then do one several actions: give the correct answer (line 03), give an incorrect answer (line 11), initiate repair on the question, for example, a repeat or paraphrase request (line 09) or the give up (line 13). When the user gives the correct answer (line 03), the agent confirms it (line 04), and when the user gives an incorrect answer, the agent disconfirms it (line 12). The following (Example 8) uses the quiz pattern for computer trivia questions.

(8) Computer Trivia (Alma)

```
01 U:  ask me a trivia question
02 A:  Who invented the hard disk drive?
03 U:  the what?
04 A:  hard disk drive?
05 U:  Microsoft?
06 A:  That's not it.
07 U:  I give up
08 A:  IBM
09 U:  ok
10 A:  Anything else for you?
11 U:  ask me another one
12 A:  What computer beat human champions at
13        Jeopardy in 2011?
14 U:  Watson!
15 A:  That's right!
16 U:  yay
17 A:  Anything else today?
```

In the Quiz module, the *agent* initiates an inquiry sequence (line 2), and the user tries to complete it with the correct answer. The user can get the answer correct (line 14), incorrect (line 5) or can abort the sequence (line 7). In addition to computer trivia, the Quiz module is used by Alma to tell question-answer jokes, as we can see in this working script (Example 9).

(9) Joke Telling (Alma)

```
01 U:  tell me a joke
02 A:  What can you hold without ever touching it?
03 U:  stocks?
04 A:  That's not it.
05 U:  a conversation?
06 A:  That's right!
07 U:  tell me another one
08 A:  Who earns a living by driving his customers away?
09 U:  Microsoft?
10 A:  Nope.
11 U:  you tell me
12 A:  A taxi driver.
13 U:  haha
14 A:  Anything else today?
```

In guessing the punchline of a question-answer joke, like answering a trivia question, the user can get it right (line 5), get it wrong (lines 3 and 9) or give up (line 11). This is how a question-answer-joke sequence works. In contrast, most of today's chatbots and virtual agents either give humorous one-liners or attempt to collapse the whole joke sequence into a single response, for example, "Why can't you trust atoms? They make up everything!," which gives away the punchline.

While the social activities are different, trivia game vs. joke telling, the underlying conversational UX patterns are identical. This is one example of how the same conversation module can be reused with different content and for different purposes. It also demonstrates the difference between content and a UX pattern. The aim of the Natural Conversation Framework is to provide a systematic set of UX patterns, not libraries of industry-specific content, such as intents, entities, questions or answers.

Story/Instructions Module

Although the action pair, or "adjacency pair," is the most prevalent type of conversational sequence, it is not the only one (Schegloff 2007). Another common sequence type is the *story*. A story is a longer unit of talk that requires multiple turns to complete. When telling a story, the speaker does not deliver the whole thing at once. The teller breaks the story into parts and waits for feedback from the recipient before continuing. The pattern for agent storytelling can also be used for giving instructions to the user (Example 10), and it can be extended to any number of parts or steps.

(10) Story/Instructions Pattern

```
01 U:  Story/Instruction Request
02 A:  Part/Step 1
03 U:  Continuer/Pause
```

```
04 A:  Part/Step 2
05 U:  Continuer/Pause
06 A:  Part/Step 3
07 U:  Repair Initiator
08 A:  Repair
09 U:  Continuer/Pause
10 A:  Part/Step 4
11 U:  Sequence Closer
---
12 A:  Story/Instruction Offer
13 U:  Acceptance
14 A:  Part/Step 1
15 U:  Story Complaint
16 A:  Stop Offer
17 U:  Acceptance
```

Storytelling or instruction-giving can be initiated by either the user (line 01) or the agent (line 12). The agent then gives the first part of the story or the first instruction in the set (lines 02 and 14) and waits for feedback from the user. The user can initiate repair (line 07) on that part of the telling, for example, a repeat or definition request, if necessary. Or the user can bid the agent to continue, using what conversation analysts call "continuers" (Schegloff 1982): "ok," "all right," "uh huh," "mhmm," etc. (lines 03, 05 and 09). In addition, the next part of the story or next instruction can also be triggered by the end of a short pause, obviating the need to produce the continuer while still giving the user a slot in which to initiate a repair on the prior part or to stop the telling (lines 15–17). The following is a simple example of using the Story/Instructions pattern for giving a set of three instructions (Example 11).

(11) Instructions (Alma)
```
01 U:  how do I meditate?
02 A:  First, sit comfortably and breathe slowly.
03 U:  ok
04 A:  Next, count each in breath and out breath
05     until you get to ten. Then repeat.
06 U:  what do you mean?
07 A:  As you breathe in, out, in, count one,
08     two, three all the way to ten.
09 U:  ok
10 A:  Finally, continue counting your breaths
11     for ten minutes.
12 U:  thanks
13 A:  You're welcome! Anything else?
```

After the initial part of the telling, in this case, the first instruction (line 2), the agent stops and waits for the user to produce a continuer (line 3). By waiting for a continuer after each part of the telling, the agent gives the user the opportunity to repair his hearing or understanding of the prior part before continuing on to the next. For example, in response to the second instruction, the user requests a paraphrase

Table 9.3 Basic navigation actions

1. What can you do?	Capability check
2. What did you say?	Repeat
3. What do you mean?	Paraphrase
4. Okay/thanks	Close sequence
5. Never mind	Abort sequence
6. Goodbye	Close conversation

(line 06) instead of bidding the agent to continue. After receiving the paraphrase (lines 07–08), the user produces a continuer (line 09), and the agent completes the set of instructions (lines 10–11). We see then that breaking an extended telling into parts and waiting for a signal to continue enables the recipient to repair hearing or understanding troubles *as the telling unfolds* instead of waiting until the end, at which point it would be more difficult to refer back to the source of trouble, as well as to comprehend the subsequent parts.

The Opening, Quiz and Story modules are just three of the 15 Common Activity modules with over 70 sub-patterns currently in the Natural Conversation Framework; however, our goal is to expand the library of UX patterns as we identify additional ones. Each module captures some aspect of conversational competence.

9.1.3 Conversation Navigation

With any computer interface, users must learn how to navigate the space. In command-line interfaces, users learn to navigate directories through cryptic commands. In graphical interfaces, users learn to drag files on a desktop to folders. In web interfaces, users learn to jump from page to page with URLs and hypertext. And in mobile interfaces, users learn to touch the screen, rotate it and "pinch" the images. But how should users navigate a conversational interface? What are the basic actions that they can always rely on at any point to navigate the conversation space or to get unstuck? Natural human conversation contains devices for its own management, as we see with sequence expansions. We propose a subset of these as basic actions for conversational interface navigation (Table 9.3).

Capability Check

Discovering the capabilities of a conversational agent can be challenging because, unlike a graphical interface, there are often no visual elements to click and explore. So users should always be able to talk to the agent about what it can do. "What can you do?" is perhaps the most general request for a description of the system's scope and functionality. This is somewhat analogous to the global help functionality of a graphical interface. The capability check should give the user enough guidance to use the app or to ask more specific questions about its capabilities, for example, "tell me more about destination recommendations" or "can you help me book a hotel?" or "do you know about restaurants?"

Repeat

In voice interfaces, unlike text interfaces, utterances are transient. Once the agent's voice response is done it is gone. Therefore, users must be able to elicit repeats of all or part of the agent's utterances. "What did you say?" is a natural conversational way to request a full repeat of the prior utterance. In voice interfaces, requesting repeats is somewhat analogous to 'going back' in visual interfaces. Although repeats are not as crucial in text-based interfaces, with their persistent chat histories, virtual agents appear dumb if they cannot understand a repeat request. The ability to repeat its prior utterance is such a basic feature of conversational competence. The NCF supports other repeat repairs, including partial repeat requests and hearing checks, but the full repeat request is the most general.

Paraphrase

While capability checks provide a kind of global help to the user, paraphrase requests provide local help on a turn-level basis. This is more analogous to tooltips in a graphical user interface, accessible by hovering the pointer over a button or icon, to get help on a particular feature. Similarly, "What do you mean?" elicits an elaboration or upshot of the prior utterance. In general, the agent's responses should be concise to increase speed and efficiency, but the paraphrase of that response should be written in simpler language, should avoid jargon and include explicit instruction where necessary. As a result, the elaboration will be longer and more cumbersome than the initial response, but will be easier to understand. Conversely, if the agent's initial response on occasion must be long and complex, then the paraphrase should be shorter and to the point, making the upshot of the prior utterance more clear. Paraphrase repairs enable users can control the level of detail they receive (see also Chap. 4) without slowing down the conversation for all users. The NCF supports other paraphrase repairs, including definition requests, example requests and understanding checks, but the full paraphrase request is the most general.

Close Sequence

Users should be able to close the current sequence when they receive an adequate response and move on to the next sequence. This is somewhat analogous to closing a document in a graphical user interface or a popup window in a web browser. "Okay" or "thanks" are natural conversational ways for the user to signal the completion of the current sequence and invite the agent to move onto any next topics. This creates a slot in the conversation in which the agent can initiate next topics, for example, offering to look up flights after recommending vacation destinations, or checking to see if the user has any last topics, for example, with "Anything else I can do for you?" Using "OK" to close a conversational sequence in third position is different from the typical use of "OK" in second position with a graphical dialog box to acknowledge a system prompt.

Abort Sequence

When users fail to elicit an adequate response from the agent, they should be able to abort the current sequence and move on to the next. "Never mind" in a conversation functions somewhat like escape in other computer interfaces. It enables the user to give up and move on. This is useful when the user has attempted to repair prior utterances, but the agent still fails to understand. Or if the agent is eliciting a series of details for a complex request (e.g., Open-Ended Request module), and upon hearing the required information, the user changes his or her mind, the user should be able to cancel the current activity by aborting the sequence. In addition, sequence aborts (e.g., "never mind," "nvm," "forget it"), provide implicit feedback that there is some kind of interactional problem, and they should be tracked.

Close Conversation

As in a human conversation, users should be encouraged to close their interaction with the agent. This is similar to closing an application or logging out of a system. "Goodbye" is the natural way to move to end a conversation. While the agent could respond with an immediate return farewell ("Goodbye!"), instead it should treat the user's attempt to close the conversation as a "pre-closing" (Schegloff and Sacks 1973). The pre-closing gives the agent the opportunity to bring up a last topic before returning the "goodbye" and ending the session. This last topic, which can be configured in the Conversation Closing modules of the NCF, might be an organization appreciation (e.g., "Thank you for contacting IBM!"), a success check sequence (e.g., "Did you find what you were looking for?"), a name request (e.g., "Can I get your name before you go?"), a promotion (e.g., "One last thing, would you like to hear about our current promotion for new customers?) or any other last topic that the designer may want to insert into the conversation before losing the user. In addition, the NCF also recognizes user utterances that are designed as pre-closings rather than farewells, such as "got to go," "are we done?" or "anything else?"

After any agent utterance in a conversation, users should be able to do any of the above six actions. At first users may need to be taught that, unlike a search engine or most of today's chatbots, your conversational agent will recognize these six basic actions and respond appropriately and *usefully*. Because they are based on human conversation, they should already be familiar to the user and natural to perform, as well as easy to remember.

For an example of how these navigation actions might work, see the following exchanges with Alma (Example 12).

(12) Conversation Navigation A
```
01 U:  what can you do?
02 A:  I haven't been trained yet. I can only make small
03     talk, answer or ask some computer trivia questions
04     and tell some jokes.
05 U:  ok who invented the hard disk?
06 A:  The hard disk was invented by IBM in 1956.
07 U:  say again
```

```
08 A:  The hard disk was invented by IBM in 1956.
09 U:  what do you mean?
10 A:  The hard disk was invented in 1956 by engineers
11     at IBM's laboratory in San Jose, California.
12 U:  thanks
13 A:  You're welcome!
14 A:  Anything else for you?
15 U:  goodbye
16 A:  Did you find what you were looking for?
```

In Example 12, the user relies on five of the basic actions to navigate the conversation. At the beginning, he checks the agent's capabilities (lines 1–4) and then does an action within the scope of that response, asking a "computer trivia question" (line 5). In response to the answer, the user then requests a repeat (line 7), followed by an paraphrase request (line 9). The user then closes the trivia-question sequence with an appreciation (line 12) and moves to close the conversation (line 15). Instead of completing the closing sequence, the agent treats it as a pre-closing and brings up a last topic, a success check (line 16). Now contrast the next Example (13).

(13) Conversation Navigation B
```
01 U:  show me flights
02 A:  What do you mean?
03 U:  show me flights from SFO to JFK
04 A:  I'm sorry, I still don't understand.
05 U:  never mind
06 A:  Whatever you say, friend.
07 A:  Want to know what I can do?
08 U:  yes please
09 A:  Okay.
10 A:  I haven't been trained yet. I can only make small
11     talk, answer or ask some computer trivia questions
12     and tell some jokes.
```

Here the user fails to check the agent's capabilities at the beginning of the conversation and instead initiates a flight request (line 1). This time the agent responds with a default paraphrase request (line 2) to which the user offers an elaboration (line 3). This still fails to enable the agent to understand (line 4) so the user aborts the attempted flight request sequence with "never mind" (line 5). In response, the agent acknowledges the abort and offers to describe its capabilities (line 7), which the user accepts (line 8). The agent then attempts to align with the user's expectations by describing its capabilities (lines 10–12).

Our first implementation of the Natural Conversation Framework was for IBM's What's in Theaters web application in 2015. What's in Theaters was built on the Watson Dialog service (the precursor to Watson Assistant) as a simple demonstration of how to integrate the service with other components. But it also demonstrates an early version of our conversation navigation method (Example 14).

(14) What's in Theaters (2015)

```
01 U: what can you do?
02 A: I can look up current and upcoming movies by Genre or
03    MPAA Rating and show you trailers for them. But I'm
04    afraid I cannot search by number of stars or by movie
05    titles or actor and director names at this time.
06 U: ok show me current movies
07 A: Are you in the mood for a specific genre?
08 U: say again
09 A: I said... Are you in the mood for a specific genre?
10 U: what are my choices?
11 A: Action, adventure, animated, comedy, crime, documentary,
12    drama, family, fantasy, foreign, historical, horror,
13    music, mystery, romance, science fiction, TV movie,
14    thriller, war movies and western.
15 U: science fiction
16 A: Do you prefer a certain movie rating?
17 U: what do you mean by movie rating?
18 A: The rating is a recommendation by the Motion Picture
19    Association of America about the suitability of a
20    movie's content for particular age groups. For example,
21    G is for general audiences, while R is restricted to
22    people 17 and older. Do you prefer a certain movie rating?
23 U: I don't care
24 A: Good choice, Bob! I found 24 results for Current Science
25    Fiction movies.
26    ((first movie results))
27 U: no I mean PG-13
28 A: Good choices, Bob! I found 1 results for Current
29    PG-13-rated Science Fiction movies.
30    ((Justice League))
31 U: thanks
32 A: Is there anything else I can help you with?
33 U: where is AMC Saratoga?
34 A: I'm sorry, I don't understand. Try What's playing?
35 U: what's the address for AMC Saratoga?
36 A: I'm afraid I don't understand. I can't recognize movie
37    titles at this time.
38 U: never mind
39 A: Okay. Whatever you say, Bob! Is there anything else
40    I can help you with?
41 U: no
42 A: Okay. Did you find what you were looking for, Bob?
43 U: yes
44 A: Great! Goodbye.
45 U: bye
46 A: Say anything to continue.
```

In What's in Theaters, we can see demonstrations of all six conversation navigation actions: capability check (line 1), repeat request (line 8), partial paraphrase request (line 17), sequence closing (line 31), sequence aborting (line 38) and conversation closing (line 45). It also supports detail elicitations (line 10), no-answer responses (line 23) and self-corrections (line 27). Although the functional scope of What's in Theaters was intentionally limited, as a proof-of-concept, it nonetheless demonstrates expandable sequences and conversation navigation.

9.1.4   Sequence Metrics

Since our Natural Conversation Framework is based on *expandable sequences*, the base sequences and their expansions can each be measured separately. This enables corresponding metrics for the effectiveness and efficiency of the conversation itself, independently of customer satisfaction. Effectiveness and efficiency are also two-way metrics: they apply to both the automated agent and to the user. The NCF offers the following three metrics.

Number of Sequences is a measure of how many action pairs, or base adjacency pair sequences, were initiated by the user or by the agent. Instead of reporting simply total number of turns, we segment the conversation logs into expandable sequences, that is base sequences with their expansions, if any. This gives a more informative measure of how many social actions the user or the agent attempted than does total number of turns. The number of user-initiated sequences is a good measure of user engagement.

Sequence Completion Rate is the percentage of initiated base sequences that were completed by the recipient: agent or user. In other words, this is a measure of the rate of success across sequences in the conversations, which is closely related to the level of mutual understanding. If agent or user do not understand what the other means or is doing, they cannot complete the sequence initiated by the other. This is critical because *mutual understanding* is one of the distinctive goals of conversation.

Interactional Efficiency is a measure of how much extra work the user or the agent had to do in the conversation. The expandable-sequence interaction model gives us a theoretical minimum number of turns a given conversation could have. That is, if every completed sequence were compact, the theoretical minimum would be double the number of completed base sequences. We can then compare that minimum to the *actual* number of turns in the conversation and get a measure of the rate of sequence expansion.

Taken together, these sequence metrics tell us different things about conversations with our agent, Alma. Using extreme sets of artificial data (Examples 15–17), we can demonstrate how the metrics vary with different kinds of conversations.

(15) Example of Set A

```
01 U:  what computer beat Jeopardy?
02 A:  An IBM computer named Watson.
03 U:  what computer beat a human chess champion?
04 A:  It was named Deep Blue.
```

(16) Example of Set B

```
01 U:  what computer beat a human chess champion?
02 A:  It was named Deep Blue.
03 U:  Deep what?
04 A:  Blue.
05 U:  what do you mean?
06 A:  The IBM computer was named Deep Blue.
07 U:  oh ok
08 A:  Is there anything else I can do for you?
```

(17) Example of Set C

```
01 U:  what's in theaters?
02 A:  What do you mean?
03 U:  what movies are playing in theaters now?
04 A:  I'm sorry, I still don't understand.
```

These examples represent the kinds of sequences in each experimental data set, A, B and C. The data sets are "extreme" in that they only contain one kind of sequence, that is, compact sequences (A), expanded, completed sequences (B) and uncompleted sequences (C). These extreme data sets better enable us to see under which conditions these metrics vary than real data do (Table 9.4).

In data set A, we included only completed sequences initiated by the user and no expansions by the user. The Sequence Completion rate for agent and user combined was 88% and the Interactional Efficiency was 92%. In data set B, we included only completed sequences initiated by the user, but also numerous expansions by the user, such as repeat requests, "what did you say?", paraphrase requests, "what do you mean?", sequence closers, "ok" and "thanks," and more. In the case of these frequent expansions, the combined Sequence Completion rate was still high, 83%, but Interactional Efficiency dropped significantly to 49%. Finally, in data set C, we included only conversations in which none of the substantive sequences initiated by the user were completed. In other words, there was almost a complete lack of understanding by the agent of what the user was saying. The Sequence Completion rate plummeted to 14% and Interactional Efficiency to 9%.

Table 9.4 Sequence metrics for extreme data

Set	Number of sequences	Sequence completion	Interactional efficiency
A	17.4	0.88	0.92
B	10.4	0.83	0.49
C	7.2	0.14	0.09

In short, if both the Sequence Completion and Interactional Efficiency rates are high, the conversations themselves are effective. If they are both very low, the conversations have failed. But if Sequence Completion is high and Interactional Efficiency is moderate, the conversations are successful, but the user or agent is doing additional work to achieve that success. This invites the conversational UX designer to explore the nature of those sequence expansions. If they are eliciting details, the topic of conversation may be inherently complex. For example, buying airline tickets involves a lot of details and decisions. Moderate Interactional Efficiency may be normal for this activity. However, if the expansions are primarily due to understanding repairs, the conversation designer should re-evaluate the terminology that the agent uses and the knowledge that it assumes and determine if the conversation can be redesigned so that it is more comprehensible from the start. With inherently complex topics or activities, expansions may be unavoidable, but at least with repair features, the user and agent can still succeed in the face of understanding troubles. This is the value of a robust conversational repair system.

The Sequence Metrics also enable us to help disentangle user dissatisfaction with the agent itself from dissatisfaction with its message, for example, company policies. If a customer reports dissatisfaction after an interaction with a company's virtual agent, and the Sequence Completion and Interactional Efficiency rates are high for that conversation, then we know that the customer did not experience trouble understanding the agent and vice versa. Rather the dissatisfaction must have come from the message delivered by the agent and not the quality of the conversation itself. In other words, if the user complains and the agent recognizes and responds appropriately to that complaint, then the problem is not in the agent's ability to understand but in the substance of the complaint itself.

How it works

In order to measure the occurrence of base sequences and their expansions in conversation logs, we label both the user's and the agent's actions inside the dialog nodes themselves. We set context variables on each node that contains an intent or response, to indicate if the user inputs and agent outputs associated with that sequence are parts of base sequences or expansions. So for example, a simple greeting exchange would be labelled with the following context data (Example 18).

(18) Labelled Conversation Log

```
01 U:  hi
02 A:  Hello.
---
01  user_input = "hi"
    user_action = "greeting"
    confidence = 1.0
    user_APR = B1PP
02  repeat = "Hello."
    agent_action = "greeting"
    agent_APR = B2PP
```

What the user says, in this case "hi," is captured by a system variable, *input_text*, and set to the variable *user_input*. The user's action is captured by recording the intent name, "greeting," using the system variable, *intents[0].intent*, and setting it to *user_action*. In addition, the confidence level for that intent is captured. The sequential function of the user's utterance is captured by a set of structural codes, *user_APR*, that we have constructed based on the adjacency pair and repair models in Conversation Analysis (Schegloff 2007), for example, "B1PP" stands for the first pair part of a base adjacency pair sequence. On the other hand, what the agent says is captured through the custom variable, *repeat*, which is also used for repeat repairs, and the agent's action is hardcoded when the response is written and captured by *agent_action*. And like the user's utterance, the agent's is assigned a sequential function with the agent APR code, "B2PP," or base second pair part. Once the dialog nodes are labeled as such, the conversation logs label themselves as users interact with the agent!

One limitation of this approach is that when a user's input is unrecognized, that is, does not match any dialog conditions, we do not know what kind of action the user did nor its sequential function. To attempt to compensate for this missing data, we provide a modifier that represents the average percentage of unrecognized inputs that are initiators of base sequences. For example, if 80% of past unrecognized user utterances are base first pair parts (B1PPs), we set this modifier to 0.8. The modifier is then based on prior data in order to provide a correction to the metrics. Unrecognized user utterances, or random samples of them, should be inspected on a regular basis both to set the modifier but also to discover any systematic problems hidden in these unclassified inputs. Furthermore, conversational UX designers and product managers can learn to interpret the sequence metrics to determine if their conversational agent is doing better or worse than it did yesterday.

9.2   Conclusion

Our Natural Conversation Framework for Conversational UX Design contains four components: (1) an interaction model based on expandable sequences, (2) reusable modules for common conversational activities, (3) a conversation navigation method and (4) a set of metrics that measure effectiveness and efficiency in terms of sequence organization (Schegloff 2007). Each component relies on models and patterns documented in the Conversation Analysis literature. So far this design framework has been implemented on two natural language platforms, IBM Watson Dialog (now shuttered) and IBM Watson Assistant (formerly Conversation), but the patterns are abstract enough to apply to any natural language platform.

While much attention has been given to the natural language classification and entity extraction, an equally important component for conversational interfaces is "sequential context" (Schegloff 1992a). The primary context for interpreting utterances produced in conversation are the prior utterances in that conversation. For example, "how about Las Vegas?" is ambiguous in isolation, but following the utterance, "Here are things to do in Los Angeles," it becomes sensible. Speakers rely heavily on previous talk to provide a context for their next utterance, which enables them to take shortcuts. For the conversational UX designer, deciding what aspects of the sequential context to persist and how to represent it through so-called "context variables," is still a challenging design problem. Creating an interaction that works like a natural conversation requires capturing the current topic of the talk, the user's prior question or request, which entities the user has mentioned so far, whether the previous user utterance was recognized or not and more. Therefore *context design* is a critical area within conversational UX design that must be advanced if virtual agents are to handle many common conversation patterns.

In addition to outlining our design framework for conversational UX, we have also attempted to demonstrate a practice for representing the user experience for natural language and conversational systems: by using simple transcripts. Transcripts can represent sequences of utterances, and who is speaking each one, for either text- or voice-based conversations. Transcripts are easy to read, easy to create and easy to share. Designers and stakeholders can quickly iterate on a mocked-up transcript before building any parts of the conversation space. And because transcripts lack any representation of a graphical user interface, they enable the developers and stakeholders to focus on the design of the conversation without getting distracted by visual elements.

Conversation analysts trade in excerpts of detailed transcriptions of naturally occurring human conversation in order to share and demonstrate their analytic discoveries. Conversational UX designers should likewise trade in transcripts in order to demonstrate the form and beauty of their designs. The practice of sharing transcripts will enable conversation designers to share tips and tricks, learn from each other and collaborate: "Here's a design I made!" "Check out this working script!" "How did you do that?" Every discipline needs standard ways of representing its phenomenon in order to progress. Transcripts are the currency of conversation analysts and should be for conversational UX designers too!

References

Luff P, Gilbert N, Frohlich D (eds) (1990) Computers and conversation. Academic Press, London
Sacks H, Schegloff EA (1979) Two preferences in the organization of reference to persons in conversation and their interaction. In: Psathas G (ed) Everyday language: studies in ethnomethodology. Irvington, New York, pp 15–21
Sacks H, Schegloff EA, Jefferson G (1974) A simplest systematics for the organization of turn-taking for conversation. Language 50:696–735
Schegloff EA (1982) Discourse as an interactional achievement: some uses of 'uh huh' and other things that come between sentences. In: Tannen D (ed) Analysing discourse: test and talk. Georgetown University Press, Washington, DC, pp 71–93
Schegloff EA (1992a) In another context. In: Duranti A, Goodwin C (eds) Rethinking context: language as an interactive phenomenon. Cambridge University Press, Cambridge
Schegloff EA (1992b) Repair after next turn: the last structurally provided defense of intersubjectivity in conversation. Am J Sociol 98:1295–1345

Schegloff EA (2007) Sequence organization in interaction: a primer in conversation analysis, vol 1. Cambridge University Press, Cambridge

Schegloff EA, Sacks H (1973) Opening up closings. Semiotica 7:289–327

Schegloff EA, Jefferson G, Sacks H (1977) The preference for self-correction in the organization of repair in conversation. Language 53:361–382

MIX
Papier aus verantwortungsvollen Quellen
Paper from responsible sources
FSC® C105338

www.fsc.org

Printed by Libri Plureos GmbH
in Hamburg, Germany